POLITICAL CONSTITUTIONALISM

Judicial review by constitutional courts is often presented as a necessary supplement to democracy. This book questions its effectiveness and legitimacy. Drawing on the republican tradition, Richard Bellamy argues that the democratic mechanisms of open elections between competing parties and decision-making by majority rule offer superior and sufficient methods for upholding rights and the rule of law. The absence of popular accountability renders judicial review a form of arbitrary rule which lacks the incentive structure democracy provides to ensure rulers treat the ruled with equal concern and respect. Rights-based judicial review undermines the constitutionality of democracy. Its counter-majoritarian bias promotes privileged against unprivileged minorities, while its legalism and focus on individual cases distort public debate. Rather than constraining democracy with written constitutions and greater judicial oversight, attention should be paid to improving democractic processes through such measures as reformed electoral systems and enhanced parliamentary scrutiny.

RICHARD BELLAMY is Professor of Political Science and Director of the School of Public Policy, University College London. He is the author of seven books, numerous articles and book chapters and has edited over twenty volumes including *The Cambridge History of Twentieth Century Political Thought* (with Terence Ball, Cambridge, 2003) and editions of Beccaria and Gramsci in the Cambridge Texts in the History of Political Thought series.

T0384579

POLITICAL CONSTITUTIONALISM: A REPUBLICAN DEFENCE OF THE CONSTITUTIONALITY OF DEMOCRACY

RICHARD BELLAMY

CAMBRIDGE
UNIVERSITY PRESS

CAMBRIDGE
UNIVERSITY PRESS

University Printing House, Cambridge CB2 8BS, United Kingdom

Cambridge University Press is part of the University of Cambridge.

It furthers the University's mission by disseminating knowledge in the pursuit of education, learning and research at the highest international levels of excellence.

www.cambridge.org
Information on this title: www.cambridge.org/9780521683678

© Richard Bellamy 2007

First published 2007
Reprinted 2010

A catalogue record for this publication is available from the British Library

ISBN 978-0-521-86510-4 Hardback
ISBN 978-0-521-68367-8 Paperback

In Memory of my Father

CONTENTS

PREFACE AND ACKNOWLEDGEMENTS

A written, justiciable constitution, incorporating a bill of rights, is widely accepted as a necessary safeguard against the abuse of power by democratic governments. This book challenges that common view and the often unexamined and erroneous assumptions about the workings of democracy on which it rests. Far from guarding against a largely mythical tyranny of the majority, the checks imposed by judicial review on majoritarian decision-making risk undermining political equality, distorting the agenda away from the public interest, and entrenching the privileges of dominant minorities and the domination of unprivileged ones. As such, legal constitutionalism can produce rather than constrain arbitrary rule, detract from the rights protection of weak minorities, and damage the rule of law in both the formal and the substantive senses of treating all as equals. By contrast, the workings of actually existing democracies promote the constitutional goods of rights and the rule of law. Party competition and majority rule on the basis of one person one vote uphold political equality and institutionalise mechanisms of political balance and accountability that provide incentives for politicians to attend to the judgements and interests of those they govern and to recruit a wide range of minorities into any ruling coalition. From the republican perspective adopted here, the procedures and mechanisms of established democracies offer adequate, if not perfect and certainly improvable, safeguards against domination and arbitrary rule. Most kinds of legal constitutionalism subvert these democratic protections, creating sources of arbitrariness and dominance of their own in the process. In sum, democracy provides a form of political constitutionalism that is superior both normatively and empirically to the legal constitutional devices that are regularly proposed as necessary constraints upon it.

In developing this thesis, I have incurred numerous debts. While controversial within the legal and political theory communities that I habitually frequent, it is far less so among political scientists. I owe much to the Government Department at Essex, where this project was originally conceived and partly written, for providing an environment where you seem to absorb the latest research on political systems and behaviour simply by walking along the corridor. Colleagues in the Political Theory group nonetheless ensured I addressed certain central normative issues, and I am particularly grateful to Albert Weale for written and verbal comments on Part I and to Sheldon Leader in the Law Department for likewise reading drafts of those chapters and judiciously reminding me that not all legal constitutionalist objections could be dealt with quite as cavalierly as I might have hoped. At University College London (UCL), I have received a similar stimulus from colleagues in Political Science, Philosophy and Laws. I am especially grateful to Cécile Laborde for her supportive and incisive comments on the chapters in Part II which provided much needed advice and encouragement. The general republican orientation of my argument incurs a deep indebtedness to Quentin Skinner and Philip Pettit, to whom I owe inspiration and support over a long period. Initially, the book had been planned as a joint monograph with Dario Castiglione, with whom I have co-authored numerous pieces exploring constitutionalism in the EU that gave rise to many of the key ideas of this work. Unfortunately, other projects prevented Dario from being a co-author on this occasion but he has been so generous in reading and discussing drafts of the book that I almost feel he has been so nonetheless. I am also grateful to many others who have read, heard or simply discussed various parts of the argument and offered helpful observations, criticisms and guidance. With apologies to any I have inadvertently forgotten, these include Larry Alexander, Luca Baccelli, Rodney Barker, John Bartle, Ian Budge, Tom Campbell, Alan Cromartie, John Dryzek, Andrew Gamble, Jason Glynos, Bob Goodin, Ross Harrison, Janet Hiebert, David Howarth, Peter John, Anthony King, Christian List, Martin Loughlin, Neil MacCormick, Peter Mair, Andrew Mason, John McCormick, Glyn Morgan, Danny Nicol, Aletta Norval, Emilio Santoro, Niamh Nic Shuibhne, Adam Tomkins, Jim Tully, Richard Vernon, Jeremy Waldron, Neil Walker, the late Iris Marion Young and Danilo Zolo. John Haslam and Carrie Cheek have been long suffering in awaiting the delivery of the manuscript and extremely helpful in seeing it though to completion. They arranged exceptionally helpful referees' reports, and I am especially grateful to Jeremy Waldron for his detailed comments on the original proposal and draft chapters. Needless to say, all the usual caveats apply, with I alone responsible for the errors and misunderstandings these friends and colleagues have valiantly struggled to save me from. The one delay that was not of my own doing resulted from my father's death in the Autumn of 2005. It's a sad truth that you often do not appreciate how important certain people are to you until they are no longer there. I really do not know how to express what I owe to Louise and Amy for helping me through that difficult period and keeping me focused on other things, not least this book. Though my father always dutifully promised to read each one of my books, it was a sobering fact that his eyes would start to droop somewhere around page 3 – if he got that far. However, I greatly miss the support and love he showed me in proudly displaying them alongside his own very different publications. Now his adorn my shelves, I'm proud in my turn to stack this one next to them and to dedicate it to him.

INTRODUCTION: LEGAL
AND POLITICAL CONSTITUTIONALISM

This book is about constitutions and democratic politics. The increasingly dominant view is that constitutions enshrine and secure the rights central to a democratic society. This approach defines a constitution as a written document, superior to ordinary legislation and entrenched against legislative change, justiciable and constitutive of the legal and political system.[1] It contends that a constitution of this kind, not participation in democratic politics *per se*, offers the basis for citizens to be treated in a democratic way as deserving of equal concern and respect.[2] The electorate and politicians may engage in a democratic process, but they do not always embrace democratic values. The defence of these belongs to the constitution and its judicial guardians. As Cherie Booth, the barrister wife of the former British Prime Minister Tony Blair, neatly put it: 'In a human rights world . . . responsibility for a value-based substantive commitment to democracy rests in large part on judges . . . [J]udges in constitutional democracies are set aside as the guardians of individual rights . . . [and] afforded the opportunity and duty to do justice for all citizens by reliance on universal standards of decency and humaneness . . . in a way that teaches citizens and government about the ethical responsibilities of being participants in a true democracy.'[3]

That the wife of a democratically elected political leader should express such a condescending view of democratic politics may be a little surprising, but it all too accurately reflects the prevailing opinion among legal constitutionalists. As Roberto Unger has remarked, 'discomfort with democracy' is one of the 'dirty little secrets of contemporary jurisprudence'. This unease is manifest in:

---

[1] E.g. J. Raz, 'On the Authority and Interpretation of Constitutions', in L. Alexander (ed.), *Constitutionalism: Philosophical Foundations*, Cambridge: Cambridge University Press, 1998, pp. 153–4.

[2] R. Dworkin, *Freedom's Law: The Moral Reading of the American Constitution*, Oxford: Oxford University Press, 1996, 'Introduction: The Moral Reading and the Majoritarian Premise', pp. 24, 32–5.

[3] C. Booth, 'The Role of the Judge in a Human Rights World', Speech to the Malaysian Bar Association, 26 July 2005.

the ceaseless identification of restraints on majority rule . . . as the overriding responsibility of . . . jurists . . . in the effort to obtain from judges . . . the advances popular politics fail to deliver; in the abandonment of institutional reconstruction to rare and magical moments of national refoundation; in an ideal of deliberative democracy as most acceptable when closest in style to a polite conversation among gentlemen in an eighteenth-century drawing room . . . [and] in the . . . treatment of party government as a subsidiary, last-ditch source of legal evolution, to be tolerated when none of the more refined modes of legal resolution applies.[4]

Ms Booth, like the writers criticised by Roberto Unger, has in mind not the obviously sham democratic regimes of autocratic dictators, but working democracies like the United Kingdom and the other twenty-two countries around the world where democratic practices have been firmly established for at least fifty years, and in some cases much longer. Of course, these are also the countries with the longest traditions of judicial independence, rights protection and a stable system of law. However, that is because the one leads to the other. After all, not all these countries have, or have always had, written constitutions, and only three have strong systems of constitutional judicial review.[5] In fact, the rule of law, in the sense of all being equal under the law, emerged from the self-same processes of economic development and social pluralism that gave rise to democracy,[6] and has only survived and developed in those societies where the democratic control of power and the socio-economic conditions that support it persist.[7] I shall argue that in such countries the concerns of legal constitutionalists about democracy and their proposed judicial and other counter-majoritarian remedies prove at best misconceived, at worst subversive of the very democratic basis of the constitutional goods they seek to secure. The legal constitutionalist's attempts to constrain democracy undercut the political constitutionalism of democracy itself, jeopardising the legitimacy and efficacy of law and the courts along the way. For a pure

---

[4] R. Unger, *What Should Legal Analysis Become?*, London: Verso, 1996, p. 72. See too J. Waldron, 'Dirty Little Secret', *Columbia Law Review*, 98 (1998), pp. 510–30 and his *Law and Disagreement*, Oxford: Oxford University Press, 1999, pp. 8–10.

[5] These figures come from R. A. Dahl, *How Democratic Is the American Constitution?*, New Haven: Yale University Press, 2002, pp. 164–5, who also notes only four have that other counter-majoritarian check, a strongly bicameral legislature.

[6] On the relationship of polyarchy to democracy, on the one hand, and modern dynamic conditions, on the other, see R. A. Dahl, *Democracy and its Critics*, New Haven: Yale University Press, 1989, Part 5.

[7] See chapter 2 section 3 below and the essays in J. M. Maravall and A. Przeworski (eds.), *Democracy and the Rule of Law*, Cambridge: Cambridge University Press, 2003.

legal constitutionalism, that sees itself as superior to and independent of democracy, rests on questionable normative and empirical assumptions – both about itself and the democratic processes it seeks to frame and partially supplant. It overlooks the true basis of constitutional government in the democratic political constitutionalism it denigrates and unwittingly undermines. To see why, let's briefly examine and compare the legal and political constitutionalist approaches.

Two related claims motivate legal constitutionalism. The first is that we can come to a rational consensus on the substantive outcomes that a society committed to the democratic ideals of equality of concern and respect should achieve. These outcomes are best expressed in terms of human rights and should form the fundamental law of a democratic society. The second is that the judicial process is more reliable than the democratic process at identifying these outcomes. This book disputes them both.

The desire to articulate a coherent and normatively attractive vision of a just and well-ordered society is undoubtedly a noble endeavour. It has inspired philosophers and citizens down the ages. But though all who engage in this activity aspire to convince others of the truth of their own position, none has so far come close to succeeding. Rival views by similarly competent theorists continue to proliferate, their disagreements both reflecting and occasionally informing the political disagreements between ordinary citizens over every conceivable issue from tax policy to health care. The fact of disagreement does not indicate that no theories of justice are true. Nor does it mean that a democratic society does not involve a commitment to rights and equality. It does show, though, that there are limitations to our ability to identify a true theory of rights and equality and so to convince others of its truth. Such difficulties are likely to be multiplied several fold when it comes to devising policies that will promote our favoured ideal of democratic justice. In part, the problem arises from the complexity of cause and effect in social and economic life, so that it will be hard to judge what the consequences of any given measure will be. But as well as the difficulty of specifying what policies will bring about given values, disagreements about the nature of these values also mean it will be difficult to identify those political, social and economic conditions that best realise them. For example, both types of difficulty are in evidence when philosophers or citizens debate the degree to which market arrangements are just or the modifications that might be necessary to render them so. How far they can or should reflect people's efforts, entitlements or merits, say, are all deeply disputed for reasons that are both normative and empirical. Similar difficulties bedevil discussions over which electoral system best embodies democratic principles so as to ensure an equal influence over government policy.

These problems with the first claim of legal constitutionalism raise doubts regarding its second claim about the responsibilities of constitutional judges. If there are reasonable disagreements about justice and its implications, then it becomes implausible to regard judges as basing their decisions on the 'correct' view of what democratic justice demands in particular circumstances.[8] There are no good grounds for believing that they can succeed where political philosophers from Plato to Rawls have failed. At best, the superior position legal constitutionalists accord them must rest on courts providing a more conscientious and better informed arbitration of the disagreements and conflicts surrounding rights and equality than democratic politics can offer. However, this shift in justification moves attention from outcomes to process and suggests a somewhat different conception of the constitution within a democratic society. Instead of seeing the constitution as enshrining the substance of democratic values, it points towards conceiving it as a procedure for resolving disagreements about the nature and implications of democratic values in a way that assiduously and impartially weighs the views and interests in dispute in a manner that accords them equal concern and respect. Rather than a resource of the fundamental answers to the question of how to organise a democratic society, the constitution represents a fundamental structure for reaching collective decisions about social arrangements in a democratic way. That is, in a way that treats citizens as entitled to having their concerns equally respected when it comes to deciding the best way to pursue their collective interests.

A political constitutionalist elaborates this second approach and makes two corresponding claims to the legal constitutionalist's. The first is that we reasonably disagree about the substantive outcomes that a society committed to the democratic ideals of equality of concern and respect should achieve. The second is that the democratic process is more legitimate and effective than the judicial process at resolving these disagreements. Judicial claims to exemplify a form of public reasoning that is more inclusive and impartial than democracy proper are disputed in both theory and practice. It is only when the public themselves reason within a democratic process that they can be regarded as equals and their

---

[8] For this sort of bold claim by a leading British judge, see J. Steyn, *Democracy Through Law: Selected Speeches and Judgments*, Aldershot: Ashgate, 2004, p. 130.

multifarious rights and interests accorded equal concern and respect. A system of 'one person, one vote' provides citizens with roughly equal political resources; deciding by majority rule treats their views fairly and impartially; and party competition in elections and parliament institutionalises a balance of power that encourages the various sides to hear and harken to each other, promoting mutual recognition through the construction of compromises. According to this political conception, the democratic process *is* the constitution. It is both constitutional, offering a due process, and constitutive, able to reform itself.

Four senses of the political underlie these claims. First, a constitution offers a response to what Jeremy Waldron and Albert Weale, among others, have termed 'the circumstances of politics'.[9] That is to say, circumstances where we disagree about both the right and the good, yet nonetheless require a collective decision on these matters. Consequently, the constitution cannot be treated as a basic law or norm. Rather, it offers a basic framework for resolving our disagreements – albeit one that is also the subject of political debate. Second, the constitution is identified with the political rather than the legal system, and in particular with the ways political power is organised and divided. This approach harks back to the republican tradition and its emphasis on self-government, on the one hand, and the balance of power, on the other, as mechanisms to overcome domination through the arbitrary rule of others.[10] Third, it draws on work in the field of public law political science, what Michael Shapiro has called 'political jurisprudence',[11] and sees law as functioning as politically as democratic politics. Finally, it offers a normative account of the democratic political system. In particular, it shows how real democratic processes work in normatively attractive ways so as to produce the constitutional goods of a respect for rights and the rule of law by ensuring legislation is framed in ways that treat all as equals.

There are elements of both legal and political constitutionalism in most constitutions. The bulk of any constitutional document is usually given over to a detailed description of the political and legal system, setting out the electoral rules, enumerating the powers and functions of different levels and agencies of government, and so on. These clauses lay out the

---

[9] Waldron, *Law and Disagreement*, pp. 107–18, A. Weale, *Democracy*, Basingstoke: Macmillan, 1999, pp. 8–13.

[10] See C. H. McIlwain, *Constitutionalism: Ancient and Modern*, revised edition, New York: Great Seal Books, 1958, ch. 2 and G. Maddox, 'A Note on the Meaning of "Constitution"', *American Political Science Review*, 76 (1982), pp. 807–8.

[11] M. Shapiro, 'Political Jurisprudence', *Kentucky Law Journal*, 52 (1964), pp. 294–345.

processes whereby citizens decide their common affairs and settle their disputes. In the first modern constitutions, bills of rights formed a mere preamble or appendix to this procedural constitution. Yet, in recent times the importance of political and legal procedures has been eclipsed by concentration on bills of rights. As the quote from Cherie Booth illustrates, it is this substantive part of the constitution that legal constitutionalists believe truly encapsulates the essence of both democracy and constitutionalism. They regard the rules describing the form of government as having no independent weight as constraints on the system they describe.[12] They fail to see how these rules structure the way decisions are taken and that procedures themselves have constitutional value as constraints upon arbitrary rule.[13] That said, I am also critical of the ways some of those sympathetic to a more processual view have been tempted to constitutionalise these procedures in a legal way.[14] Not only do such accounts have a tendency to collapse into the substantive, rights-based view, with a 'due process' becoming defined in terms of conformity with constitutional rights, but they also overlook the constitutive as well as constitutional aspect of democracy.

Legal constitutionalists acknowledge that no constitution will survive long unless citizens can identify with it. Joseph Raz remarks how a constitution must serve 'not only as the lawyers' law, but as the people's law', its main provisions commanding general consent as the 'common ideology' that governs public life.[15] In a similar vein, Jürgen Habermas talks of the members of a democratic society being bound together and to their country by means of a 'constitutional patriotism'.[16] However, once again these theorists locate this moral glue in the 'thin' constitution of rights as determined by judicial review, rather than the 'thick' constitutional processes of democratic law-making. But if we disagree about the basis and bearing

---

[12] Raz, 'On the Authority and Interpretation of Constitutions', p. 153 and G. Sartori, 'Constitutionalism: A Preliminary Discussion', *American Political Science Review*, 56 (1962), p. 861.

[13] For brief accounts of the historical antecedents of political constitutionalism as a form of government, see W. H. Morris-Jones, 'On Constitutionalism', *American Political Science Review*, 59 (1965), p. 439. See too Maddox, 'A Note on the Meaning of "Constitution"', p. 807.

[14] E.g. J. H. Ely, *Democracy and Distrust: A Theory of Judicial Review*, Cambridge, MA: Harvard University Press, 1980 and, in a different way, J. Habermas, *Between Facts and Norms: Contributions to a Discourse Theory of Law and Democracy*, Cambridge: Polity, 1996, both of whom are discussed in chapter 3.

[15] Raz, 'On the Authority and Interpretation of Constitutions', p. 154.

[16] J. Habermas, Appendix II: 'Citizenship and National Identity', *Between Facts and Norms*, p. 500.

of rights, then the imposition of such a view is more likely to divide than unite citizens – witness the divisions created in the United States by the judicial determination of abortion rights. By contrast, political constitutionalism addresses the task of building a democratic public culture by viewing all citizens as equal participants in the collective endeavour to frame a just social order. Citizens are far more likely to identify with laws in which they have had some say. Of course, that say may be very small and be outweighed by what most others say. But the entitlement to have as equal a say as everyone else is the essence of being viewed as a bearer of rights. In sum, a democratic society in the inclusive, rights and equality respecting sense desired by legal constitutionalists comes from the political constitution embodied in democracy itself.

The following chapters elaborate this critique of legal constitutionalism and defend political constitutionalism. The critique occupies Part I. Chapter 1 explores the constitutional rights project at the heart of legal constitutionalism. It indicates why and how rights belong to the 'circumstances of politics' through being subject to reasonable disagreements. It then details the weaknesses of judicial review as a fair process for resolving these disputes. Courts turn out to suffer from many of the same vices legal constitutionalists criticise in legislatures, though with fewer of the compensating virtues these bodies possess for overcoming them. Meanwhile, many of the advantages claimed for courts are revealed as bogus.

Chapter 2 turns to the rule of law. Though sometimes straightforwardly if mistakenly identified with rights, the defence of the integrity and equity of law provides a distinct argument for a legal constitution. However, there is no canonical form law can take that ensures that it is 'good' or 'just' law, nor can law *per se* rule. Law too lies within the 'circumstances of politics' and requires appropriate processes to certify that persons frame it in ways that treat citizens with equal concern and respect. While judges play a necessary role in upholding legality, so that those laws that are so enacted are applied in consistent and equitable ways, they cannot ensure the laws themselves are not arbitrary. That only comes through a system of popular self-rule in which all citizens enjoy an equal status. Only then can they determine as equals the ways laws will treat them alike or unalike.

Chapter 3 then enquires whether it might not be necessary nonetheless to protect the preconditions of democracy within a constitution. I start by examining the substantive version of this thesis, evident in the above quote from Cherie Booth, whereby a bill of rights is seen as encapsulating democratic values. I then look at arguments that seek to defend equitable democratic processes. Both are found wanting. The second collapses into the first, which returns to the already criticised constitutional rights thesis. I then investigate whether it makes a difference for the constitution itself to have been democratically enacted. I cast doubt on the democratic credentials of such self-binding constitutional moments and contrast unfavourably the populist constitutional politics most proponents of this thesis espouse to the genuinely constitutional and constitutive qualities of normal politics.

This critique sets the scene for defending a democratic political constitutionalism in Part II. Chapter 4 outlines the normative case for a political constitutionalism in terms of the republican notion of freedom as non-domination. Following other republican theorists,[17] I dispute the coherence of the liberal view of negative liberty whereby constitutional government is identified with limited, in the sense of less, government. Rather, constitutionalism seeks to prevent arbitrary rule – that is, rule that can avoid being responsive to the interests of the ruled and fail to provide for the equal consideration of interests. I argue that taking rights out of politics, as legal constitutionalism attempts to do, gives rise to arbitrary rule – criticising along the way those republican theorists who have believed otherwise. The reason is that we have no method – including certain idealised accounts of democracy – for objectively ascertaining those outcomes that will treat all equally. Instead, we can only give individuals equal political resources to determine and contest the collective policies that should apply equally to all and employ processes they can recognise as promoting equal concern and respect.

Chapter 5 investigates the type of processes that might serve this purpose. Following the republican tradition, I argue their chief quality must be to encourage citizens and governments to 'hear the other side'. However, once again I take issue with certain contemporary republican theorists. A number of these have espoused deliberative democracy, on the one hand, and the separation of powers, on the other, as the appropriate means to achieve republican ends. Deliberative democrats assume that disagreements over rights and other matters of public policy can be resolved through a carefully structured form of rational debate. This model mirrors the claims made about the public reasoning of the judiciary by legal theorists. However, like the apologists of judicial deliberation, deliberative theorists provide flimsy epistemological grounds for their claims that

---

[17] Q. Skinner, *Liberty before Liberalism*, Cambridge: Cambridge University Press, 1998 and P. Pettit, *Republicanism: A Theory of Freedom and Government*, Oxford: Clarendon Press, 1997.

such debates can produce the 'best' argument. Though deliberation can sometimes, though not always, improve arguments and move people to a fuller appreciation of their opponents' position, it is unlikely to produce consensus on the most rationally defensible view. On the contrary, deliberation may serve to polarise positions even more by highlighting the points of disagreement. A public reasoning process can only treat all equally through being inclusive and providing a transparent way of treating all views fairly. In other words, public reasoning has to be by the public and employ an impartial decision-making procedure for resolving their disputes. The separation of powers is often seen by legal constitutionalists and certain republican theorists as a necessary check on arbitrary power. By contrast, I argue it too produces arbitrary rule. Not only do its counter-majoritarian checks unfairly favour the *status quo*, potentially entrenching the unjust privileges of historically powerful minorities, but it also offers no incentives for those running these different branches to be responsive to citizens. Instead, I argue for a balance of power between competing aspirants for office. This arrangement creates accountability of the rulers to the ruled, while encouraging citizens to collaborate and compromise with each other. The result of combining procedural public reasoning with the balance of power is to produce both an attentiveness to rights and incentives to legislate in ways that treat all in relevant respects as equal under the law.

Chapter 6 sums up the foregoing argument by showing how the actually existing democratic systems of the main established democracies satisfy the requirements of non-domination. Taken together, majority rule, competition between parties in free and fair elections, and parliamentary government, provide an appropriately constitutional process of public reasoning and the balance of power. Defending majority rule against the critiques of public choice theorists, I argue it offers a fair and impartial procedure that is unlikely to produce either irrational or tyrannical decisions. Rather, it provides an open way whereby all citizens can feel their views and interests have received equal consideration. Meanwhile, competition between political parties in elections and parliament offers a balance of power that renders governments attentive and answerable to the electorate, and citizens tolerant of each other and willing to reciprocate and collaborate. I conclude by exploring a number of potentially hard cases, where the mechanisms that for the most part render legislation equitable and attentive to rights might fail to operate. As I show, legislatures neither perform so poorly nor courts so well for these exceptional cases to provide the basis for a general argument for rights-based judicial review.

Legal and political constitutionalism have often been identified with the American and British political systems respectively. The tendency to take an idealised version of the US Constitution as a model has been particularly prevalent among the highly influential generation of liberal legal constitutional theorists who grew to intellectual maturity under the Warren Court.[18] As a result, despite subsequent research revealing its role to have been atypical and its influence much exaggerated,[19] decisions such as *Brown*[20] have attained a certain iconic status in the legal constitutionalist literature, with the many less congenial Supreme Court judgements simply put to one side.[21] Likewise, parliamentary sovereignty and the Westminster model – no doubt often similarly idealised, if less influential – has frequently provided the model for political constitutionalists.[22] For that reason, I will often illustrate aspects of my argument with examples drawn from these two systems. However, it would be misleading to characterise my argument as a critique of US-style judicial review and a defence of the UK system pre-Human Rights Act. For a start, as I noted above, these two types of constitutionalism exist within most constitutions. There has always been a legal constitutionalist strand within British constitutional culture, and historians have long stressed the republican and political thread running through the American as well as the British constitutional tradition.[23] As a result, I cite evidence to back my criticisms of legal constitutionalism and its supporters from both systems, and align myself in each case with those who have stressed the merits of the political constitutionalist aspects of the American as well as the British polity.[24]

---

[18] For example, the influence of the Warren era is discernible in Dworkin, 'Introduction: The Moral Reading and the Majoritarian Premise', e.g. p. 16, and – in a different way – even more in Ely, *Democracy and Distrust*, pp. 73–5. Though Rawls does not cite either *Brown* or *Roe*, his *Political Liberalism*, New York: Columbia University Press, 1993 is as much an idealisation of US constitutional arrangements and the role of the Supreme Court within them as is, in different ways, Dworkin's theory of judicial interpretation in *Law's Empire*, Oxford: Hart, 1998.

[19] E.g. G. Rosenberg, *The Hollow Hope: Can Courts Bring About Social Change?*, Chicago: University of Chicago Press, 1991.

[20] *Brown v Board of Education* 247 US 483 (1954), 349 US 294 (1955).

[21] For comments on this tendency, see L. Kramer, *The People Themselves: Popular Constitutionalism and Judicial Review*, New York: Oxford University Press, 2004, pp. 229–30; I. Shapiro, *The State of Democratic Theory*, Princeton: Princeton University Press, 2003, pp. 20–21.

[22] E.g. J. G. A. Griffith, 'The Political Constitution', *Modern Law Review*, 42 (1979), pp. 1–21.

[23] E.g. J. G. A. Pocock, *The Machiavellian Moment: Florentine Political Thought and the Atlantic Republican Tradition*, Princeton: Princeton University Press, 1975.

[24] On the US context, I have been most influenced by M. Tushnet, *Taking the Constitution Away from the Courts*, Princeton: Princeton University Press, 1999, Dahl, *How Democratic*

At the same time, my concern is to criticise the very idea of legal constitutionalism and not just its US and British versions.[25] After all, it might
be objected that in many European countries, notably Germany, constitutional judicial review operates rather differently, for example in being
more appreciative of social rights, and so avoids certain of the problems I
identify in British and US judgements. Though I think these substantive
differences are overdrawn, particularly as the European Union promotes
both economic liberalisation and a more adversarial and legalistic regulatory style on the Continent,[26] my main focus is with the procedural
legitimacy of constitutional courts striking down democratically enacted
legislation. In this regard, Continental European courts have been even
more proactive than the US Supreme Court, with French, Italian and
German courts invalidating more national laws in the past thirty years
than it has over the course of its entire history.[27] As in the United States,
the justification for such actions comes from counter-majoritarian arguments – often inspired by British and American practices – that largely
predate modern democratic processes, being established during the nineteenth and early twentieth centuries. Meanwhile, as Unger observes in the
quote cited above, those who have tried to give legal constitutionalism a
democratic foundation have tended to do so in relation to a somewhat
idealised form of democracy that similarly antedates mass electorates and
contemporary party systems.[28] Indeed, this propensity is shared by many
of the scholars behind the republican revival whose writings have to some

Is the American Constitution?, and, with the caveats expressed in chapter 3, Kramer, *The
People Themselves*. For the British context, I draw on the work of Griffith, 'The Political
Constitution' and his *The Politics of the Judiciary*, London: Fontana, 1977, the work of K.
Ewing and C. Gearty in *Freedom under Thatcher: Civil Liberties in Modern Britain*, Oxford:
Oxford University Press, 1990 and *The Struggle for Civil Liberties: Political Freedom and the
Rule of Law in Britain 1914–1945*, Oxford: Oxford University Press, 2001, and A. Tomkins,
Our Republican Constitution, Oxford: Hart, 2005.

[25] In this respect, I follow the approach taken by Waldron in *Law and Disagreement* and 'The
Core of the Case Against Judicial Review', *The Yale Law Journal*, 115 (2006), pp. 1346–406.

[26] See R. D. Kelemen and E. C. Sibbitt, 'The Globalisation of American Law', *International
Organization*, 58 (2004), pp. 103–36.

[27] A. Stone Sweet, 'Why Europe Rejected American Judicial Review. And Why it May Not
Matter', *Michigan Law Review*, 101 (2003), p. 2780.

[28] For example, Habermas's influential arguments, that idealise German constitutional
arrangements in a parallel manner to the way Rawls idealises those of the United States,
contrast 'normative' with 'empirical' accounts of democracy (Habermas, *Between Facts
and Norms*, ch. 7), a distinction that clearly harks back to his account of the eighteenth
century 'public sphere' and its undermining in the nineteenth century in his very first
book on the *Structural Transformation of the Public Sphere: An Inquiry into a Category of
Bourgeois Society*, Cambridge: Polity, 1989. I discuss his arguments in chapter 3.

degree inspired this project. Yet, in arguing that we must look instead to the constitutionality of 'actually existing democracy' I do not wish to idealise these arrangements in their turn and suggest any, least of all the British, are by any means perfect. Rather, just as the critique of legal constitutionalism centres on the inner rationale of constitutional judicial review, so my defence of democracy relates to the underlying logic of existing practices. Because political theory is often divorced from political science, many theorists have failed to explore the mechanisms of democratic politics and so appreciate their normative qualities. The chief aim of this book is to draw attention to these virtues of the democratic process and suggest that the constitutional goods of rights and the rule of law would be better served by developing rather than curtailing them via less effective and legitimate legal constitutional constraints.

PART I

Legal constitutionalism

Constitutional rights and the limits of judicial review

Central to legal constitutionalism is the idea of constitutional rights. Constitutions do many things beyond enshrining rights. But probably nothing has been so influential in driving constitutionalism along the paths of legal rather than political thought than the emphasis on rights, their entrenchment in a constitutional document and their interpretation and elaboration by a supreme or constitutional court. It is this rights focus that gives contemporary constitutionalism its whole juridical cast, whereby a constitution's task is viewed as being to embody the substance of fundamental law rather than to provide a fundamental structure for law-making.

Of course, few people would deny that individuals have certain fundamental interests that should be legally and politically protected. However, a commitment to rights is different to assuming their protection requires their entrenchment in a bill of rights overseen by a constitutional court. Three reasons standardly motivate this position and lie at the heart of legal constitutionalism.[1] First, rights-based judicial review is said to guard against majority tyranny and fecklessness. Though democracy offers a vital mechanism for citizens to pursue their interests and throw out governments that wilfully or negligently override them, prejudice, self-interest or simple thoughtlessness can lead majorities to pass legislation that oppresses minorities or even unwittingly works against their own concerns. Second, the integrity of law is said to depend on rights. Laws often allow more than one interpretation when applied to a given case, or have to be adapted to novel circumstances. In such hard cases, rights are said to provide the principles needed to guide judges towards a decision consistent with the basic values underlying the legal system as a whole. Third, certain rights are said to be implied by the democratic

---

[1] For a useful summary of these arguments, see R. Dworkin, *Freedom's Law: The Moral Reading of the American Constitution*, Oxford: Oxford University Press, 1996, 'Introduction: The Moral Reading and the Majoritarian Premise'.

process itself. Consequently, for a democracy to infringe rights would be self-defeating and inconsistent with its very rationale.

The three chapters comprising Part I of this book will challenge respectively all three arguments of this current orthodoxy. I shall question their underlying assumption that democracy and judicial review are best seen as the means to realise a particular account of rights – be it the account derived from a given, supposedly ideal, theory of justice, that allegedly held by the community, or one presumed to underlie the very idea of a constitutional democracy. Rather, these two mechanisms offer procedures for fairly adjudicating between alternative and occasionally conflicting accounts of rights. Seen in this light, democratic decision-making, including majority rule, is revealed as buttressing rather than threatening rights, as is often assumed. Meanwhile, judicial review performs the more modest, if no less vital, role of maintaining consistency through both the casuistical interpretation of the law and by supplying a means of challenging failures to apply it in an equitable manner.

The need for this alternative and more political approach arises from the contested nature of rights. Despite widespread support for both constitutional rights and rights-based judicial review, theorists, politicians, lawyers and ordinary citizens frequently disagree over which rights merit or require such entrenchment, the legal form they should take, the best way of implementing them, their relationship to each other, and the manner in which courts should understand and uphold them. These are often reasonable differences that are liable to arise in most open and democratic societies. They stem not from any neglect or carelessness about rights but from taking them very seriously indeed. Such disputes rarely involve a questioning of rights *per se*. In fact, there is often broad agreement at the level of abstract principle at which bills are usually framed, though dissent can arise here too.[2] But the interpretation and application of rights to particular circumstances are frequently the source of profound debate and conflict. In these circumstances, ambitious schemes of judicial review that ignore, unduly minimise or somehow seek to trump such disagreements over the meaning and bearing of rights prove hubristic. They risk making judicial decisions appear arbitrary, thereby threatening the legitimacy of the constitution.

This chapter explores the reasons behind disagreements about rights and the weaknesses of judicial review as a forum for resolving them.

---

[2] See R. Bellamy and J. Schönlau, 'The Normality of Constitutional Politics: An Analysis of the Drafting of the EU Charter of Fundamental Rights', *Constellations*, 11:1 (2004), pp. 412–33.

The first section outlines the nature of the constitutional rights project and certain tensions within it. The second section then considers the sources and types of disagreement about rights, locating them within the circumstances of politics. The third section casts doubt on the legitimacy and effectiveness of judicial review as a mechanism for fairly adjudicating these disagreements. Many of the alleged advantages over democratic processes prove on further investigation to be disadvantages. Finally, the fourth section questions whether a bill of rights is necessary to create a culture of rights. This discussion sets the scene for investigating in chapters 2 and 3 how far judicial reasoning and the rule of law depend on constitutional rights, and whether democracy implies a set of rights requiring constitutional protection.

I Constitutional rights and 'the circumstances of justice'

We need rights because of what John Rawls, elaborating on David Hume, termed 'the circumstances of justice': namely, 'the normal conditions under which human cooperation is both possible and necessary'.[3] If there was a superabundance of resources and human beings were unfailingly altruistic (and, it should be added, omniscient too, and so not prone to inadvertently doing the wrong thing), there would be no need for rights.[4] Everyone could pursue their own plans in their own way while avoiding hindering the similar pursuits of others. However, when resources are even moderately scarce and people prone to careless and sometimes malicious behaviour, then, given the inevitability of social coexistence, it becomes necessary to have some common rules capable of coordinating individual activities. Of course, any social and legal rules will stabilise human relations to a degree and create certain rights of either a customary or institutional character. After all, it is ordinary legislation that details what rights we can claim in particular circumstances, indicates precisely who is entitled to a given benefit, such as social security, and lays down when and how it can be requested and provided. Yet, as we shall see in the next chapter, legal rules may not be that just or fair. They can unjustifiably discriminate against (and implicitly or explicitly unduly favour) certain groups of people, even if whatever stability of expectations they do offer helps promote an individual's ability to plan and act freely.

To avoid the possibilities of unjust or unfair law, constitutional bills of rights aspire to operate as a higher law that can be deployed to ensure

---

[3] J. Rawls, *A Theory of Justice*, Cambridge, MA: Harvard University Press, 1971, pp. 126–30.
[4] R. Bellamy, *Rethinking Liberalism*, London: Pinter, 2000, pp. 152–5.

the rules are equitable and protect those vital interests without which humans would lack the capacity to act at all. Laws that fail these tests can be blocked or overturned and, where the absence of law is itself a cause of unfairness or injustice, new laws initiated. Contemporary legal and political theorists – at least those of a liberal disposition – have generally interpreted such bills as aiming less at promoting particular goals and more at enabling citizens to pursue whatever goals they choose in a manner that shows equal concern and respect for the possibility of others – including future generations – doing likewise.[5] Even those measures found in certain constitutions that seek to entrench a value especially dear to a particular community, such as certain national languages or religious faiths, have been defended, albeit contentiously, as necessary to ensure equal recognition to different cultures and forms of human flourishing.[6] Such rights certainly constrain how people pursue their goals and rule out certain of them as incompatible with any plausible form of equitable social existence. But their underlying purpose is to foster the autonomy of individuals to choose their own way of life without unjustifiably constraining or being constrained by others. In sum, for liberals at least, a rights-based constitutionalism offers not a vision of the good life but a necessary framework for each person freely to pursue his or her own vision.[7]

Most constitutions contain three types of rights in order to achieve this objective.[8] The first type concerns human well-being in a general sense. These rights protect bodily integrity and what many Continental bills refer to as human dignity, for example through provisions against torture; promote individual liberty of thought and action, notably freedom

---

[5] E.g. J. Rawls, *Political Liberalism*, New York: Columbia University Press, 1993, Lecture 5 and B. Barry, *Justice as Impartiality*, Oxford: Clarendon Press, 1995, pp. 83–5.

[6] Most notably by Will Kymlicka, *Multicultural Citizenship: A Liberal Theory of Minority Rights*, Oxford: Clarendon Press, 1995.

[7] Obviously, not everyone accepts this liberal neutralist argument for rights, and certain criticisms of this approach made by communitarians and perfectionists will be rehearsed and partly endorsed below. I single out this approach because it alone insists that rights must be primary, regardless of one's other beliefs and concerns, at least among those who accept certain basic premises of a democratic regime – particularly some version of political equality. I adopt very similar assumptions but argue they lead to quite different conclusions.

[8] I have adapted these categories from Ronald Dworkin's account of the values underlying a constitutional democracy in his *Law's Empire*, London: Fontana, 1986. Of course, I am not suggesting that any constitution actually groups rights in this way. Moreover, although the first and usually the second categories often, if not always, appear in a specific bill of rights, many in the third category are detailed in the body of the constitution describing the workings of the political system and its institutions.

of conscience; defend private property, often work and welfare too; and in many cases marriage and the family. This type of right offers the supposed prerequisites for individuals to make the autonomous and responsible choices that enable them to secure their livelihoods and engage in a range of meaningful relationships. The second type includes rights relating to the rule of law, notably the need for due process and equality before the law. Finally, the third type refers to rights of a more strictly political character. These are the rights entailed by a functioning democracy. Some of them may be peculiar to the regime of the country concerned, such as the dates when elected federal politicians' terms end specified in the Twentieth Amendment of the US Constitution. However, they standardly sit alongside more abstract protections for freedom of expression, association and assembly.

These three types of rights relate respectively to the three arguments supporting rights-based judicial review noted at the start of this chapter. Broadly speaking, the first set emphasise justice, the second consistency and the last fairness.[9] All three are valuable qualities that promote individual autonomy and political legitimacy. Justice ensures people receive their due and have their interests respected, consistency lets them know where they stand, and fairness gives everyone the chance to be consulted and assures they are dealt with in an even-handed manner. Each of these factors can and frequently does support the others. Nevertheless, though these rights form a package, there are certain tensions between them. Justice can require discrimination to recognise a special case or be procedurally unfair. Consistency may be a necessary feature of law but, as I noted, is insufficient to yield either fairness or justice. Fairness, in the procedural senses of giving everyone a say and possibly ensuring decisions are proportionate to the views of those concerned, need not always result in consistent or just outcomes.

Most defences of constitutional rights recognise the various claims of each of these three considerations yet seek to harmonise them in some way. A common position, which I shall focus on here, has been to stress the primacy of the first set of rights over the other two, usually by suggesting that it is in some way implied by or intrinsic to them. For example, justice may be equated with (or deemed necessary for) coherence or a sophisticated form of legal consistency,[10] or be seen as the outcome of

---

[9] E.g. see Dworkin, *Law's Empire.*
[10] In different ways, L. Fuller, *The Morality of Law*, revised edition, New Haven: Yale University Press, 1969, F. A. Hayek, *Rules and Order*, London: Routledge, 1973 and Dworkin, *Law's Empire* emphasise this aspect.

(or a precondition for) a fair procedure, reflecting an implicit consensus amongst democratic citizens required by the very process of democracy itself,[11] or be associated with some combination of all these positions.[12] In these accounts, judicial review is justified as providing a less biased and more stable procedure for adjudication, one that more closely approximates an idealised form of public reasoning, than could be supplied by any legislature. Such claims are partly empirical, though as we shall see the evidence for them is far from unequivocal. However, the main focus will be on their normative grounding. Underlying them is the belief that at some level the role of a constitution must be to promote an agreed account of justice – indeed, that the very integrity as well as the rationale of a constitutional system depends on its doing so.[13] By contrast, I shall maintain that no such agreement is likely to be available. If so, then the character and task of a constitution is radically different. Its purpose cannot be to preserve a certain pattern of just relations among citizens. Rather, it offers them fair procedures to work through their disagreements about justice and, where necessary, come to collective decisions that can be equitably enforced. In other words, instead of reading the rights regarding fairness and consistency through those defining justice, we need to reverse this perspective and see this latter set of rights as emerging from (and being challengeable by) the processes associated with the former two sets. As I noted, how substantive the rights implied by these legal and democratic procedures are, and whether they should be constitutionalised and judicially protected in their turn, will be addressed in later chapters.

II Constitutional rights and 'the circumstances of politics'

Though people may agree that the circumstances of justice render rights necessary, they disagree about which rights these are, their nature, bearing and relations. Does the right to life rule out abortion; how far does the right to property restrict transfer payments for welfare; when, if ever, should freedom of speech give way to privacy? The list of potential divisions over the meaning and application of rights appears potentially endless. This

---

[11] Rawls, *Political Liberalism* and J. Habermas, *Between Facts and Norms: Contributions to a Discourse Theory of Law and Democracy*, trans. W. Rehg, Cambridge: Polity, 1996 both adopt this sort of argument, albeit with important differences and nuances.

[12] Probably most accounts that prioritise constitutional rights, including those cited in earlier footnotes, can be seen as synthesising some form of all these positions, though they emphasise different ones and interpret them in differing ways.

[13] As Rawls puts it, a 'well-ordered society' is one 'in which everyone accepts, and knows that everyone accepts, the very same principles of justice'. Rawls, *Political Liberalism*, p. 35.

predicament poses a problem for the constitutional rights project. For if we need rights because of the circumstances of justice, it appears that we have to identify and interpret them in what Jeremy Waldron and Albert Weale, among others, have called the circumstances of politics: namely, a situation where we need a collectively binding agreement, because our lives will suffer without it, yet opinions and interests diverge as to what its character should be and no single demonstrably best solution is available.[14] If rights form part of the subject of politics, then their ability to constitute the political sphere will be seriously limited. We will not be able to define or interpret rights on the basis of their congruence with an agreed account of truth and justice. Instead, the legitimacy of any constitutional or legislative rights will rest on the fairness of the procedures employed to resolve people's disagreements about them and their coherence as a package. Instead of constitutional rights legitimating the political system, the constitution of the political process will be the guarantor of the acceptability of the system of rights.

It is sometimes objected that disagreements over rights occur solely due to self-interest, ignorance or prejudice leading people to seek to perpetuate various sources of injustice. Wittingly or unwittingly this is no doubt often the case. Yet, as John Rawls has observed, they also arise from what he calls 'the burdens of judgement . . . the many hazards involved in the correct (and conscientious) exercise of our powers of reason and judgement in the ordinary course of political life'.[15] Rawls lists the following six 'more obvious' (and, in his view, least controversial) factors as contributing to a divergence of judgement amongst reasonable people:[16] (1) the difficulty of identifying and assessing often complicated empirical evidence with regard to any given case; (2) disagreement about the weighting of different considerations even when there is agreement about which are relevant; (3) the vagueness and indeterminacy of our concepts, which makes them subject to hard cases; (4) the effect of the different life experiences of people, which in complex societies vary widely, on the ways they assess evidence and weigh moral and political values; (5) the different kinds of normative consideration, each with different force, on both sides of an issue, which make overall assessments problematic; and (6) the impossibility of any social and political system being able to accommodate all values.

---

[14] J. Waldron, *Law and Disagreement*, Oxford: Oxford University Press, 1999, pp. 107–18, A. Weale, *Democracy*, Basingstoke: Macmillan, 1999, pp. 8–13.
[15] Rawls, *Political Liberalism*, pp. 55–6.   [16] Ibid., pp. 56–7.

Rawls cites these six factors as making it impossible to base a stable political settlement on a consensus around a comprehensive conception of the good. Yet, as a number of commentators have remarked, they raise equal doubts about a consensus on the right.[17] For example, think of the debates over whether freedom of speech can be restricted in the case of 'pornography'. First, it is notoriously difficult to assess the evidence concerning the harm pornography may cause in inciting violence against women or lowering the esteem in which they are held and hold themselves. Second, even were there agreement on some of these facts, not everyone would weigh them in the same way because of the other four factors. Third, the concept of 'speech' has proved infamously slippery and vague, producing long discussions over the degree to which a performance or figurative art count as 'speech' and so on. This vagueness is not just superficial nit-picking about the ordinary usage of words, but can extend to the core normative assumptions involved in certain key terms – for example, over whether 'speech' suggests some form of reasoned argumentation and what that entails. Disputes at this level can render terms 'essentially contestable',[18] with a number of rival conceptions of a concept in play, each of which will highlight a different (if often overlapping) sphere of applicability for any right. Fourth, different life experiences are no doubt an important factor in explaining why most women – even those who do not agree with a ban – feel more strongly about, or have greater understanding of the feelings raised by, this issue than most men. Fifth, this is a matter where focusing on different types of moral claim can produce different assessments and make an 'overall', 'on balance' judgement hard to make. An assessment that looks at the consequences for social attitudes towards women is likely to be more sympathetic to restrictions than one focused narrowly on the deontological claims of particular parties. After all, speech is restricted in the case of tobacco advertising in part because widespread smoking is regarded as socially as well as personally harmful. Glamorising smoking is also seen as encouraging young people to take it up. Sexually explicit advertising on TV is limited for partly similar reasons related to public morality and its effects on children. Finally, the issue potentially raises a clash of rights of either a logical or contingent character. In such cases, we are forced to compare incommensurable goods and whichever decision we take entails some loss. We may decide, say, that the risk to a woman's

[17] E.g. B. Bower, 'The Limits of Public Reason', *Journal of Philosophy*, 91 (1994), p. 21.
[18] See W. B. Gallie, 'Essentially Contested Concepts', *Proceedings of the Aristotelian Society*, 56 (1955–6), pp. 167–98 and more generally W. E. Connolly, *The Terms of Political Discourse*, Oxford: Blackwell, 1974.

right not to be discriminated against is less than the problems and possible consequences of restricting freedom of speech. But the comparison of the values involved is always going to be contentious because there is no metric for saying the one is more important than the other. After all, some would counter even a small risk of gender discrimination is worse than a greater than necessary curtailment of free speech.

The burdens of judgement reflect the practical limits of human reason rather than any meta-ethical or epistemological thesis regarding pluralism or scepticism. They do not entail that no agreement on the right might be reached in principle, merely that they are unlikely in practice – whatever theory of rights one might employ. Indeed, it should be noted that the burdens of judgement operate to create differences not only over how an agreed conception of rights might be applied in a particular case, but also between rival accounts of rights, as in the debate between 'choice' and 'benefit' approaches.[19] As Rawls notes, none of these differences need be attributed to self-interest, lack of knowledge, bias or bad faith.[20] The complexity of the issue, the distinctiveness of people's standpoints and the diversity of their perspectives are sufficient to explain why people disagree in these various ways. Moreover, these circumstances can largely be ascribed to the very interests and values rights theorists are generally concerned to protect: namely, autonomy of thought and action, openness and pluralism. For it is only in an open society that allows freedom of thought and action that the plurality of views, attachments and ways of life that give rise to the burdens of judgement will develop. Some theorists argue that in this case we need rights that will protect the preconditions for autonomy. Yet, these too will be subject to dispute on exactly the same grounds. For example, whereas some see market outcomes as potentially inhibiting the capacity for autonomy of those who lose out, others regard them as the products of entirely autonomous choices that could only be altered at the expense of autonomy. Whereas the first see socio-economic rights as autonomy promoting, the second regard them as diminishing autonomy by undercutting, rather than complementing, the basic civil rights on which it depends.

A number of features of the resulting disagreements over rights serve to place them firmly within the 'circumstances of politics'. First, as the last example indicates, debates over the nature or interpretation of rights

---

[19] For good overviews of these debates see J. Waldron's 'Introduction' to his edited collection *Theories of Rights*, Oxford: Oxford University Press, 1984 and P. Jones, *Rights*, Basingstoke: Macmillan, 1994, ch. 2.

[20] Rawls, *Political Liberalism*, p. 58.

often mirror many political arguments amongst the wider public, such as those between conservative libertarians and social democrats. This feature might lead to the suspicion that these arguments over rights are not 'genuine' but are in some sense politically motivated and so suspect. However, this suggestion misses the point that people's political preferences are intimately related to their principled judgements over what individuals and groups are entitled to. In other words, their political divisions result from principled differences about rights as much as conflicts of interest and policy preferences.

Second, these disagreements about rights not only give rise to political differences but also produce different accounts of the nature of the political. The various dimensions of rights are tied up with how we define the 'polity' and 'regime' of a given state. At the 'polity' level, they demarcate both who is a subject or citizen, to and from whom certain special obligations are owed by the state, and the territorial and functional spheres over which it holds sway. At the 'regime' level, they delineate both the accepted styles of politics, for example the type of electoral system and the permissibility of various sorts of protests, such as political strikes and demonstrations, and the scope of government activity, such as whether it is merely regulatory or distributive as well. Thus, the rights implied by different policy proposals will also have implications for how the political realm is to be configured.[21] The conservative libertarian's disagreement with the social democrat over welfare spending, say, is also linked to a different conception of the scope of politics, since he will tend to be less interventionist; its sphere, as he will probably wish to exclude many aspects of the economy; and even its subjects, who he may regard largely as economic agents and consumers rather than as citizens in the political sense. As a result, rights cannot constitute the political sphere within which arguments over policy may take place. Indeed, the desire for a change in the structure of the polity and/or the regime may be at the heart of the policy dispute. Thus, debates between libertarians and social democrats are not within a political framework of rights, they are about that framework. Nor can we, as some suggest, separate out 'normal' and 'constitutional' politics.[22] The very constitution of the political will always

---

[21] For a full analysis of the debates over these dimensions of rights, see R. Bellamy, 'Constitutive Citizenship versus Constitutional Rights: Republican Reflections on the EU Charter and the Human Rights Act', in T. Campbell, K. D. Ewing and A. Tomkins (eds.), *Sceptical Essays on Human Rights*, Oxford: Oxford University Press, 2001, especially pp. 17–21.

[22] E.g. B. Ackerman, *We the People: Foundations*, Cambridge, MA: Harvard University Press, 1991, pp. 3–33.

be at issue within any normal political debate. Of course, there can still be exceptional 'constitutional moments' when a particularly momentous transformation is proposed, such as the secession of a particular territory. Yet these revolutionary changes are frequently the cumulative result of a series of incremental reforms having produced a gradual alteration in public opinion. After all, Ronald Reagan and Margaret Thatcher aimed at changing the role and nature of the state rather than just giving a New Right twist to government policy for the duration of their administrations. Most politicians inevitably end up with similar ambitions, even if they are less successful or desire less dramatic changes.

Third, different accounts of rights may be not just contrasting but also incompatible and incommensurable. For example, I noted above how social democrats see social rights as promoting autonomy, whereas libertarians regard the taxation required to support them as 'on a par with forced labour'.[23] One cannot overcome this dilemma by trying to identify either a minimal set of 'core' rights all should adhere to, as libertarians sometimes claim, or a maximal set that somehow finds a place for all combinations of rights, as social democrats often attempt to do. Their views of coercion and interference not only differ, they also conflict. Moreover, because of the 'burdens of judgement', no agreed metric or common currency exists for saying which view is superior. Rather, each highlights a different perspective on the nature of rights arising from differing world views and moral concerns all of which can claim, in their own terms, some degree of validity. Indeed, even within an agreed account of the substance of rights, we will be faced with the fact that not all rights prove compossible and the 'burdens of judgement' make it hard to agree the right balance between them in particular cases. People may still differ about a right's sphere and scope, and hence when it is infringed and what is required to secure it. To the extent a society requires a collective agreement, therefore, it will have to be on some other basis than citizens convincing each other of the truth of a given position.

These points suggest that rights form part of the 'circumstances of politics' in three related ways. First, disagreements about rights inform normal political debates no less than conflicts of interest. Therefore, a consensus on rights cannot be said to stand somehow outside politics. Second, these normal political debates extend to the very constitution of the political. So we cannot see an agreed constitutional framework of rights as somehow offering the basis and limits for the ordinary political process. Third,

---

[23] R. Nozick, *Anarchy, State and Utopia*, Oxford: Blackwell, 1974, p. 169.

people's views of rights are often incompatible and incommensurable and so cannot be simply combined into a single all-encompassing position that overcomes the very need for politics.[24] Even if such a position might in principle exist, the 'burdens of judgement' mean that we are unlikely ever to overcome our perceived conflicts and agree on it. In the meantime, we must confront a situation where despite our disagreements we nevertheless need to agree on a common view.

There seems little alternative in these circumstances than to search for a procedure that all accept as either legitimising one of the views in contention prevailing over all others, regardless of their own opinion as to its substantive merits, or that manages to secure some sort of mutually acceptable accommodation or compromise between the different views. Such a procedure must treat the different perspectives and persons who hold them fairly, showing individuals equal concern and respect not just as rights holders but as autonomous agents who have their own reasoned and reasonable views about rights, but not be itself biased towards favouring, or derive its legitimacy from, any given account of rights – for the validity of the various possible theories and conceptions is what is in dispute. The next section discusses the suitability of judicial review for this role.

III The tyranny of the minority: why judicial review fails to take rights seriously

That rights belong to the 'circumstances of politics' need not necessarily mean that politics *per se* offers the best means for resolving the reasonable disagreements surrounding them. If the disputes are too divisive for the parties involved to treat each other fairly, then third-party arbitration might provide the best solution. These sorts of grounds are often adduced in support of judicial review. It is defended almost by default as supplying a necessary counter to the supposed failings of democratic politics. Common assumptions about the inadequacy of democracy in promoting and protecting rights, such as that it rests on self-interested bargaining and leads to tyrannous majorities, will be challenged in Part II, particularly chapter 6. Here I want to explore whether judicial review escapes these failings and offers compensating strengths of its own.

---

[24] This possibility might be viewed as an idealist version of K. Marx, 'On the Jewish Question', in *Early Writings*, Harmondsworth: Penguin, 1975, whereby the ideational as opposed to the structural sources of political conflict are removed, so that the sole legitimate role of the state is the efficient administration of things in accordance with an agreed account of justice.

The comparative assessment of democratic and judicial processes is generally made in terms of their respective merits as mechanisms for treating individuals with equal concern and respect with regard to 'input', on the one hand, and 'output', on the other.[25] 'Input' considerations relate to who participates in a given decision procedure. These may be quite distinct from, and pull in opposite directions to, 'output' considerations – as when we regard someone as entitled to go their own way, even at the cost of making mistakes. In politics, the main 'input' related reasons concern the right for all citizens to participate in political decision-making on an equal basis to others through some form of democracy. By contrast, 'output' considerations relate to designing a procedure so that it produces good or right decisions. As I noted above, given that we disagree about rights, these considerations cannot be orientated towards favouring a particular, controversial outcome. Rather, they are driven by more general thoughts about the likelihood of certain types of procedure to treat the issues at hand in a conscientious and even-handed manner so as to get at the true substance of the matter.

Conventionally, democracy has been viewed as overwhelmingly stronger than courts with regard to 'input' criteria, with courts doing better on 'outputs'. Indeed, some defenders of judicial review have been inclined to dismiss the relevance of 'input' measures altogether, or to view them as secondary.[26] In Part II, particularly chapter 4, I shall show why we should take these 'input' considerations seriously when it comes to constitutional questions, arguing against those who ignore or undervalue them. There and in chapters 3 and 5 I shall also question one rather strong version of the 'output' argument: namely, that we should see constitutional rights as implied by, and the products of, an ideal democratic procedure that structures judicial reasoning.[27] As advocates of judicial review rightly note, 'no political procedure is an instance of perfect procedural justice'.[28] They need to acknowledge the same can be said of courts.[29] This

---

[25] See. J. Waldron, 'The Core of the Case Against Judicial Review', *Yale Law Journal*, 115 (2006), pp. 1372–5. Waldron calls them 'process-related' and 'outcome related' reasons, but given both are processes I find the first term not entirely satisfactory (though I confess to not being completely satisfied with 'input' either).

[26] E.g. J. Raz, 'Disagreement in Politics', *American Journal of Jurisprudence*, 43 (1998), pp. 45–6.

[27] As we shall see, this is the argument adopted by Rawls, *Political Liberalism*, Lecture 6.

[28] S. Freeman, 'Constitutional Democracy and the Legitimacy of Judicial Review', *Law and Philosophy*, 9 (1990), p. 327.

[29] J. Waldron, 'Freeman's Defense of Judicial Review', *Law and Philosophy*, 13 (1994), pp. 27–41.

section considers a more modest and realistic version of the 'output' case, whereby courts simply offer a corrective to certain potential drawbacks of democratic decision-making about rights.

Its worth noting that at a general level democratic and judicial processes employ similar standards of what best conduces to good 'outputs'. Each seeks to weigh relevant views and evidence in a fair, impartial and equitable manner that is not biased towards any given outcome. Of course, where a bill of rights exists, courts are expected to give a judgement in accord with it. But so are legislatures when they pass laws or make policy. Like them, a court can only express what most of its members think the relevant bill dictates in a given case. And even in the absence of a bill of rights, rights-based arguments figure not just in courts but also in legislatures and electoral campaigns. So, the alleged superiority of courts cannot be said to consist of their considering rights whereas democratic processes do not. Rather, their supposed advantage will have to lie in their processes being somehow more scrupulous in considering them than democratic ones.

Why might this be so? As I noted, the standard argument is that whereas a system of equal votes and majority rule treats all the same with regard to 'input' it often fails to treat them as equals when it comes to 'output'. This weakness allegedly arises for three main and interrelated reasons. First, democracy aggregates votes and so risks sacrificing individuals to the collective welfare. Second, democratic decisions are said to be swayed by those who shout the loudest or can apply most pressure at a given time, rather than treating each argument on its merits according to set-tled criteria. Third, both these problems reflect the danger of democratic majorities oppressing minorities and not engaging with their concerns at all. By contrast, courts are assumed to possess three compensating features. First, they focus on individuals rather than the collectivity. Second, they are independent and bound by legal norms and precedent. Third, both these characteristics provide a counter-majoritarian check that serves to protect the rights of minorities. According to this picture, courts and democracy offer complementary qualities that neatly balance utility and rights.[30] However, in the event of a clash, those of the courts should always take precedence because they defend the long-term interest all individuals have in ensuring their basic rights are upheld in ways that treat them as worthy of equal concern and respect.

[30] As H. L. A. Hart, 'Between Utility and Rights', *Columbia Law Review*, 79 (1979), pp. 828–46 noted, this desire forms a *leitmotif* of much contemporary analytical jurisprudence, particularly that of figures such as Rawls and Dworkin who inspire many of the arguments for rights-based judicial review of the kind criticised here.

In what follows, I shall dispute this argument. As I said, I reserve the direct defence of democracy to Part II. However, it is as important to consider the positive arguments for judicial review in their own terms and assess how far courts do indeed manifest these allegedly superior qualities and whether they yield the benefits their proponents hope for.[31] I shall argue that they are often absent and to the extent they are not their presence is frequently detrimental rather than beneficial to rights. In fact, constitutional courts have a disturbing tendency to have many of the vices attributed to democracy without any of the virtues of those processes. And the reason is precisely that these judicial checks constitute blocks on democracy and, as a consequence, on political equality. To employ the republican language to be introduced in Part II, they operate as sources of domination – not just with regard to 'inputs', but also with regard to 'outputs'. Only mechanisms that view all individuals as entitled to the same 'input', because each person is considered an equally valid source of reason and information, end up treating everyone as equals when it comes to 'outputs'. The two types of procedural consideration turn out to be related. To the extent democracy promotes this goal and judicial review undermines it, the latter rather than the former offers the main source of danger with respect to tyranny.

To see why, let us explore in turn each of the three supposed advantages of courts enumerated above. The first relates to rights being attached to individuals. It is sometimes argued that it goes against the very rationale of at least basic human rights to treat them as subject to the bargaining and horse-trading that typically characterises political decision-making. Such processes are said to be fine when dealing with policy matters that aspire to serve some collective goal of the community as a whole. In these cases, it is legitimate to expect people to modify their personal goals to fit in with what is best for all. However, rights are 'individual political goals' that should not be subordinated to notions of the 'general interest'.[32] As such, rights must stand outside the weighing of the different demands and concerns of the community that is the appropriate sphere of politics.[33] They mark the boundaries of what any individual can ever be expected

---

[31] As Aileen Kavanagh, 'Participation and Judicial Review: A Reply to Jeremy Waldron', *Law and Philosophy*, 22 (2003), pp. 451–86, rightly notes, citizens have as much an interest in 'good governance' as participation. However, I dispute her claims that judicial review proves superior to democracy in achieving it.

[32] R. Dworkin, *Taking Rights Seriously*, London: Duckworth, pp. 91, 269.

[33] As I have noted, some theorists also place the rights they hold to underpin democracy in this category. I presented some objections to this view at the end of section II and shall deal with these arguments more fully in chapter 3.

to trade, and so may justifiably 'trump' these sorts of decisions.[34] The advantage of courts, therefore, lies in their focusing on the rights of specific individuals in particular cases.

There are a number of problems with this argument.[35] For a start, the cases tried by courts may relate to individuals but they create public policy. By the time cases come to the higher courts debate turns almost entirely on the matters of constitutional principle they raise rather than the specific concerns of the individual rights holders involved. Indeed, these cases often have been selected by advocacy groups precisely because they offer an appropriate test case for a given general issue. However, if more is at stake than a specific individual's entitlement under the prevailing law, then courts no longer offer an appropriate forum. To devise a collective policy on some abstract question of rights on the basis of a single case produces all sorts of distortions, for the contrast between individual rights and the collective good proves misleading.

The portrayal of rights as a two-term relation, whereby x has a right to some y, has a peremptory quality. However, the specification of rights is always a three-term relation that involves identifying the duty holders who must give effect to x's right and takes into account the consequences of so doing on their rights and hence the correlative duties of x to them. This whole process of specification will involve making choices from amongst various reasonable alternative conceptions of rights and their bearing within particular circumstances. These choices largely determine the patterns and character of human development and interaction within a society. They structure the behaviour of all individuals. Consequently, in deciding how to overcome conflicts between different conceptions of rights or the enjoyment by different persons of the same or different rights, one is in effect always making a judgement about the common good of the community.[36] A sort of utility of rights will be necessary precisely in order to ascertain what balance of rights most accords with the 'general interest'. Indeed, rights charters often refer to the legitimacy of limiting certain rights 'for the purpose of securing due recognition of and respect for the rights of others and of meeting the just requirements of morality, public order and the general welfare in a democratic society'.[37]

---

[34] E.g. Dworkin, *Taking Rights Seriously*, p. 191.
[35] See Waldron, 'The Core of the Case Against Judicial Review', pp. 1379–80.
[36] J. Finnis, *Natural Law and Natural Rights*, Oxford: Clarendon Press, 1980, pp. 214, 219.
[37] E.g. Articles 8–11 of the European Convention for the Protection of Human Rights and Fundamental Freedoms (1950).

In fact, many rights are better seen as defending public goods than as individual entitlements *per se*.[38] For example, freedom of speech is rarely exercised by most citizens. It is valued mainly by journalists and politicians, with others having little direct interest in it. Yet everyone benefits from living in the kind of society where speech is not subject to political or other forms of censorship. For all gain from the ways the criticism and dissent voiced by politicians and journalists helps combat tyranny, corruption or mere incompetence and complacency by governments and other powerful groups. Thus, freedom of speech operates as a public good. We measure the limits of the individual exercise of this right by its tendency to undermine that good, for to uphold it in the face of that diffuse benefit would seem perverse. Notions of libel, for example, largely draw on this understanding – giving out misleading information benefits nobody. Likewise, 'official secrets' consists of information that would damage the public interest if such matters as the location of nuclear weapons were generally known. In other words, rights can be seen as supporting a certain kind of social environment. Rights do not 'trump' notions of the collective good because they only make sense in so far as they contribute to that good and provide a suitable range of individual opportunities for all members of the community.

When it comes to considering this sort of general issue, legislatures have the advantage of numbers. Rights legislation will affect millions of individuals in a myriad of different ways. As I shall detail in chapter 6, legislatures can claim to represent the views and experience of all citizens on such questions. By contrast, the need to decide constitutional questions in the context of a single case means not all interested parties will have standing before the court, notwithstanding the opportunities for multiple-party suits and an *amicus* brief for non-parties. As a result, they are less able than legislatures to assess the impact of a particular view of rights on the community as a whole and to anticipate its potential consequences for the social, political and economic system.[39] There is also the possible atypicality of the case itself. In fact legislatures can also pass legislation that responds to individual cases. However, they are often rightly criticised for doing so. Laws like the notorious UK Dangerous Dogs Act

---

[38] I take this argument from J. Raz, 'Rights and Individual Well-Being', in his *Ethics in the Public Domain: Essays in the Morality of Law and Politics*, Oxford: Clarendon Press, 1994, ch. 3, though I draw different conclusions regarding judicial review to his.

[39] See C. Eisgruber, *Constitutional Self-Government*, Cambridge, MA: Harvard University Press, 2001, pp. 165–73, cited in Waldron, 'The Core of the Case Against Judicial Review', p. 1380, n. 93 and A. Tomkins, *Our Republican Constitution*, Oxford: Hart, 2005, pp. 27–30.

of 1991, passed in the wake of some vicious attacks on children by certain breeds of dogs, have a way of backfiring because they attempt to formulate general policy to address a small number of specific and possibly uncommon cases. As the phrase goes, hard cases make bad law.

What about those rights that charters usually treat as having no limitations, such as the rights not to be tortured or enslaved? These are surely moral absolutes that brook no compromise, often being stated in the negative form that 'no one shall be' (as opposed to the positive form that 'everyone shall be entitled to') in order to underline their unconditional status.[40] It is certainly not part of my argument to deny either that torture and slavery are inconsistent with the very idea of viewing individuals as being equal bearers of rights, or that retrospective criminal legislation – the other Article the European Convention on Human Rights states in this unequivocal form – is likely to be at odds with a legal system that treats all as equal under the law. On the contrary, as chapter 4 explains, the basis for the democratic approach advocated in this book is to prevent the domination exemplified by slavery and with it the capacity to rule others in arbitrary ways. Nevertheless, even granting the importance of these rights, it is far from obvious that constitutional judicial review provides the best way to protect them.

For a start, it is not clear that our reasons for viewing these kinds of rights as so important are ones that mechanisms that might be biased towards the collective rather than individual good will fail to appreciate. True, there could be countervailing 'greater good' arguments for torturing individuals, such as to secure information from terrorists about the whereabouts of a ticking bomb that places many innocent people in imminent danger. However, such arguments are motivated by a concern to maximise the number of individual rights that are protected that is itself rights-based. To appeal to the right of an individual to 'trump' the rights of many other individuals has seemed to many somehow self-contradictory.[41] As Charles Fried remarks, 'it seems fanatical to maintain the absoluteness of the judgement, to do right even if the heavens will

---

[40] This argument is made by Finnis, *Natural Law and Natural Rights*, pp. 211–12, who notes how, for example, Article 3 of the European Convention for the Protection of Human Rights and Fundamental Freedoms (1950) states that 'no one shall be subjected to torture or to inhuman or degrading treatment or punishment'. Articles 4 and 7 are also stated in this form and are the only Articles from which there can be no derogation (Article 15.2).

[41] As V. Bufacchi and J. M. Arrigo, 'Torture, Terrorism and the State: A Refutation of the Ticking-Bomb Argument', *Journal of Applied Philosophy*, 23 (2006), pp. 355–73, to whom the following argument is indebted, note, many of those making rights-based arguments against torture have been willing to accept this possibility as a hypothetical exception to

fall'.[42] Rather than appealing to the absolute right of an individual to override the basic rights of many others, even when he or she may be responsible for their infringement, it seems more appropriate to challenge the consequentialist reasoning on which such logical possibilities are based and point to the collective costs of adopting such policies – even *in extremis*.[43] Torture is a notoriously unreliable method for extracting information and to break the resistance of hardened individuals can be a lengthy process. As a result, there is a low probability such measures would work, while the danger of their being abused is high. They allow a degree of arbitrariness and moral insensitivity that can infect key social institutions, from the police and security services to the legal, medical and governmental establishments, thereby endangering the rights of all citizens. Historically, it was something like this mixture of rights-based and utilitarian considerations rather than straightforward rights-trumping arguments that prompted moves for the abolition of both torture and the death penalty.[44] As with other rights, there are good reasons for thinking the collective aspects of these morally urgent rights are likely to be treated more adequately in a legislative than a judicial setting precisely because the collectivity is represented.

Certain other weaknesses of the judicial process, explored below, may also make it a less appropriate mechanism than ordinary legislation for safeguarding these rights. Though these rights merit absolute protection, there will still be grey areas as to what actions precisely they cover – what counts as 'torture' or, in the case of slavery, 'forced and compulsory labour'. Focus on the legal interpretation of a form of words may unnecessarily narrow and distort the full range of moral arguments that need to be raised. Think of the way the US debate on the death penalty has been warped in this way, centring attention on devising mechanisms for humane killing rather than the utility and justification of such punishments in the first place. By contrast, in Britain capital punishment, which legal constitutionalists have a habit of blithely assuming the popular masses overwhelmingly support, was abolished by the legislature in part because juries had begun to rebel against the instructions of hanging

---

the general prohibition. E.g. H. Shue, 'Torture', in S. Levinson (ed.), *Torture: A Collection*, Oxford: Oxford University Press, 2004, p. 57, though he has since changed his mind (the original article was published in 1977).

[42] C. Fried, *Right and Wrong*, Cambridge, MA: Harvard University Press, 1978, p. 10.

[43] Bufacchi and Arrigo, 'Torture, Terrorism and the State', pp. 362–7.

[44] See, for example, the classic discussion in C. Beccaria, *On Crimes and Punishments*, ed. Richard Bellamy, Cambridge: Cambridge University Press, 1995, ch. 16.

judges and refuse to convict, not least because they doubted its efficacy and worried about its abuse.[45] In other words, they did so not simply to uphold the individual criminal's right but out of a legitimate concern for the consequences of such practices for the rights of all people.

These points lead neatly to doubts about the advantages of the second quality that supposedly means judges consider the question of rights more scrupulously than legislators: namely, their assumed isolation from populist pressures and consequent ability to deliberate and reason on the basis of moral principle and the law, rather than simply bargaining to maximise their constituents' interests so that the majority view rather than the best argument wins out. A number of assumptions underlie this argument, all of them problematic. First, it ignores the links that often justifiably exist between interests and rights. For example, the struggle by women and workers to obtain the franchise was precisely so that their interests would be represented and their rights acknowledged. Thus, in Britain the achievement of political rights through popular pressure in the late nineteenth and early twentieth centuries was the route to obtaining important social and economic rights regarding working conditions through the ordinary legislative process. By contrast, during the same period in the United States, roughly from 1885 to 1935, the state and federal courts struck down some 150 pieces of similar labour legislation.[46] In this respect, the fact that interests are represented in the legislature in a way they are not in courts counts in its favour, not against it. The need to represent broad constituencies enlarges the range of experiences with which law-makers must acquaint themselves and seek to address, so that it is less likely they will ignore – through ignorance or prejudice – the impact of certain policies on underprivileged groups from outside the elite classes. Consider, for example, the blocking of legislation outlawing child labour in the United States. Passed by Congress in 1916, the Supreme Court deemed it unconstitutional in 1918 by a 5:4 vote, leading Congress to pass new legislation that was invalidated in its turn in 1922. A proposed constitutional amendment just failed to get the necessary 2/3 majority to succeed, but overwhelming popular support for such measures led Congress to legislate again in 1938, though the Supreme Court only endorsed it in 1941.[47] This sorry tale of judicial blocking indicates

[45] V. A. C. Gatrell, *The Hanging Tree: Execution and the English People 1770–1868*, Oxford: Oxford University Press, 1994.

[46] Waldron, *Law and Disagreement*, p. 288.

[47] See R. A. Dahl, *Democracy and its Critics*, New Haven: Yale University Press, 1989, p. 359, n. 8.

how a putatively 'principled' stance, deriving in this case from the infamous *Lochner* decision repudiating legislation limiting working hours on the grounds of upholding freedom of contract,[48] can in fact merely reflect an obtuseness to certain fundamental interests of a kind that is less likely to be found among a more popularly responsive set of officials who are forced to engage with a broad range of social concerns. Indeed, in this example those immediately affected are not even enfranchised, though by the time it passed both their parents were. In similar ways, the New Deal, deregulation and the environment are all areas where Congress has made the running precisely because the relevant interests found a voice and were able to shed new light on the principles involved, challenging the hegemonic views of the dominant classes who benefited from the prevailing system.[49]

Second, there is no compelling evidence for assuming that self-interest or blind prejudice motivates most or even many members of the electorate and their representatives. After all, it is one of the paradoxes of social choice that the purely self-interested voter would not bother voting. The costs of doing so far outweigh the very slight likelihood that his or her vote might bring about the desired legislative change.[50] As I noted above, the enfranchisement of women and before that employment and other social legislation favouring both women and children, were often enacted by male legislators against resistance from the courts. Moreover, on many matters of 'principle', such as abortion or the death penalty, legislators are often given a free vote because opinion cuts across the party divide. Even on those issues where self-interest might be thought to be a more potent factor, such as the economy, it proves difficult to predict people's view simply from their socio-economic position, especially in developed societies. Interest may structure people's understanding of rights, but the reverse is also true. The consequences of many public policy decisions prove so hard to predict, especially in the long term, that they are often taken behind the veil of ignorance. Nobody knows what decision would best foster their own interests, so they seek instead to go for what seems fair and right as they see it.

Parallel considerations undermine the arguments relating to the assumed benefits of courts being bound by law. Court decisions are said

---

[48] *Lochner v New York* 198 US 45 (1905), which struck down as unconstitutional a law limiting bakers to a maximum sixty-hour week.

[49] G. Rosenberg, *The Hollow Hope: Can Courts Bring About Social Change?*, Chicago: University of Chicago Press, 1991.

[50] A. Downs, *An Economic Theory of Democracy*, New York: Basic Books, 1957, p. 265.

to be more likely to be stable and consistent over time due to the pressure of precedent.[51] Courts are claimed to respect *stare decisis* in a way legislatures do not. This may be true of lower courts, for reasons explored in chapter 2, but it proves an inaccurate description of constitutional courts. The US Supreme Court, for example, regularly overturns constitutional precedents that it had set only a few years previously.[52] Indeed, the fact that a new appointment can lead a court to overturn a previous decision creates considerable uncertainty. Major constitutional changes are far harder to get through legislatures, though, which are much less prone to oscillating majorities. Time constraints, the scope for delaying tactics that can hold up an entire legislative programme and mobilise popular support and influence against the government outside the chamber, and the difficulty of building a majority for radical measures in most systems where governments have very small majorities or are dependent on coalition partners, all tend to make legislatures relatively conservative bodies that rarely go beyond incremental reform unless there is an overwhelming popular mandate for change.[53]

To the extent courts are bound by law, this may also be disadvantageous so far as treating the full moral implications of an issue are concerned. As I noted, they can only consider the legal points that are raised by those with standing before the court. A plaintiff may need to take certain of the broader considerations off the table in order to strengthen or present their case in law, even though these may involve the key constitutional issues. As an example of such narrowing, Adam Tomkins cites the way the *Prolife* case in the UK came before the House of Lords.[54] Prolife is a political party that campaigns against abortion. In the 2001 general election it fielded sufficient candidates in Wales to be entitled to a party election broadcast there. However, the broadcasting authority deemed the pictures of aborted foetuses included in the proposed broadcast to breach their statutory obligation to show nothing 'offensive to public feeling'. These were duly

---

[51] L. Alexander and F. Schauer, 'On Extrajudicial Constitutional Interpretation', *Harvard Law Review*, 110 (1997), pp. 1371–81.

[52] E.g. *Payne v Tennessee*, 501 US 808 (1991) and *Agostini v Felton*, 117 S. Ct. 1997 (1997), where the Supreme Court overruled respectively important death penalty and establishment clause precedents set just four and twelve years earlier, discussed in the course of a critique of Alexander and Schauer, 'On Extrajudicial Constitutional Interpretation', in M. Tushnet, *Taking the Constitution Away from the Courts*, Princeton: Princeton University Press, 1999, p. 28.

[53] Tushnet, *Taking the Constitution Away from the Courts*, pp. 28–30.

[54] Tomkins, *Our Republican Constitution*, pp. 27–8, discussing *R (Prolife Alliance) v British Broadcasting Corporation* [2004] 1 AC 185.

removed, with Prolife broadcasting their soundtrack along with a blank screen with the text 'censored'. Prolife asked for judicial review of the broadcaster's decision. The Court of Appeal originally decided in Prolife's favour, deeming the decision unnecessary and disproportionate. However, when the broadcasters appealed to the House of Lords this judgement was overturned – in part at least because the general question of whether the prohibition on broadcasts 'offensive to public feeling' complied with the principle of freedom of expression was conceded not to be at issue, leaving the Lords merely to consider the narrower legal point of whether or not the broadcasters had correctly applied this prohibition in this particular case.

Finally, making principle a matter of law can be to the detriment of both. On the one hand, as I argue in chapter 2, it may make law more uncertain. It invites judges to employ their potentially eccentric or debatable moral judgements rather than to be guided by narrower legal considerations that allow citizens to know where they stand with regard to laws by making it more likely they will be interpreted and applied in consistent ways. On the other hand, codifying morality as law, as a bill of rights does, may circumscribe moral debate into a discussion of the correct doctrinal meaning of given legal terms, thereby preventing a full discussion of the moral implications of a given policy or action. Legality is not morality. Most citizens obey many laws they find morally dubious or contentious because they accept they are the law and have been passed and applied by due procedures. As I noted at the end of the last section, it is agreement on legal and political procedures that allows us to live with our moral disagreements. To ignore that distinction risks engulfing the very system and rule of law in profound moral controversies.

What about the tyranny of the majority and the need for a counter-majoritarian check? The third supposed advantage of courts is usually assumed to be the strongest and most necessary of all. Yet, this non-majoritarian quality proves the most controversial and dubious of the three. As I remarked at the outset, it simply will not do to regard legislatures as ignoring rights and courts as upholding them. More often than not, what gets weighed and traded in the political process are not mere preferences or selfish interests but different arguments about rights. Talk of courts employing rights considerations to 'trump' legislative decisions seems misconceived if we consider that rights considerations have already figured in the legislature.[55] For, can trumps trump trumps? True,

---

[55] Waldron, *Law and Disagreement*, p. 12.

the legislative decision may well have been taken by majority rule. But then, so may the court's. For example, the US Supreme Court routinely decides key constitutional issues 5:4. As in a legislature, so in a court the need for majority decision-making arises because everybody believes they hold trumps, so that nobody does. In both cases, majority rule is a closure device for reaching a decision when all trumps have been played. However, a major difference exists between majority voting in legislatures by contrast to courts. In the former, it operates as a fair way for deciding between the equally weighted views of the people. No such consideration of fairness applies with regard to a court. Both the case under discussion and the views expressed by the judges may be entirely arbitrary so far as representing the full range of citizen concerns about rights in a given area is concerned.

Meanwhile, courts are as prone as legislatures, if not more so, to the very democratic pathologies they are supposed to rectify. As with voting in legislatures, numbers are what matter and a badly argued case counts for as much as a well-argued one. Invariably a bare majority suffices. It is extremely rare in legislatures for a rogue vote to carry the day. As we shall see in chapter 6, representatives generally follow the broad views of the millions of voters who elected them, and under the proportional representation (PR) systems that characterise most advanced democracies policy decisions are likely to reflect the views of an overwhelming rather than a bare majority of the population. By contrast, a single and somewhat eccentric view can be crucial within a judicial vote.

This possibility is related to fears about the potential irrationality and manipulability of majority rule due to the phenomenon known as voting cycles – the likelihood, given more than two options, that in a pair-wise comparison of all the alternatives none will beat all others (so that A beats B beats C beats A . . .).[56] As a result, any majority winner will be arbitrary – the product of the particular voting system chosen or the way the votes on the various alternative options have been structured.[57] However, and as chapter 6 will document, though logically possible, cycles turn out to be empirically rare because of the preference shaping effects of democratic competition, while the sheer size of legislatures and their responsiveness to a vast electorate makes manipulation extremely difficult.[58] However, there is no reason to suppose courts are less susceptible to voting cycles

---

[56] W. Riker, *Liberalism against Populism*, San Francisco: W. H. Freeman, 1982.
[57] For a clear guide to this problem, see Weale, *Democracy*, pp. 137–46.
[58] For details see G. Mackie, *Democracy Defended*, Cambridge: Cambridge University Press, 2003.

than legislatures. Yet their small size and the fact that by and large a chair will know his or her colleagues preferences well, and so can structure the voting schedule to deliver his or her preferred outcome, renders them much easier to manipulate.[59]

It might still be argued that a court offers an important source of contestation for those individuals whose concerns have been overlooked by a legislature. Though all views are respected via the act of voting, and there is the possibility of campaigning for change through lobbying, demonstrating and using the threat of withdrawing support for a government at the next election, some views may fail to be adequately represented. Legislation may also have unintended effects for a particular individual or group of individuals, or their concerns simply be overlooked because of ignorance or unfounded assumptions or unconscious prejudice. Again, chapter 6 presents reasons for thinking such possibilities rather rarer than is often supposed. However, even if a break on majority oppression was necessary, it is not clear that courts do or should offer an alternative, counter-majoritarian force. They tend to be less independent than is often supposed or can be justified; access to them is more limited and prone to reflect inequalities of power than majoritarian voting; while their influence on the legislative process may be malign as well as benign.

For a start, courts form part of the political system and the more general culture of the polity. It would be not only impossible but also inappropriate to seek to isolate them from such influences entirely. A parallel is sometimes drawn between constitutional judicial review and delegation to other non-majoritarian regulatory bodies, such as central banks. However, in neither case is such isolation so clear-cut nor as beneficial as is often assumed, though the grounds for it are if anything stronger with banks than with constitutional courts. The delegation of the setting of interest rates to banks is usually justified on the grounds that politicians lack the expertise and, more crucially, the incentives to make sound long-term decisions about interest rates. Banks are said to be more expert and independent. Yet, the truth of both contentions is debatable.[60] After all, politicians are professionals and come from a wide range of backgrounds, including finance. They also can and do choose congenial experts to advise them. So informed, they prove able to formulate very

---

[59] I. Shapiro, *The State of Democratic Theory*, Princeton: Princeton University Press, 2003, pp. 13–14.

[60] On the politics of interest rate and other decisions by banks, see K. McNamara, 'Rational Fictions: Central Bank Independence and the Social Logic of Delegation', *West European Politics*, 25:1 (2002), pp. 47–76.

sophisticated policies in such sensitive and technical areas as taxation. Nor is it the case that politicians could get away for long with purely short-term economic policies that manipulate pre-electoral booms. Not only is such manipulation hard to pull off given the numerous economic factors outside any politician's control, but also the high electoral salience of the economy gives politicians a clear incentive to acquire a reputation for good management if they wish to retain power. Meanwhile, though there is broad agreement that low inflation is desirable, economists still debate, for reasons as much ideological as technical, which measures might best achieve it in given circumstances, or how far it should be pursued at the expense of weakening manufacturing industry or rising levels of unem-ployment. Banks also form part of the domestic public sphere, and as such are subject to pressure from the media and politicians on these matters. If there is widespread and sustained clamour for a hike or drop in interest rates, they generally respond. Indeed, in countries such as New Zealand, the inflation target is set by politicians and the Governor can be held accountable if the Bank fails to meet it. That said, politicians may have an interest in making them seem more independent than they really are in order to shift blame away from themselves when difficult decisions need to be made or the economy performs badly. In these cases, independence merely serves to undermine responsibility and accountability.

When it comes to rights, there is even less reason to defer to experts. Though democratic citizens may be as united, if not more so, in their approval of rights as they are of low interest rates, they are also better placed to express a view on their nature and interpretation than on the technicalities of financial markets and so are likely both to disagree more and be more entitled to have a say in how such disagreements should be resolved. Indeed, as chapter 5 shall show, claims to moral expertise rest on dubious foundations and are far less well-grounded that expertise in economics. We have also seen already how isolating judges from popular prejudices does not necessarily guarantee their impartiality and indepen-dence from all social biases and prejudices. It may merely mean that they reflect those of the privileged classes. In any case, it is a basic aspect of the rule of law that all should be both subject to and equal under it. Mak-ing judges a class apart threatens that equality. To insulate courts from prevailing public opinion and give them the resources to impose their decisions against the determined will of elected majorities would risk their becoming tyrannical and undermine their legitimacy. Fortunately, courts, like banks, tend not to be out of step with the popular will for long and there is little evidence of constitutional courts holding out for an extended period against sustained, national majorities.[61] In both Britain and the United States, for example, a degree of direct political control is exercised by the appointment process, which will bring courts roughly into line with persistent political trends. Courts are also dependent on governments to abide by and implement their judgements. They cannot oppose them too frequently or persistently, since measures can be undermined as much by administrative inertia, a lack of resources and a failure to abide by the spirit rather than the narrowly construed letter of a ruling, as by outright defiance. As with banks, courts are also subject to indirect pressures through the press and other sources of influence. Their standing and authority gets questioned when they are consistently at odds with the public, making most judges highly reluctant to be so. Meanwhile, as will be explored below, judicial independence can be exploited by politicians to duck their responsibilities and, where real, may damage rather than foster good legislation.

The emphasis on the counter-majoritarian role of courts also overlooks their function as national institutions in *upholding* the majority view against minorities. This task is especially important within federal systems, where they overwhelmingly support unitary forces against individual member states that may be moved by a majority within their own jurisdiction to pull away from a given national measure. More generally, administrative review also works to remove local discretion. Such favouring of the national majority is usually sound. It prevents free-riding or selective defection from public interest arrangements and helps guard against arbitrary or corrupt practices. Indeed, progressive rights-based judicial review in the United States in the 1950s and 60s broadly reflected federal majorities in favour of some relaxation of abortion laws, desegregation and so on against certain regional majorities that resisted such reforms. For example, liberal legislation in most states meant that well before *Roe v Wade* some 600,000 lawful abortions were performed a year.[62]

---

[61] R. A. Dahl, 'Decision-making in a Democracy: The Supreme Court as National Policy-maker', *Journal of Public Law*, 6 (1957), pp. 279–95, W. Mishler and R. S. Sheehan, 'The Supreme Court as a Counter-majoritarian Institution? The Impact of Public Opinion on Supreme Court Decisions', *American Political Science Review*, 87:1 (1993), pp. 87–101 and Tushnet, *Taking the Constitution Away from the Courts*, pp. 134–5. These studies all deal with the US Supreme Court, where most work on this issue has been done, but are largely confirmed by comparative studies, e.g. M. Shapiro, *Courts: A Comparative and Political Analysis*, Chicago: University of Chicago Press, 1981.

[62] C. Sunstein, *The Partial Constitution*, Cambridge, MA.: Harvard University Press, 1993, p. 147.

Significantly, the main exception to the rule that the courts follow the polls is the aforementioned sustained anti-majoritarian decisions of the US Supreme Court pre-1937 favouring the property rights of powerful vested interests. This fact indicates problems with the contestatory argument for judicial rule. The pursuit of constitutional rights via litigation in the courts is sometimes justified as an alternative avenue of political participation. Advocates of this view point to the ways differences in financial and organisational resources can undermine political equality, giving those who are better situated a larger influence over legislation. They defend judicial review as a mechanism whereby these inequalities might be mitigated.[63] It is more likely, though, that they will get reinforced. For these same inequalities apply to the mounting of court cases. These too favour those with deep pockets and the skills, time, money, influence and capacity to muster concerted support. The big difference is that in electoral politics all citizens are equal in at least one important respect – they all possess the same decisive political resource, a single vote. That places limits on how far even very powerful elites can distort the political agenda, for in the final analysis they will only attain and retain power by wooing the majority of voters. That countervailing factor is not present when it comes to litigation. As such, it can give these same groups a second vote under less equitable conditions to defend their interests.

In fact, counter-majoritarianism is usually bad for minorities and the underprivileged because it is biased towards the privileged and well-organised. To the extent judicial review obliges proponents of change to amass a supermajority to overcome objections on constitutional grounds, it is more likely to entrench injustice rather than uphold justice. For a start, it favours the *status quo* by awarding it more votes than any proposed change.[64] Though reforms may be less just or efficient than what already exists, they are as likely to be improvements aimed at overcoming current injustices and inefficiencies – indeed, probably more so since many problems cannot be perceived or anticipated when any set of arrangements is enacted but only become evident over time as people's preferences and circumstances change. In that case, majority rule offers more protection to the worst-off minority than other systems because it maximises the ability to overcome unfavourable outcomes. For a start, if there is a more than 50% chance that any proposed change will be an

---

[63] Kavanagh, 'Participation and Judicial Review', pp. 480–81.
[64] A. J. McGann, 'The Tyranny of the Supermajority: How Majority Rule Protects Minorities', *Journal of Theoretical Politics*, 16 (2004), pp. 56–70.

improvement on what exists, then it should be at least as easy to alter the *status quo* as to remain with it. Any scheme that requires more than a majority to change matters will favour those with a vested interest in retaining the currently unfair or inefficient arrangements. It is also biased towards minorities that are concentrated and well-organised, allowing them to form blocking coalitions. By contrast, as Dahl has long showed, democracy is the product of pluralist societies in which majority rule is rarely the result of a single, homogeneous group dominating the rest, but a coalition among a heterogeneous grouping of minorities.[65] The need to maintain such a majority from fragmenting fosters inclusion, since those who are disaffected can threaten to desert to a rival grouping.[66] Indeed, the likelihood due to majority cycling that this will happen eventually works against permanent losers. The only way to ensure stability will be to make excluded parties indifferent to being out of or in power by governing as consensually as possible. As Lijphart has noticed, in countries where PR means majority rather than plurality rule prevails, such consensual politics is usually the norm.[67] Ironically, courts tend to be most successful in striking down legislation when majorities are weak and unstable, formed of ever-changing coalitions. In these cases, it will often be hard to reassemble the original majority in support of the affected measure. Yet what the court may have done is simply exploit a cycle – that is, substitute a possible for the actual winning coalition. Indeed, their own fluctuating judgements, as in the case of the death penalty in the United States, may themselves be the product of a cycle.

The general alignment between courts and politics should not be taken to mean that judicial review only influences the democratic process at the margins. On the contrary, it can change its character in numerous ways. However, it frequently does so in a manner that distorts democracy so as to produce the very problems its advocates seek to correct.[68] For a start, it raises the stakes for winners and losers alike. If losers wish to alter a measure, they will have to gain overwhelming support for their view. However, as I noted, that raises the threshold not only for those wanting to pass unjust measures but also for those wishing to overturn certain dominant forms of injustice. In the process, it places all the focus on a single

---

[65] Dahl, *Democracy and its Critics*, ch. 17.
[66] McGann, 'The Tyranny of the Supermajority', pp. 70–71.
[67] A. Lijphart, *Democracies: Patterns of Majoritarian and Consensus Government in Twenty-One Countries*, New Haven: Yale University Press, 1984.
[68] Rosenberg, *The Hollow Hope* and Tushnet, *Taking the Constitution Away from the Courts*, ch. 6.

issue rather than a package of policies, where trade-offs might be possible that create a broad coalition of support. Effort will go into capturing the judiciary rather than constructing a legislative majority by reaching a mutually acceptable compromise with one's political opponents. As a result, both sides become ever more polarised. To some degree, abortion has come to be handled this way in the United States, with all the attendant drawbacks. Thus, we saw how *Roe v Wade* came in the wake of a general shift by most states towards more liberal abortion legislation. Yet, taking it out of the hands of legislatures has not resolved the issue once and for all but rather raised it to undue prominence. On the one hand, anti-abortion groups have striven to make it the defining concern of the anti-progressive opposition, and the key question when it comes to judicial appointments – seemingly above even legal competence, integrity, fairness and other desirable qualities. On the other hand, pro-abortion groups, having initially moved on to other issues, have now found it necessary to give overwhelming importance in their turn to abortion. For winning in law is rarely the end of the matter. It proves largely empty unless the decision also wins political support – and to the extent that it may either galvanise opposition or divert the activities of supporters elsewhere, may even work against political success.

Real change only comes with legislation, and judicial review may hinder as much as it promotes that process. To take the other defining modern US constitutional decision, a decade after the 1954 ruling in *Brown v Board of Education* no more than 1.2% of black children in the south attended desegregated schools. Change only began to occur with the civil rights movement and the passage by Congress of the Civil Rights Act and the Voting Rights Act in 1964 and 1965. *Brown* may have helped energise support for such measures but popular protest against racial discrimination would undoubtedly have arisen anyway. Yet, it also motivated a shift to the right by white southern politicians and staunch, and occasionally violent, opposition to reform. Moreover, whatever its positive or negative effects, *Brown* failed to alter the material conditions of most African-Americans. Only getting a majority to pay for extensive social reforms can tackle the racial poverty gap.[69]

Meanwhile, judicial 'overhang' may lead a legislature to adopt precisely the sort of pure interest-based politics proponents of judicial review seek

[69] For details, see Rosenberg, *The Hollow Hope*, J. Hochschild, *The New American Dilemma: Liberal Democracy and School Desegregation*, New Haven: Yale University Press, 1984 and Tushnet, *Taking the Constitution Away from the Courts*, pp. 147–50.

to guard against. There are several variations of this phenomenon. A legislature might leave a particularly divisive or contentious issue to be decided by the court. The danger here is that politicians and ordinary citizens feel no responsibility for or allegiance to whatever gets decided, while the judiciary risks being discredited as elitist or biased. Legislatures may also be led to concentrate more on anticipating the judiciary's likely view than debating the merits of the case. As Alec Stone Sweet has ruefully remarked, governing with judges can in this respect become governing like judges.[70] This is unwarranted not just because courts, as we have seen, have no greater claim to get rights 'right' than legislatures, but also because in many respects they often get it 'wrong'. In particular, whereas legislatures do consider the public dimension of rights, including their knock-on effects for other rights and the social policies needed to resolve them, courts tend to focus on the individual case and the actions of identifiable persons against others. However, the case may in social policy terms prove a perverse instance of the problem to be tackled, while the issue may be more structural than individual. Thus, a decision requiring expenditure on school bussing may have adverse effects on other education policies or those in other areas, such as housing and health, which are actually more effective in tackling the issue of low educational attainment in particular groups.[71]

These observations also suggest difficulties with the argument that constitutions provide gag rules that take certain socially divisive issues off the agenda.[72] Such arrangements are likened to a tacit agreement among neighbours of diametrically opposed ideological convictions never to discuss politics, thereby facilitating convivial social relations between them. The separation of church and state provides the paradigm case. If communities are too polarised to be able to strike a compromise on an issue, then this tactic may appear the sensible solution. Once again, though, the danger is that it prevents them ever moving together. Instead, of seeking a mutually acceptable solution, they insist on their respective views of their rights and condemn those who oppose them, including the courts, of acting unjustly. Alternative solutions, such as multiculturalism or state support for various religious schools, never get explored.

Do matters change if judicial review comes about through a democratic process? After all, bills of rights and constitutions are often brought

[70] A. Stone Sweet, *Governing with Judges: Constitutional Politics in Europe*, Oxford: Oxford University Press, 2000, p. 204.
[71] Sunstein, *The Partial Constitution*, pp. 147–9.
[72] S. Holmes, 'Gag Rules or the Politics of Omission', in J. Elster and R. Slagstad (eds.), *Constitutionalism and Democracy*, Cambridge: Cambridge University Press, 1988, ch. 1.

into being by specially elected conventions to draw up their constitutions and many use supermajorities within the legislature and/or in popular referenda to ratify and amend them. In Britain, the Human Rights Act was enacted as a piece of ordinary legislation and is arguably capable of being amended or withdrawn by the legislature in an ordinary vote. These origins seem to provide judicial review with a democratic foundation whereby a responsible people binds itself. It is argued that judicial review offers a pre-commitment strategy,[73] through which the electorate seeks to be bound by judicial decisions on rights so as to guard against those occasions when they might be tempted to act unjustly. The court can then be portrayed as enacting the people's will, with only a very special set of democratic procedures allowing it to change its mind.[74]

As I shall show in chapter 3, the democratic credentials of such acts of self-binding are dubious.[75] Here I simply want to ask whether the advantages of courts compared to legislatures are such as to justify such a step. The analysis thus far suggests they are not. Historically, the cases of democracies being tempted by tyranny are few and far between, and it is doubtful that a constitutional court could save them on those occasions when it is. As the example of Nazi Germany reveals, widespread popular prejudices against a minority are likely to be shared by a significant proportion of the ruling elite, including the legal establishment and where they are not the judiciary is unlikely to be able to withstand sustained popular and governmental pressure.[76] The standard case is rather of members of the legislature disagreeing about rights and settling their dispute with a vote. What reason do we have for giving a court, which also disagrees on the issue and must decide by a vote, the power to overturn the decision of the legislature in this case? It is not that the legislature has suddenly been moved by mass hysteria to some perverse position that in its calmer moments it would abjure in favour of the court's alternative ruling. Many will calmly and in a reasoned way wish to dispute the court's decision. Indeed, as we saw, so will a number of judges – possibly almost half – on the court. How can this situation be judged as the court saving the legislature from some sort of excess of populism? Indeed, we have seen there are grounds for fearing the danger of a perverse or eccentric view carrying

[73] For the best discussion of this issue, see S. Holmes, 'Precommitment and the Paradox of Democracy', in Elster and Slagstad (eds.), *Constitutionalism and Democracy*, ch. 7.

[74] The development of this second aspect is a distinctive feature of Ackerman's theory in *We the People*, and will be discussed in ch. 3.

[75] See too Waldron, *Law and Disagreement*, ch. 12.

[76] Dahl, *Democracy and its Critics*, p. 173.

the day is much more likely in courts than in legislatures. Moreover, there is no chance in the latter case for the decision to be challenged at the next election.

Nor, as some have claimed, can the court's decision be viewed as some sort of democratic supermajoritarian device which temporarily locks the demos into one position, but allows through constitutional amendment for its being overturned should a large majority choose to do so in the future.[77] Given we have seen how courts themselves decide by bare majorities, having them bind legislatures in this way is hard to defend. As we noted, the bias it gives to a given arrangement is unjustifiable if there is a genuine division on this matter among the population. But the fact is, it is not the 'people's' own earlier view that gets entrenched, but the court's (or a majority on the court's) interpretation of what that view is.[78]

Does it make any difference if, as in the UK and some Commonwealth countries, a bill of rights is simply an ordinary piece of legislation?[79] In these systems, the executive and parliament have a duty to evaluate the rights implications of legislation. In New Zealand, Britain and the Australian National Territory, courts cannot strike down primary legislation but only declare it 'incompatible' with the statutory bill of rights and send it back to the legislature for consideration. Like the Canadian national and provincial legislatures, in these jurisdictions parliament and the executive may choose nonetheless to let the contested legislation stand 'notwithstanding' the declared incompatibility. Some analysts have regarded this as a new 'commonwealth model of constitutionalism', quite different to the American model, in which the tensions between democracy and constitutionalism are overcome by bringing constitutional courts and parliaments into dialogue with each other.[80] In practice, though, the lack of entrenchment seems to make little difference to the role or influence of judicial review *vis-à-vis* the legislature.[81] For example, although the UK Bill obliges ministers to issue a declaration of compatibility of legislation with the Act, and there are provisions for prior legislative scrutiny of such claims, it is ultimately judicial review by the judges sitting in the relevant

---

[77] Freeman, 'Constitutional Democracy and the Legitimacy of Judicial Review', p. 364.

[78] Waldron, 'Freeman's Defense of Judicial Review', pp. 39–41.

[79] The first such bill was the New Zealand Bill of Rights Act 1990 (NZ), 1990/109, followed by the Human Rights Act 1998 (UK) 1998 c. 42 and the Australian Capital Territory's Human Rights Act 2004 A 2004–5 (ACT).

[80] See S. Gardbaum, 'The New Commonwealth Model of Constitutionalism', *The American Journal of Comparative Law*, 49 (2001), pp. 707–60.

[81] For an empirical assessment to this effect, see J. L. Hiebert, 'Parliamentary Bills of Rights: An Alternative Model?', *Modern Law Review*, 69 (2006), pp. 7–28.

court which decides the issue.[82] As a result, legislators come under pressure to anticipate the court's ruling rather than to elaborate a view of their own. Of course, they can override the court by invoking a 'notwithstanding' clause or by enacting new rights legislation. However, the experience of Canada and Britain suggests legislatures are very reluctant to employ either of these mechanisms. The first places them in a position where it appears they are putting rights to one side. That is very different to arguing they have an alternative view of how they should be interpreted. The second raises similar problems, despite occasional blustering by Labour politicians and a recent, and much ridiculed, plan by the Conservative opposition to amend the Act. Such moves always risk being condemned for playing fast and loose with rights rather than as offering a different account of them – a risk all the more likely because the dominant view has been that even statutory bills of rights have committed them to something like the American model.[83] It is also not easy for governments to find the necessary parliamentary time for such major changes. Real legislative control and consideration of rights come not from abstract declarations that are then passed to others to interpret but through the detailed discussion and scrutiny of specific pieces of legislation.

IV The culture of rights

It is often alleged that bills of rights help create a rights culture – they lead citizens and legislators to see things in more principled terms. As Dworkin has put it: 'It encourages each individual to suppose that his relations with other citizens and with his government are matters of justice, and it encourages him and his fellow citizens to discuss as a community what justice requires these relationships to be.'[84] I doubt this proposition. As Mary Anne Glendon has remarked of the rights-based judicial politics of the United States, it has produced a rights culture characterised 'by its starkness and simplicity, its prodigality with the rights label, its legalistic character, its exaggerated absoluteness, its hyper-individualism,

---

[82] In the UK the number depends on the jurisdiction and the issue.

[83] See J. L. Hiebert, 'New Constitutional Ideas: Can New Parliamentary Models Resist Judicial Dominance When Interpreting Rights?', *Texas Law Review*, 82 (2004), pp. 1980–85. In Britain, Dworkin's ideas have been highly influential in the campaign to have a Bill of Rights – see Dworkin, 'Does Britain Need a Bill of Rights?', in *Freedom's Law*, ch. 18 and the Dworkinian reading of the British constitution offered by T. R .S. Allan, *Law, Liberty and Justice: The Legal Foundations of British Constitutionalism*, Oxford: Clarendon Press, 1993.

[84] R. Dworkin, 'Political Judges and the Rule of Law', in *A Matter of Principle*, Oxford: Clarendon Press, 1986, p. 32.

its insularity, and its silence with respect to personal, civic and collective responsibilities'.[85] True, she notes how many of these features arise from American political culture more generally and the type of rights the US Constitution enshrines. In other contexts, rights-based judicial review can operate very differently. This finding reinforces my earlier observation that judicial review broadly reflects the weaknesses and virtues of the social and political system within which it is embedded. Yet, notwithstanding that some bills may be better than others, bills of rights and judicial review *per se* have distorting effects.

As Glendon also observes, 'the language of rights is the language of no compromise'.[86] This uncompromising view of rights proves particularly potent when they are treated as entrenched constitutional principles designed to protect individuals against appeals to the public good. From this perspective, there appears to be no room for acknowledging reasonable disagreements about them and looking for ways to accommodate different points of view. The collective simply has no business expressing an opinion or interfering with the individual's legitimate sphere of personal choice. The role of the courts becomes the defender of the individual against the illegitimate incursions of the collectivity. I have argued that this is an implausible view of rights. They may apply to individuals but they also always have to be contextualised within a scheme of competing rights and varying, yet equally reasonable, interpretations of them, not to mention important moral considerations other than rights. These are all matters where a collective view is necessary and it is not clear that the judiciary is better placed than ordinary citizens to decide what that view is. When we see rights as shaping and being shaped by our collective life through a decision process in which we all take part, then the need to respect our disagreements and address people's different concerns and experiences through the search for mutually acceptable compromises becomes more compelling. As I shall argue in chapter 4, equal participation in this process forms the right to have rights,[87] and it is through acknowledging that basic entitlement and engaging in decision-making with others that we are brought to see our fellow citizens as autonomous rights-bearers deserving of equality of concern and respect.

Would this collective process be itself improved if it was undertaken with regard to a bill of rights? Would not political debate be enhanced by having some sort of statement of public standards as a reference point?

---

[85] M. A. Glendon, *Rights Talk: The Impoverishment of Political Discourse*, New York: The Free Press, 1991, p. x.
[86] Ibid., p. 9   [87] Waldron, *Law and Disagreement*, ch. 11.

I doubt it. To the extent such mechanisms work, then it is probably at the beginning of a regime. Constitutions commonly come into being after a period of general political collapse, frequently following military defeat and often involving civil war. In this situation, a bill of rights can provide a statement of intent not to commit the errors of the past and to deal equitably with former opponents. However, the beneficial effects mainly derive from the very act of drafting and endorsing the bill, which forces the contending parties to come together and find common ground through compromise. The Italian constituent assembly following the Second World War, and the compromises forged there between Communists, Socialists, Liberals and Christian Democrats, are exemplary in this respect.[88] Thereafter, though, the effects of such a bill can be unfortunate. Charters are necessarily phrased at a high level of abstraction in order to promote agreement. That leaves the disagreements over the substance, scope, sphere and subjects of rights, the best means to secure them, and so on still to be decided. It is not always particularly profitable to discuss all these issues in terms of which formulation best interprets the wording of the right in a given document. Think, for example, of the way American debates concerning defamation, incitement, libel, pornography, commercial advertising and the like all get distorted by terminological disquisitions over what counts as 'speech'. It would seem much more fruitful to discuss the pros and cons of particular policies head on in terms of the interests and values at stake. Only then are the complexities of the issues likely to be appreciated along with the reasonableness of the disagreements they provoke, often reflecting as they do different experiences and moral considerations.[89] Only then will compromise be possible, which will invariably be good policy and not just good politics because all dimensions of a problem will have been considered and addressed. Indeed, focus on a right can often have harmful effects. Thus, tackling poverty, say, through meeting a 'right to subsistence' may mean overlooking the key ways to get the poor out of their position through training and employment programmes. The language of rights offers an apparently simple relation between something being wrong and giving individuals an entitlement that it be put right. Yet

---

[88] See P. Pombeni (ed.), *Potere costituente e riforme costituzionale*, Bologna: Il Mulino, 1992 and, for a parallel finding for the drafting of the EU Charter of Fundamental Rights, Bellamy and Schönlau, 'The Normality of Constitutional Politics'.

[89] Glendon, *Rights Talk*, provides numerous examples of how focusing on the way rights are framed in a given document actually leads to the real moral issues in the policy being overlooked. For example, see her discussion of *Bowers v Hardwick* 478 US 186 (1986) at p. 151.

the connection between the moral wrong and the best way of addressing it is rarely as simple as this.[90]

Conclusion

Implementing any rights-based policy requires the acquiescence and often the active cooperation of the whole population of a country. As we have seen, all rights have both a collective dimension and raise matters over which we disagree. Even those rights which reflect what practically everyone recognises as great moral wrongs, such as murder or rape, can still involve disagreements over how they should be interpreted and interact with other rights. For example, the role played by mitigating circumstances, including self-defence, in murder cases, or the nature of personal responsibility, the desirability of victims being able to remain anonymous and the relevance and means of identifying consent in rape cases – these and other issues can all be matters of dispute on which a settled view is needed if trials are to be equitable. Any decision will often be controversial and affect a large number of people who dissent from it. A procedure that allows all views to be expressed, seeks to a degree to integrate them and show equal concern as well as respect to the various issues different perspectives raise, and allows decisions to be challenged and amended to take into account new information and changing values and circumstances, should have a greater chance of securing the assent and collaboration of the political community than one that devolves this decision to a group that is neither representative of, nor directly accountable to, popular opinion. For what touches all should surely be decided by all. Of course, the political process is not foolproof. Yet neither is the judicial process. Indeed, we have seen it suffers from some of the self-same problems. Paradoxically, judicial review is itself dependent on democracy. It is only accepted in democratic pluralist societies where the tyranny of the majority is unlikely due to the polyarchical and pluralist character of social relations, and proves most effective when either supporting the majority against a minority or where there is no consistent majority. However, as the next two chapters detail, it risks undermining the integrity of both the legal and the democratic process.

[90] Waldron, *Law and Disagreement*, pp. 217–19.

2

The rule of law and the rule of persons

When judges criticise legislatures and governments they typically do so in the name of the rule of law. Unfortunately, politicians do likewise when they attack judicial activism. The first identify the rule of law with the judiciary's authority to determine the state of the law in a given case, to pass sentence and to review legislation for its compatibility with prevailing legal norms, including constitutional rights. They see attempts by politicians to contest or interfere with these powers as undermining the integrity of the legal system.[1] The second, however, associate the rule of law with the right of a legally authorised government to pass laws according to the due formalities and to have them obeyed. They regard judicial moves to reinterpret or question duly passed laws as usurping the government's right to legislate. On this view, the prime danger to consistency in the legal process comes from courts aspiring to make the laws rather than simply applying them. Meanwhile, people's ability to influence and contest legislation via the ballot box also gets eroded.[2] Given the often self-serving and apparently incompatible character of these two positions, it is perhaps small wonder that many theorists have regarded the concept as at best 'essentially contested',[3] at worst no more than a 'meaningless . . . self-congratulatory rhetorical device'.[4]

As the two accounts outlined above indicate, different views of the respective powers of the legislature and the judiciary, and of the nature of their separation, lie at the heart of debates regarding the rule of law. Any

---

[1] In Britain, for example, the Lord Chief Justice has criticised plans for legal and asylum reform as undermining the rule of law. See Lord Woolf, 'The Rule of Law and a Change in the Constitution', Squire Centenary Lecture, University of Cambridge, 4 March 2004.

[2] See the round-up of press reactions to Woolf's remarks in 'His Ambition is Rule by Lawyers', *The Guardian*, 6 March 2004.

[3] J. Waldron, 'Is the Rule of Law an Essentially Contested Concept (in Florida)?', *Law and Philosophy*, 21 (2002), pp. 137–64.

[4] Judith Shklar, 'Political Theory and the Rule of Law', in Allan C. Hutcheson and P. Monahan (eds.), *The Rule of Law: Ideal or Ideology*, Toronto: Carswell, 1987, p. 1.

theory has to somehow reconcile their rival claims and show whether there is any meaningful and valuable sense in which the law, rather than judges or politicians, might be said to rule. Section I explores the nature of law and its relationship to political power. I shall argue that the rule of law has to be distinguished from both the rule of good law and rule by law. Because notions of the good and just are subject to political disagreement, the rule of law cannot be associated with some notion of the good or just that lies outside the circumstances of politics and is not the product of any political or legal authority. However, merely to rule by law proves insufficient to curtail the arbitrary use of power. Consequently, both court-centred and legislature-centred approaches must confront what I dub the Hobbes challenge: namely, how can they avoid empowering either courts or legislatures as a sovereign power, able to act in an arbitrary way? The former seek to do so by offering what might be called 'a third theory of law', lying midway between natural law and legal positivism.[5] They have to show how the very nature of law implies certain norms that can guide in all cases, directing judicial discretion so that law can indeed rule and legal forms bind those governments committed to employing them. I explore two attempts at such a theory in section II. The latter have to indicate how the political process itself might lead legislators not to rule in their own or their supporters' interests alone. They must also explain how and why judges and other officials might follow their lead. I defend a version of this position in section III. The legal, court-centred view attempts to distinguish law *strictu sensu* from legislation. The political, legislative-centred view suggests no such distinction can be made. Judges and politicians think and act in similar ways. The key is to provide each side with the motivation to treat all as equals under the law when making their decisions. This approach tackles the problem of arbitrariness at its source by so dividing power that it cannot be employed in a sovereign, and hence potentially arbitrary, manner. As with the protection of rights, the crucial factor in this regard turns out to be the social and political conditions fostering democratic rule more generally. In many respects, the rule of law simply is rule by democracy.

---

[5] I take this term from J. Mackie, 'The Third Theory of Law', *Philosophy and Public Affairs*, 7 (1977), pp. 3–16. Though intended as a characterisation of Dworkin's theory, it captures the goal of a range of theorists, such as L. Fuller, *The Morality of Law*, revised edition, New Haven: Yale University Press, 1969 and F. A. Hayek, *Law, Legislation and Liberty*, 3 vols., London: Routledge, 1973–9, with whom Dworkin otherwise disagrees.

I The idea and value of the rule of law

The rule of law and the circumstances of politics

If we were ruled by philosopher kings, who simply discovered the law through their devotion to truth and justice, and could be counted on to apply it with an angelic rectitude and a divine omniscience, then the rule of law would be unproblematic. The law's agents, whether we called them monarchs, legislators or judges, would be free from the uncertainties as well as the biases that animate politics. They would act as the mere mouthpieces of a superior wisdom offering infallibly just solutions that harmonised the individual's interest with that of the public. Clearly this is a fantasy, yet many versions of the rule of law have a tendency to embrace it. The danger lies with potentially bad political rulers. Enshrine good laws in the constitution and entrust a special caste of legal guardians to oversee them, and the rule of persons can be subordinated to the rule of law.

Unfortunately, this solution simply begs the very questions that lie at the heart of the problem. As Joseph Raz has noted, some accounts of the rule of law use the term as a catch-all slogan for every desirable policy one might wish to see enacted. He cites as an instance of this approach the International Commission of Jurists' (ICJ) equation of the rule of law with the creation and maintenance of 'the conditions which will uphold the dignity of man as an individual' – a requirement that includes 'not only recognition of his civil and political rights but also the establishment of the social, economic, educational and cultural traditions which are essential to the full development of his personality'.[6] However, we saw in the last chapter how people reasonably disagree over the nature of the right and the good. Though most people will find the general aim of the ICJ's declaration unexceptionable, many will differ over what human dignity consists in and requires. Likewise, they will dispute the various ways such aims might be achieved by making all equal under the law – including what formal and substantive procedures and entitlements would need to be in place. These differences also lie at the heart of the different views of the rule of law outlined earlier – where some see human dignity and equality promoted through democracy, others will regard it as best protected via the courts and bills of rights.[7] In other words, the rule of law lies within the circumstances of politics – it represents a necessary collective agreement

---

[6] J. Raz, *The Authority of Law*, Oxford: Clarendon Press, 1979, pp. 210–11.
[7] Waldron, 'Is the Rule of Law an Essentially Contested Concept', pp. 140–48.

in an area where there is deep disagreement over what its character might be and no demonstrably best solution available.

A more formal approach attempts to overcome these difficulties.[8] This strategy focuses on the benefits, values and constraints inherent in the very existence of legal forms and procedures. After all, people often obey laws with which they disagree simply out of respect for the advantages of living in a law-governed environment. Law facilitates social interaction and helps curb the abuse of power. It can even provide regular procedures for contesting and changing laws and decisions that they dislike. None of these considerations need involve substantive agreement with the good-ness of the law. Yet, as we shall see in the next part of this section, legality *per se* can only play a limited role in protecting against oppression and domination. To achieve this end, we may need good laws. Moreover, it is not clear that even good laws can rule in and of themselves – covering all possible eventualities and infallibly guiding those entrusted to uphold them towards the right answer.

Does this return us to the original dilemma of relying on good men to give us good laws? This question brings us to what can be termed the Hobbes challenge. Stated crudely, Hobbes argued that in circumstances of conflicting interests and deep disagreements about values and judge-ments, laws would only be equitably and coherently drafted and applied by all individuals being equally in awe of a sovereign who was outside the law and whose power was indivisible. For a start, the meaning of laws is rarely clear, so that 'all Laws, written and unwritten, have need of Inter-pretation' and these interpretations are usually controversial. Even when the meaning of laws is clear, their bearing on particular situations often is not – producing another source of controversy. Indeed, even if laws could be defined in an absolutely clear manner as to both their meaning and application, self-love, partiality and passion can lead people to employ them in self-serving ways and hence into conflict with each other. Hobbes believed these difficulties arise as much with the hypothetical impera-tives of the Law of Nature as human laws. Therefore, laws or rules do not themselves provide the basis for social cooperation. Rather, a peaceful society results from having a political authority vested with the power to formulate, interpret and apply the laws and, crucially, to overrule rival views of their bearing in any given case. The claim that laws could be

---

[8] For the contrast between 'formal' and 'substantive' approaches, see P. Craig, 'Formal and Substantive Conceptions of the Rule of Law: An Analytical Framework', *Public Law* (1997), pp. 467–87.

set above those sovereign person or persons empowered to enact and implement them was incoherent for Hobbes. It could only mean to set up another power able to judge and enforce these laws 'which is to make a new Sovereign' leading to an infinite regress with the need 'for the same reason a third, to punish the second; and so continually without end, to the Confusion, and Dissolution of the Common-wealth'.[9] On this view, law is not only subject to political contestation but intrinsically political by virtue of being the creation of political authority.

Of course, as H. L. A. Hart observed, the sovereign's rule is recognised in part because it has legal foundations. In his terminology, we need 'secondary' rules of recognition to identify what counts as law as well as the 'primary' rules or laws that are created within a recognised legal system.[10] Among these secondary rules are those identifying the sovereign as authorised to decide what the law is. Such rules do place a legal constraint on personal rule, but not necessarily a very strong one. It is not just that tyrants have a habit of securing legal legitimacy for their rule after, rather than before, seizing power. Political rulers of all stripes habitually claim that the rule of law simply requires obedience to their commands as the legally recognised authorities. Yet if government is by definition the agency authorised by law to issue laws, then on this interpretation the rule of law barely constrains the rule of persons. To say all acts of government must have a foundation in law becomes almost a tautology. If law is merely (and only) what the lawful government decrees, then anything the lawful government decrees is authorised by law and what is not authorised or so decreed is illegal and so cannot be an action of the government.[11]

All the same, it would be wrong to dismiss this view completely. After all, British courts have frequently done a valuable job in restraining ministers and officials from acting beyond their remit. A government (or other body) that has to act within and according to its legally defined powers can be held to account in ways bodies or people that are not so constrained cannot. The rule of the socially influential and wealthy, of the mafia or of the mob reveal in their different ways the disadvantages of lawless compared to lawful government. However, the Hobbes challenge emerges again since some body of people, be they judges or other politicians, have to decide if the government has breached the rules. And although they too will be legally constituted, at some point some person or persons possesses the competence to decide questions regarding its

---

[9] T. Hobbes, *Leviathan*, ed. Richard Tuck, Cambridge: Cambridge University Press, 1991, p. 169.

[10] H. L. A. Hart, *The Concept of Law*, second edition, Oxford: Clarendon Press, pp. 94–5.

[11] Raz, *The Authority of Law*, pp. 212–13.

own competence.[12] Meanwhile, an underlying set of problems remains: namely, why should the powerful have accepted to be rule-bound in the first place, unless it had somehow become in their interest to do so, and how can the legal forms of legislation and judging ensure that the law prevails rather than the will of those authorised to make decisions?

Therefore, the central dilemma posed by the rule of law is how to enjoy the benefits of legality while overcoming the Hobbes challenge. The law cannot rule without legislators and the judiciary. Can the rule of persons be modified by the rule of law if they are necessarily the instruments through which it governs? Legal constitutionalists claim that by ruling through law, those who make and enforce it are somehow led to be ruled by it in their turn. Fidelity to law is an intrinsic aspect of a coherent legal system, and for that to obtain the laws and judging must possess certain desirable qualities.[13] I shall dispute this view, arguing that it ends up perilously close to the fantasy of a system of good laws under the jurisdiction of beneficent philosophical kings. By contrast, I contend a political constitutionalism tackles the Hobbes challenge at its source – the problem of the sovereign ruler. Turning rule by law into the rule of law is in large part a matter of the process of legislation rather than the form or nature of law *per se*. It is the political system that de-sovereigntises sovereign power. Of course, the issue of how judges and others interpret and apply the law remains. Here too the solution largely lies in their place within the political system and the incentives it offers. However, the result is a less heroic view of judging than many jurists suppose: one much more sensitive to the disagreements of ordinary citizens and the political mechanisms they employ to resolve them.

Arbitrary rule and rule by law

No theorist of the rule of law believes that rule by persons can be avoided in all respects – merely that certain types of personal rule can be placed outside, or in certain respects are simply incompatible with, any workable

---

[12] The issue of whether a democratic account of the rule of law requires a constitutional or other court to uphold the rights and procedures intrinsic to democracy, as is argued by J. H. Ely, *Democracy and Distrust: A Theory of Judicial Review*, Cambridge, MA: Harvard University Press, 1980 and, in more qualified terms, by R. Dworkin, 'Political Judges and the Rule of Law', in *A Matter of Principle*, Oxford: Clarendon Press, 1986, ch. 1, is bracketed here to be dealt with in the next chapter. However, at least one reason why this proposal proves unsatisfactory is that these criteria are as disputable as any other law or right, so that placing their protection in the hands of a court suffers from parallel difficulties to them and is itself subject to the Hobbes challenge.

[13] Fuller, *The Morality of Law*, ch. 2.

system of law. Similarly, no critic of the rule of law denies that there are many advantages to rule by law – merely that these in themselves pose only mild constraints on personal rule, not least because they are inseparable from it. Therefore, to assess the respective merits of political and legal constitutionalism, we need to identify the specific dangers posed by the rule of persons, on the one hand, and the attributes, benefits and potential weaknesses and lacunas of rule by law, on the other.

The chief danger associated with the rule of persons is the possibility of arbitrary rule.[14] Arbitrariness in this context involves the capacity of rulers to coerce, obstruct, manipulate or otherwise impact upon the ruled without consulting their diverse views or interests and showing them equal concern and respect. As a result, not all are equal before the law either formally or substantively. Such arbitrariness manifests itself in three main ways. First, arbitrary rule can involve wilful or capricious government. As a result, there will be no consistency or coherence to policy, so that people will not know where they stand. For example, an act that had hitherto appeared unexceptional might suddenly, and for no apparent reason, attract a severe penalty simply because the ruler has taken a dislike to it or become unusually attentive. Indeed, arbitrariness in this sense can result from unconstrained judgement more generally. Even a good decision to reform a poor or unfair practice, say, can be the cause of injustice in its turn if it can be acted on at will and without any warning or consultation in ways that unsettle established expectations. Second, arbitrariness can stem from oppression, as when people's legitimate expectations and needs are overridden or ignored out of pure maliciousness or for the sake of another's self-interested ends. Finally, the presence of a ruler capable of acting arbitrarily in a systematic way entails domination.[15] The capacity for arbitrary interference is never absolute. No agent can always choose when, where, how and with who to interfere. However, so long as there is the potential for regular, if not total, interference we will be dominated by the ruler.[16] The ruled become permanently in awe of the power of their rulers, attempting to second-guess their next move – either to escape their wrath or win their favour.

---

[14] Raz, *The Authority of Law*, p. 219.

[15] As Philip Pettit, *Republicanism: A Theory of Freedom and Government*, second edition, Oxford: Clarendon Press, 1999, pp. 52–8 has shown, we owe the highlighting of this third aspect of arbitrariness to the republican political tradition.

[16] Obviously the possibility of very occasional arbitrary acts by individuals could never be eliminated within the circumstances of justice. Attempting to do so for all but a race of angels would inevitably involve the use of arbitrary power.

Although linked, one kind of arbitrariness can be present without necessarily involving the others. For example, an enlightened despot may not act capriciously or oppress people's interests, but by virtue of his comparatively unchecked power will still exert domination over them. Likewise, bureaucratic machines may not be wilful yet nonetheless be both oppressive and dominating. Indeed, to avoid this situation may require an occasional wilful disregard of the rules on the part of an official. Yet, that ability places him in a potentially dominating role in his turn. As we shall see, this tendency for the solution to one form of arbitrariness to generate a different form proves a general problem. The effect of all three kinds of arbitrary rule, whether singly or in combination, is to reduce the ruled to slaves of their ruler by removing their ability to act as free and equal citizens. Individuals lose the capacity to act autonomously and plan ahead on terms they can accept as fair for all. Instead, they have the anxiety of being subject to unpredictable, possibly malicious and usually prejudiced and unfairly discriminatory interference by the public authorities and their supporters and/or the inadvertent, yet preventable, or deliberately malign actions of others.

How far does law *per se* mitigate arbitrariness? Law can be broadly defined as a set of authoritative coordinating rules, regulations, directives and constraints that are backed by punitive sanctions and, less commonly, preventive restraints.[17] When designating what is required to rule by law, most commentators offer elaborations on, or synthetic summaries of, the desiderata listed by Lon Fuller as expressing the 'internal morality of law'.[18] These conditions consist of certain largely formal characteristics that are used to distinguish a system of laws from either a number of *ad hoc* directives or a collection of customary practices. Some of these qualities relate to the form of law, others to the form of the legal system. With regard to the first, standard criteria include that laws should be general and apply equally to all (though, as we shall see, they may need to take into account relevant differences), be prospective (only invoking retroactivity as a curative measure), public (albeit often through publicly funded experts), clear (avoiding vague terminology open to wide discretionary

---

[17] J. Finnis, *Natural Law and Natural Rights*, Oxford: Clarendon Press, 1980, p. 266.

[18] Fuller, *The Morality of Law*, p. 39 offers eight criteria, which Finnis, *Natural Law and Natural Rights*, p. 270 reorders and Raz, *The Authority of Law*, pp. 214–16 extends and elaborates. J. Rawls, *A Theory of Justice*, Oxford: Oxford University Press, 1971, pp. 236–9 is content with four, which Margaret Radin reduces to two (that 'there must be rules' and that 'those rules must be capable of being followed') 'Reconsidering the Rule of Law', *Boston University Law Review*, 69 (1989), p. 785, the second of which Raz also sees as capturing 'the basic idea' of the doctrine (p. 218). My analysis draws on all these accounts.

interpretation) and relatively stable (but not so as to ossify). So far as the second is concerned, laws should be consistent with each other, feasible, and congruent with official action. Most importantly, the promulgation, execution and ability to contest the laws should be guided by general, equal, public, clear and relatively stable rules.

These formal qualities of the law and the legal system are exemplified in numerous familiar legal norms and practices, such as the notion that there can be no crime without a law, or the view that the court system should be free from extraneous pressures, independent of all authority but the law and operate according to settled and open procedures that are the same for all citizens. These features give law the regularity needed for it to be a system in any moderately well-functioning sense. Without at least some of these elements, neither those subject to the laws nor those appointed to implement them will be able to follow and administer the law respectively in any sort of systematic way.

To the degree rule is by laws that satisfy these criteria, then rule by law will generate a weak form of the rule of law. At least for much of the time, people will comply with the law not out of deference to (or fear of) the persons who have made or are upholding it, nor necessarily because they agree with it, but simply because it is the law. Law so understood will be necessary to some degree in societies of any complexity that are characterised by the circumstances of justice and of politics encountered in the last chapter. It satisfies the need for common decisions that can coordinate the collective life of the community in conditions of reasonable disagreement over the nature of the good or just society. There are many aspects of social life where having almost any rule outweighs the perils or inconvenience of having none. Those with sharp elbows may not like the rule of first come first served in shops, but most people benefit from the arrangement and have a less stressful time as a result. Continuous white lines may annoy those drivers who claim to 'know' the road or to possess super-fast reactions, but the rest of us have an interest in such people being severely deterred from acting on this belief and in obeying the law. Even in areas which are not collective action problems and involve more contentious moral issues, the need for a common rule so that we know where we stand can lead us to accept laws we dislike – though, as I noted earlier, the place of that law within a more general system of legality, that usually includes mechanisms for changing or challenging it, also influences our acceptance.

A regular legal system generates a degree of predictability in social life by stabilising, regulating, securing and even constituting numerous valuable relationships. Most obviously, the presence of law reduces certain risks by protecting us from various potentially harmful, yet unforeseeable, acts by others. Criminal law achieves this reduction by attempting to deter specific wilfully harmful acts. However, by coordinating activity laws can also help prevent those harms that would otherwise arise simply from operating in an unregulated environment. For example, a traffic regulation directing that we all drive on one side of the road rather than the other undoubtedly reduces accidents by virtue of authoritatively deciding the issue and removing uncertainty. Indeed, without law, many social relationships and interactions would be insecure, prone to collapse, liable to develop in erratic and unpredictable ways, or simply not exist. Thus, marriage law promotes and to some extent creates a certain kind of social bond, shaping its development and shoring it up against those social forces that might erode or destabilise it, as well as partly regulating behaviour within it. Partners are given a clear understanding about what happens should they separate, one of them dies unexpectedly and so on. People are secured against various potential pitfalls of joint property ownership, merging their incomes, starting a family and the like, and so acquire the confidence to enter into such relations in the first place. Likewise, much commercial law not only protects us against fraud and particular sorts of economic loss, it actually facilitates trading and trust between buyers and sellers by informing each party as to the terms of their contract and holding them to it. One does not have to know the prevailing social customs of a given locality or learn and pander to the whims of the individuals with whom you are dealing in order to know one's rights and obligations. In a world where much human interaction is with numerous strangers and rather faceless yet powerful institutions – from state bureaucracies to big corporations – these qualities offer significant benefits. Indeed, as the case of marriage shows, even in the most intimate relationships a clear understanding of one's basic entitlements and duties should things come unstuck can be important.

Plainly, a certain complementarity obtains between the promotion of stability and predictability through law and the reduction of arbitrariness. To the extent officials and other power holders follow prearranged rules, arbitrariness in all three senses is diminished because these rules will restrict their room for manoeuvre. Keeping a government by and large within legal bounds protects against the 'lawless authority' Dicey famously associated with the Bastille,[19] where a figure such as Voltaire could be imprisoned solely at royal whim. Indeed, even if rulers (or our

---

[19] A. V. Dicey, *Introduction to the Study of the Law of the Constitution*, tenth edition, London: Macmillan, 1959, pp. 189–91.

fellow citizens) possess good judgement on a given matter that is superior to the prevailing law, we can still prefer that they abide by the comparatively imperfect rule and only improve upon it by following established procedures. Forcing policy changes to be made by a due process gives people warning of any new regulations and time to adapt to them. It also guards against those occasions when even good and well-intentioned rulers make mistakes. To the extent wilfulness promotes oppression and domination, then constraining this form of arbitrary rule will also reduce the others. Even under a tyrant, one may be able to avoid falling foul of the law, while a regard for legality, however superficial, will make the persecution of a particular individual more cumbersome if the due formalities are to be observed. Law also embodies a certain rough and ready form of equality. If we are to know how to react to the law so that it can guide our actions and interactions with unknown others, then we have to assume that it will have the same implications for everyone to whom it applies. Nevertheless, how deeply equality before the law reaches is a moot point.

The question of whether law is just an instrument that can be employed for any purpose, or whether oppressive and exploitative regimes are incompatible with law, has spawned a huge literature.[20] Clearly, even a tyranny within a modern society will need laws to regulate many of the activities that are incidental to its purposes, such as traffic. But some theorists believe tyrants seek to act in ways that prove antipathetic to a working legal system – they want discretion to do whatever they want, to be able to show partiality towards their supporters and to persecute whomever they dislike. All these activities are said to involve not placing themselves on a par with their fellow citizens as equals under the law. As a result, they end up undermining law because it ceases to offer a reliable guide to action. Why should I even stop at red traffic lights if many of my fellow drivers can flout them with impunity? If waiting for a green light gives me no greater assurance that I won't be crashed into and blamed for the incident than going through the red, I might as well rely on my own judgement and go whenever I think the way is clear. It cannot be doubted that tyrants typically use the law for largely cosmetic purposes when pursuing their evil ends. Nor do they usually see all, if any, of their fellows as equals. Nevertheless, the general benefits of legality as a system of coordination

---

[20] The *locus classicus* of this discussion in the Anglo-American literature is the debate between Hart and Fuller in H. L. A. Hart, 'Positivism and the Separation of Law and Morals', *Harvard Law Review*, 71 (1958), pp. 593–629 and L. Fuller, 'Positivism and Fidelity to Law: A Reply To Professor Hart', *Harvard Law Review*, 71 (1958), pp. 630–72.

and legitimation may make them wary of departing from its forms too obviously for fear of so undermining respect for law that people only act when ordered to do so by armed officials. For rule by coercion-backed commands alone is highly inefficient and makes much of social life difficult to sustain. In other words, even tyrants will want traffic laws to be obeyed. They will also wish to provide citizens with regular incentives to comply with some of their more iniquitous policies and to coordinate the actions of the officials responsible for their implementation. Of course, tyrannical regimes standardly possess an army of secret police, loyal only to the ruler and operating outside the rules governing the ordinary forces of law and order. However, they would cease to be 'regimes' if they relied on these agencies alone to enforce their will (and even these groups usually operate to a degree within the (admittedly despicable) laws of the land).[21] Moreover, it is not obvious that operating outside the law, or according to different rules, in some areas, necessarily precipitates a general decline of law-abidingness throughout the legal system. After all, no legal system is perfect.

Part of the problem is that some version of the tyrant's use of discretion, discrimination and special laws seems unavoidable if the law is not to be arbitrary in its turn. Take the simplest expression of the notion of equality before the law – the idea, that held sway for a long time in British law, that there be 'one law for all'.[22] This notion seems to neatly encapsulate the ideal of the rule of law. If law covers all, is the same in both content and application for all, then surely none is above it and law rules. Bias and self-interest should be ruled out because a tyrant who genuinely believed in law would have to apply it as severely to himself and his followers as those he wishes to persecute. Unfortunately, matters are not so neat. Let's start with discretion. The almost mechanical application of rules, however well-formulated, will not always be a good thing. An officious insistence on the letter of the law is often itself arbitrary and productive of injustices, even when the rule itself is well-motivated and just. As anyone

---

[21] On the issue of whether a tyranny could be organised without law, see the debate between Kramer and Simmonds, the latest round of which can be found in M. H. Kramer, 'On the Moral Status of the Rule of Law', *Cambridge Law Journal*, 63 (2004), pp. 65–97 and N. E. Simmonds, 'Straightforwardly False: The Collapse of Kramer's Positivism', *Cambridge Law Journal*, 63 (2004), pp. 98–131. Kramer rightly notes how Simmonds' ingenious examples of Taliban-like authorities operating entirely outside the rule of law depend on the implausible assumptions that the rule of law is an all-or-nothing affair and that a regime could be concerned solely with achieving its ideological goals to the neglect of all other areas of social life.

[22] Dicey, *Introduction*, p. 193, J. Waldron, *The Law*, London: Routledge, 1990, pp. 40–41.

who has ever had to deal with a bureaucracy knows full well, rule-bound procedures that appear excessive, or in some way inappropriate to the task at hand, exert a stultifying domination over administrators and their clients alike. The domination of arbitrary impersonal rules may be less degrading than that of an arbitrary ruler but it can prove as irksome, if not more so through being all-pervasive. Indeed, turning an unjust or plain inept policy into law may make its enforcement all the more regular. If the consistent application of unjust laws means that one can learn how to get around or evade them,[23] consistency also prevents sympathetic judges and officials quietly bending the rules to avoid injustices.[24] Within an evil regime, obedience to the law may allow officials to excuse themselves of any moral responsibility for the acts they commit. Moreover, its not just bad rules that are the problem. There can also be an absence of rules – after all, it's hard to anticipate all eventualities. In many cases the discretionary exercise of good judgement will be preferable to no decision or the attempt to adapt an unsuitable existing rule.

The universality requirement is sometimes thought to rule out discrimination. Certainly it would be hard, if still possible, to formulate a general law, applying equally to all, that is aimed solely at a particular individual. It is fairly easy, though, to construct such laws so that they discriminate against groups. Nazi race laws and South African apartheid laws had this form, applying as they did to all Jews and non-whites. It's true that if the laws apply also to the rulers, they may make them less harsh or allow for exemptions that benefit others beside themselves. It all depends how ideologically pure and committed they are – after all, prominent Italian Jewish fascists were not spared the rigour of Mussolini's late conversion to Hitler's Aryan ideal. Meanwhile, though racist and suchlike laws are rightly condemned, it's unclear all laws singling out groups as different are to be criticised. Surely, the fact all cases are *not* alike may often require laws that do differentiate between groups in order to avoid discrimination. For example, rules regarding maternity leave have been generally placed in this category.

What about the special laws governing party members and the political police? Or those laws that place the leader outside the law? Once again, these exceptions to 'one rule for all' do not appear unjustified in themselves. Officials often undertake tasks one would not wish ordinary citizens

[23] Rawls, *A Theory of Justice*, p. 59.
[24] J. Waldron, 'The Rule of Law in Contemporary Liberal Theory', *Ratio Juris*, 2 (1989), p. 82.

to be allowed to do – such as being able to detain and interrogate those suspected of criminal activities. Don't we need special laws to regulate such special powers, granting dispensations from ordinary legal constraints but setting possibly higher standards according to which such powers must be exercised? Indeed, having literally the same laws for everyone in all situations seems absurd. Most laws are framed in a conditional form so as only to apply to all those engaged in a given activity in certain circumstances, not everyone all the time. Health and safety standards in private houses are different to those in hotels, adults and children are treated differently and so on. As to there being some powers literally outside the law, executives are standardly accorded exceptional powers in an emergency that allow them to go beyond – even suspend – the law in order to preserve it.

We seem faced with a paradox. The capacity of law to avoid the arbitrariness of the rule of persons seems to rest on its being a rule-bound system that makes everyone equal before the law. Yet, without discretion, laws that treat different people differently, and specials laws that place some under different laws to others, it risks becoming arbitrary in its turn. Law has to be flexible enough to make morally or pragmatically justified distinctions and discriminations, without becoming so flexible that even a tyrant can use it. The key is whether the form or inner morality of law can guide the legitimate use of such differential treatment in ways that preserve the consistency and integrity of law as a system. If so, then law may be said to rule. Underlying the notion of the rule of law, though, is arguably a set of values that go deeper than anything law in itself can provide. It is an inherent property of rules that they treat people in the same way. As we saw, this feature can yield many desirable benefits. But there is more to equal treatment than treating everyone the same. We need to see other people as equals.

There are elements of impartiality and of reciprocity involved here. On the one hand, we should endeavour to avoid prejudice or self-interest in our judgement of others. On the other hand, we should only engage in collective enterprises all could accept and undertake to do our bit in sustaining them. Both these notions seem bound up with the ideal of equality before the law: we want the law to be not only blind and free from partiality but also in the public interest. Each of these qualities gives us faith in, and promotes fidelity to, the law. However, the second proves especially important. Procedural fairness alone will not generate a responsibility to abide by and uphold the law. We must see the law as in some sense ours – a feeling that flows in large part from the law being a public good, depending upon and making possible mutually beneficial cooperation. Yet, seeing ourselves as on a par with our fellows and bound in reciprocal ties to them is a fundamentally political ideal, linked to democratic citizenship. This ideal literally has the rule of a tyrant as its antithesis. Indeed, it points to why authoritarianism would also be incompatible with the rule of law. Theoretically, an authoritarian regime could be a benevolent rather than a tyrannical dictatorship. Obviously, there are prudential reasons for doubting this would ever be so in practice. But if we see the rule of law as subject to the circumstances of politics, so that there is no agreement on which cases are different and how they should be treated differently, then the only way to treat people as equals under the law will be to allow them to decide this issue. In this case, authoritarianism proves incompatible with the rule of law in theory as well. Put another way, authoritarianism will always be arbitrary by virtue of being dominating.[25] No privileged evaluative viewpoint, be it of a judge or some other third party arbitrator, can decide whether government action serves public rather than sectional interests and so shows equal regard for all. The only available heuristic is a political process that allows people to speak for themselves and to contest the proposals of others. In other words, only democracy is capable of promoting laws that are fairly framed and applied. Before exploring this thesis further in Part II, we need to investigate more fully the problems of legalistic conceptions of the rule of law.

II Legal rule

F. A. Hayek and Ronald Dworkin have offered two of the most important defences of the legal view of the rule of law in recent times. Superficially, their theories could not be more different. Hayek adopts a largely formal and rule-based approach of a kind Dworkin sees as ultimately vacuous. By contrast, Dworkin's principled approach appeals to a sense of moral community in a way that Hayek regards as pernicious. Though both see the rule of law as a bulwark of individual freedom, Hayek believes it defends the market against redistributive measures while Dworkin considers the equitable distribution of resources as a condition of, rather than a constraint on, liberty. However, there are also certain similarities between their theories. Both distinguish law proper from ordinary legislation, which they perceive as tainted through being particularistic and goal orientated. In their view, the former prioritises the individual, the

---

[25] Pettit, *Republicanism*, pp. 56–7.

latter the collective and a prime function of the rule of law is to ensure the one is never sacrificed to the other. They also claim law never runs out, so that judges can always be guided by it. In what follows, each of these points will be disputed.

Hayek: going by the rulebook

Hayek conceived the rule of law as being diametrically opposed to the arbitrary rules of a Hobbesian sovereign, a form of governing he associated with totalitarian regimes of right and left. Hayek counterposed 'law' as a system of general rules to 'legislation' seen as the commands of the sovereign ruler – including a democratically elected sovereign parliament.[26] Legislation was appropriate to organisations, such as an army, that had clear and determinate goals. However, he contended society at large has no such common purposes, just the very diverse and evolving ends of the individuals who compose it. Consequently, to govern all social life as if it was an organisation is an impossible task that leads all who attempt it towards tyranny. Rather, a well-ordered society needs clear and general rules designed to provide everyone with the maximum possible freedom to act and think without infringing the freedom of others to do likewise. As he put it, the law should operate like a Highway Code: it should provide the rules of the road needed for people to drive about with a reduced risk of accidents, not a set of orders directing people where to go, when and how.[27] The rule of law consisted in the primacy of such rules over legislation. If legislation was subordinated to law, citizens would no longer be made to serve the momentary purposes of government policy but would be free to pursue their own ends on equal terms with others and in ways that avoided mutual interference.

Hayek developed this thesis most clearly with regard to the economy. To run an entirely planned economy, the state would have not only to know what people currently want and need and the best way to satisfy these requirements, but also to second-guess a whole range of unpredictable events, including the conceptual innovations individuals undertake, that alter supply and demand in the future. Since no human agency can do this, planning inevitably proves inefficient and, to the extent it necessarily constrains human choice and experimentation by forcing all to conform to the plan, coercive as well. Consequently, social justice, interpreted as an

---

[26] F. A. Hayek, *Rules and Order*, London: Routledge, 1973, ch. 2.
[27] F. A. Hayek, *Road to Serfdom*, London: Routledge, 1944, pp. 55–6.

ideal distribution of goods that accords with every individual's needs and deserts, is a mirage.[28] Unfortunately, democracy encourages the pursuit of this very idea since it offers the perfect legitimation for organised groups seeking various benefits from the state.[29] As a result, state legislation was gradually encompassing all spheres of life and moving Western democracies along 'the road to serfdom'.[30] Upholding the rule of law would curb this shift.

In Hayek's view, rules arise not from human agency but spontaneously, through individuals trying to adapt to each other and their environment. Rational appraisal involves weeding out poor conventions through trial and error, not assessing their fit within a supposed rational system of law.[31] To continue the Highway Code analogy, it is custom rather than *a priori* reasoning that determines whether one drives on the right or left, and experiment that tends to fix the most appropriate speed limits. Nevertheless, laws had to have certain formal features to avoid becoming instruments of arbitrary power. They had to be fixed, general, abstract, universal and above all independent of any given policy goal. Hayek believed these criteria are sufficient to distinguish law from legislation.[32] Their very generality and abstractness make it impossible to know how they might affect particular people. As a result, law-makers have an incentive to ensure legal rules and procedures are as fair as possible. Moreover, he maintained that rules of this nature cannot be used to pursue a particular purpose. Laws so conceived only provide a framework for human interaction that prevents others, especially governments, seeking to employ us as means to their ends.

I noted in the last section how a working system of law needs to possess some formal rule-like qualities and that these reduce certain kinds of *ad hoc* and discretionary decision-making. However, Hayek's account of the rule of law is a radical version of this thesis. He maintains we can literally rule through formal, general rules – indeed, that this is the only way for a complex society to be governed without degenerating into an inefficient tyranny. How true is this argument? Hayek certainly underscores the ways general rules can overcome many of the informational, psychological and political costs of substantive, case-by-case decision-making.[33] Obtaining

---

[28] F. A. Hayek, *The Mirage of Social Justice*, London: Routledge, 1976, chs. 7 and 9.
[29] Hayek, *Rules and Order*, p. 2.   [30] Hayek, *Road to Serfdom*, chs. 5 and 6.
[31] Hayek, *Rules and Order*, ch. 1.   [32] Ibid., p. 6.
[33] For an excellent account of the advantages of rules, see F. Schauer, *Playing by the Rules: A Philosophical Examination of Rule-based Decision Making in Law and in Life*, New York: Oxford University Press, 1991, especially ch. 7, and Cass Sunstein, *Legal Reasoning and Political Conflict*, New York: Oxford University Press, 1996, pp. 110–15.

all the relevant information imposes a massive administrative burden and may not be possible in any case. It also places a huge responsibility on officials and citizens, obliging them to constantly exercise their judgement. Getting substantive political agreement on a given matter is often much harder than agreeing on a general rule. In the former case, people's different concerns and interests are likely to play a much greater role. Consequently, decision-making takes much longer and the incentives for rent-seeking behaviour increase as each group seeks some pay-off for giving its assent. The result can be incoherent and expensive legislation. By contrast, people can often agree on the reasonableness of a rule without entering into debates over its ultimate rightness and wrongness. Indeed, a procedural or formal rule, such as first come first served, can be a fair way of resolving an issue without judging the merits of each case. A rule in an uncontentious area may even be extendable as a solution to resolve contentious cases in other areas. Even if agreeing on the rule does have informational, psychological and political costs of its own, it may produce savings overall by deciding many cases at one go. Rules also guard against myopia, carelessness, bias or weakness of will. The burden of making judgements is lifted from citizens and officials alike. Moreover, both are enabled as well as constrained. For example, they can be emboldened to confront the rich and powerful by being able simply to insist that the rule be followed rather than having to challenge their actions on the basis of a personal judgement. In similar ways, by increasing visibility, rules enhance accountability. Citizens and officials alike can hold each other to the rules. The impersonality of rules can also reduce the feeling of humiliation felt by those to whom they are applied. They need not feel the hapless victims or fawning beneficiaries of an individual's discretion.

All these features, along with the others I explored earlier, diminish the scope for wilfulness, oppression and domination. However, we also saw that rules have various drawbacks. In many respects, Hayek's formalist approach highlights these shortcomings rather than overcoming them. Two of his criteria for law prove particularly problematic – the insistence that there be no reference to specific people or policy outcomes, and his desire to eliminate discretion, so that the law always guides what judges and officials should do. Both restrictions are crucial to his attempt to distinguish law from legislation, yet neither appears tenable.

Formal properties alone do not define the appropriateness of a rule. Their generality and blindness to particulars often proves a vice rather than a virtue.[34] As we noted, rules that are reasonable in some contexts

---

[34] See Sunstein, *Legal Reasoning*, ch. 5.

may be inappropriate in others – health and safety rules suitable for large establishments may be excessive for small concerns. Circumstances can also change in unforeseen ways that make a nonsense of prevailing general rules – it would be absurd to apply regulations imposing catalytic converters on 'all cars' to electric vehicles that were unimagined at the time the law was passed. Rules can also entrench certain biases and injustices. I remarked how racial laws can satisfy the criteria of generality and universality. But I observed too how not discriminating can be problematic. In general, formal equality of treatment promotes rather than reduces substantive inequalities. That can often be a legitimate goal. To discover who can run the fastest in given conditions, the rules of the race must be the same for all. However, equity often requires that we ensure the rules do not treat differently situated individuals in inappropriately similar ways. By treating all in the same way, rules can harm those who ought to be treated differently or, worse, legitimate practices that exploit those differences. Thus, feminists have criticised equal opportunities law for including a covert (and sometimes overt) male comparator test that overlooks relevant differences such as pregnancy or the structural factors that have relegated women to low-paid, casual employment.[35] Instead of rethinking work and gender roles in ways that are compatible with shared child-care duties, family responsibilities become a disqualification for certain jobs.

As a result of these difficulties, it seems impossible for laws not to deal either with policy outcomes or persons. Hayek is no doubt correct to observe that legislators rarely set out to frame laws in formal terms *per se*. But that is because it would be nonsensical to do so. They devise laws with particular ends in mind and then give them a certain form in order to obtain the law-like characteristics which enable these purposes to be achieved. Although this means laws can be turned to immoral purposes, it also enables them to avoid the pitfalls outlined above. Thus, traffic regulations have elements of generality to secure fairness and the benefits of cooperation but are also determined in part by notions of expediency and various substantive purposes. Of course, Hayek did not dispute that legislation was required in certain areas and presumably thought in these cases judges should be guided by the policies governments laid out. However, he did believe that in deciding cases where the law was unclear or when determining whether legislation was appropriate or not, then only

[35] C. MacKinnon, 'On Difference and Dominance', in *Feminism Unmodified: Discourses on Life and Law*, Cambridge, MA: Harvard University Press, 1989, p. 36.

law-like considerations should prevail. Yet it is not clear that even this more limited position is feasible. Once we admit that there can be occasions when a rule like 'nobody can drive faster than thirty miles per hour in a built-up area' might admit of exceptions – as when an ambulance, or possibly a private car, is rushing an emergency patient to hospital, then it becomes hard not to assess the rule in the light of its justification. If that occurs, the rule loses its rule-like character and becomes a piece of advice or a weighty consideration that has to be judged in terms of its relevance for the individuals in the case at hand and the likely effect of making a precedent of the exception or given reading of the rule. After all, notions of 'reasonableness' and 'proportionality' are standardly invoked in these sorts of cases and usually involve attention to particulars and some calculation of social harms and benefits. In other words, the judge begins to act in ways Hayek deems appropriate to the legislator.

This brings us to Hayek's belief that rules could ever eliminate judicial discretion. The problem is that rules almost never operate in the manner Hayek proposes – as mid-level generalisations that settle all cases in advance. A degree of vagueness that requires the exercise of judgement on those who follow or apply them is built into their very nature. Wittgenstein famously noted how easy it is to misread a rule.[36] The reason is that rules build on far more assumptions than can ever be expressed in the rule itself. Is a rule about the size of 'trunks' referring to trees, a person's body, the luggage compartment of a car, male swimming shorts, an elephant's nose? Only context and certain shared understandings will enable us to know. In these cases, most people probably could fix on a determinate meaning without too much difficulty. However, harder cases are not difficult to come up with. For example, does an 'electric' bike come under the rules relating to pedal cycles or mopeds – should the rider wear a motorcycle crash helmet, say? Or take the references to 'equality' or 'freedom of speech' in bills of rights. As we saw in the last chapter, interpreting these terms raises substantive disagreements stemming from contrasting moral, political and epistemological positions. Sometimes the assumptions that come to guide judicial understanding of these sorts of terms end up being of a highly technical character, making law-abidingness by citizens tricky when these technical definitions depart considerably from lay understandings. But often, there simply is no totally settled view – making rule following even harder and official discretion all the greater.

---

[36] L. Wittgenstein, *Philosophical Investigations*, Oxford: Blackwell, 1953, pp. 87, 185, 219.

It's doubtful that tightening up the rules or providing a glossary of definitions, as law books often attempt to do, will ever remove all ambiguity. Rules will always seem either too narrow or too broad when faced with the unanticipated case, leading those charged with enforcing them to consider whether or not it is sufficiently different in relevant ways for them not to apply. Indeed, some vagueness in the rules may even be desirable at times. I noted earlier how sticklers for the rules can sometimes seem overly rigid and officious. In fact, strict rules that seem insufficiently discriminating can lead to people surreptitiously bending or selectively ignoring them, as occasionally occurred when British juries refused to convict certain classes of murderers in cases where the death penalty was compulsory. While such deception may be warranted, transparency of decision-making can be lost in the process. Rules that are too fixed and predictable can also aid evasion. Loopholes will always exist that can be exploited and people can learn to play the rules, as tax accountants are paid to do. In these sorts of cases, it might be better to have a flexible standard rather than a fixed rule.

In sum, the model of a system of general rules seems unable to deliver the goal-independent, impartial and fixed set of prospective judgements Hayek seeks from it. Many of the difficulties become apparent if we turn to Hayek's two main claims with regard to the rule of law – that rules will operate against redistribution and economic planning, while protecting the freedom of individuals from interference by others. He assumes the formal properties of rules will exclude the pursuit of particular goals. However, there are no particular purposes that cannot be framed within some general description that applies to them alone or be derived from some suitably designed general rule. 'All persons earning above £100,000 pay supertax' is a general, equal rule. Likewise, stable prices and plans announced well in advance may also be consistent with a purely formal view of the rule of law. Far from being incompatible with the pursuit of social purposes, rules help promote them by moving officials and citizens consistently towards that objective without the need for continuous commands. The point in such cases is whether these policies are socially or economically sound – often they are.[37] For example, Hayek suggests that 'measures designed to control the access to different trades and occupations, the terms of sale, and the amounts to be produced and sold' require reference to particular goals and so 'involve arbitrary discrimination against persons' thereby contravening the rule of law as he conceives

---

[37] Raz, *The Authority of Law*, p. 228.

it.[38] Yet he immediately backtracks, admitting it is sensible to ensure doctors are suitably qualified before being allowed to practise, pilots pass eye tests, and even that sellers of firearms and poisons should be 'persons satisfying certain intellectual and moral qualities'.[39] In fact, most government regulations – including much social legislation – arise not as part of a rational plan but as responses to particular problems, being progressively modified through the trial and error mechanism Hayek approves.[40]

These problems prove even more acute in the case of liberty. Hayek's central contention is that 'when we obey laws, in the sense of general abstract rules laid down irrespective of their application to us, we are not subject to another's will and are therefore free'.[41] At times, he appears to suggest that so long as everyone is similarly affected by a rule, it is not aimed at anyone personally, and infraction is avoidable, then no coercion is involved. Lawgivers do not know the particular cases where their rules will be applied and the judge is simply applying that law. Consequently, law is like a natural obstacle. But this leads to absurdities. As Hamowy has observed,[42] by these criteria a gangster-ridden neighbourhood – being like a plague-infested swamp, neither aimed at me personally nor unavoidable – represents no limit on my freedom. This is a serious problem given that his purely formal criteria not only offer no guidance as to which rules should apply to what sorts of activity, but also are consistent with all kinds of hidden or overt biases that can discriminate against particular groups. Hayek partially acknowledged this difficulty in accepting that it can be misguided to apply the same rules to everyone in all circumstances. As we have noted, law frequently discriminates on grounds of age or sex, for example. The key is to discover when such discrimination is reasonable or not. His response to this problem is extremely suggestive: 'Such distinctions will not be arbitrary', he wrote, 'will not subject one group to the will of others, *if they are equally recognised as justified by those inside and those outside the group.*'[43] However, this criterion makes the test of the rule of law not its formal qualities but its capacity to evince reciprocity and hence obtain mutual assent from citizens. Equality before the law involves the content of legal rules taking everyone into account and giving equal weight

[38] F. A. Hayek, *The Constitution of Liberty*, London: Routledge, 1960, pp. 227–8.
[39] Ibid., p. 228.
[40] N. MacCormick, 'Spontaneous Order and the Rule of Law: Some Problems', *Ratio Juris*, 2 (1989), pp. 41–54.
[41] Hayek, *Constitution of Liberty*, pp. 153–4.
[42] R. Hamowy, 'Law and the Liberal Society', *Journal of Libertarian Studies*, 2 (1987), pp. 287–97.
[43] Hayek, *Constitution of Liberty*, p. 154, emphasis added.

to different points of view. Put another way, Hayek appears to be suggesting that law must reflect the general rather than any particular will. Yet, this argument pushes us towards the political conception of constitutionalism, since such mutual acceptance is only likely from a political process in which all must actually consult the interest of others. Before exploring that possibility, though, we need to see if an alternative view of legal integrity to the Hayekian rulebook might be capable of leading law to rule.

Dworkin: judging on principle

Among contemporary jurists, Ronald Dworkin has probably mounted the boldest defence of the judiciary's role in upholding the moral integrity of the law. However, he focuses on principles, which he largely identifies with constitutional rights, rather than general, abstract rules. He contends law's principles can be consistently and prospectively applied to every possible case, securing individual rights in the process. As a result, he believes law's empire can be legitimately and coherently extended to cover all persons so as to render everyone, including the courts, equally subject to it.

Although Dworkin shares Hayek's view of legislation as policy orientated and designed to promote the general welfare, he grants it a broader scope and sees democracy as the fairest mechanism for aggregating individual interests in ways likely to promote the public good. Still, he too believes it needs to be supplemented and circumscribed by law. Legislation suffers from the sorts of problems we identified with rule by law. Somewhat contentiously, Dworkin maintains that legislative rules tend to be quite specific, applying to any given instance in an 'all-or-nothing' manner that lacks the possibility of 'weighing' different considerations.[44] As a result, a rule's bearing in an unforeseen case is not just hard to fathom but literally non-existent – there simply is no relevant rule to apply. Even if this contention goes too far, legal positivists would agree that legislation frequently contains 'gaps', albeit often arising from its deliberate vagueness rather than its overspecificity. These 'gaps' present judges and officials with 'hard cases'. The legal positivist argues that in this instance law runs out, so that they must use their discretion to decide the matter, though this is usually guided in various ways by prevailing legal norms and parallel cases from which analogies might be drawn. By contrast, Dworkin believes a 'right answer' may be discerned by consulting the moral principles that

---

[44] R. Dworkin, 'The Model of Rules', in *Taking Rights Seriously*, London: Duckworth, 1978, pp. 24, 26.

underpin the legal system.[45] These principles consist of rights rather than policy goals.[46] As such, they constrain ordinary legislation by protecting individual interests from being overlooked or curtailed for the benefit of the collective welfare. Moreover, by not being tied to the needs of the moment, they allow a consistent and prospective application of the law.

How does this work? In the most developed version of his thesis, Dworkin argues that judges must interpret the law so that it both achieves a 'fit' with generally accepted aspects of legal doctrine and has the most justificatory 'appeal' from a moral point of view. In a pre-interpretative phase, judges collect the available legal materials. Then, within the constraints of 'fit', they seek to interpret the law in a way which offers the morally 'best constructive interpretation of the political structure and legal doctrine of their community' by reference to a 'coherent set of principles about people's rights and duties'.[47] Finally, in the post-interpretative phase they develop the law by adjudicating upon its bearing in particular cases in the light of their interpretation. Dworkin believes this procedure constrains judicial discretion by promoting consistency of judgement and removing 'gaps' – even in hard cases. For in every case the judge is simply 'discovering' the existing entitlements of the different parties. Though judges necessarily employ a 'weak' form of discretion given that there is no clear-cut decision-making procedure, they do not have discretion in the 'strong' sense of being able to decide a case as they wish. Such discretionary judgement is ruled out not only by the need for 'fit' with settled and relatively uncontroversial aspects of the law, but also by Dworkin's contention that the rights and principles that best justify it will supply, theoretically at least, determinate answers that it is the duty of the judge to uncover. Nevertheless, these justificatory moral values are not simply those a legal positivist would recognise as legally valid because they have been explicitly incorporated into the law, as is the case with bills of rights, or expressly referred to by it, as arises with notions of fairness in contracts. In giving the 'morally best' justification of the law, judges must draw on their own moral views and not just take account of conventional morality. It is not simply that settled social rules may not exist in all areas and bills of rights can be compatible with more than one theory of morality. Dworkin also believes the law's integrity rests on its reflecting certain objective moral considerations.

---

[45] R. Dworkin, 'Hard Cases', in *Taking Rights Seriously*, p. 81.
[46] Dworkin, 'Model of Rules', pp. 22–3 and 'Hard Cases', p. 82.
[47] R. Dworkin, *Law's Empire*, London: Fontana, 1986, p. 255.

For Dworkin, therefore, law rules by virtue of its 'fit' with 'a coherent set of principles about justice and fairness and procedural due process'.[48] Indeed, he believes that by giving law a degree of moral and practical integrity, these principles promote faith in the legal system as a whole, generating an obligation to abide by it on the part of citizens and officials alike. I dispute both these claims. Law is too complex and, due to 'the burdens of judgement' explored in the last chapter, capable of being given too many conflicting moral readings, for any such principled 'fit' to appear anything but arbitrary. In this case, fidelity to law is more likely to arise from allowing the expression of principled disagreement through the legislature than through promoting a non-existent consensus via the courts.

First, Dworkin's holistic approach to the law can often be arbitrary, encouraging the application of principles and considerations in settled parts of the law that are remote from, and inappropriate to, the case at hand. Dworkin concedes that constructing a coherent picture of law, let alone providing it with a principled justification, requires an almost Herculean effort beyond the capacity of ordinary judges. The law contains many branches, and he accepts the time and intellectual effort involved makes it unlikely that any real judge could hope to construct a comprehensive picture of the law in each area and an overarching general theory to unite them all. Instead, real judges necessarily operate with an understanding of the law that is partial. However, he believes that for all their limitations, they still strive for as coherently principled a view as they can.[49] But this may not be available. Different parts of the law give different weights to different goods, values and types of moral claim. Civil and criminal cases tend to operate with different standards of evidence and notions of responsibility, for example. Even similar areas of the law may involve quite different criteria. Principles and considerations relevant to cases of sex discrimination, say, may be quite inappropriate to issues of race. Dworkin's holistic approach may force a coherence that does not and should not obtain, by treating very different areas as if they were the same. He partly hides these difficulties by arguing at the level of very abstract principle. But when one descends from considering equality as such to equality in particular cases and areas, dissimilarities as well as similarities soon emerge. Moreover, it may be that the moral considerations involved are of quite diverse and incommensurable kinds. In these circumstances,

---

[48] Ibid., p. 243.   [49] Ibid., p. 265.

to appeal from rights in one part of the law and apply them to quite another could be incoherent.[50]

Second, and related to this last point, decisions based on rights need not yield a right answer. There may be two or more answers that could be seen as being, in very different ways, equally right. Of course, Dworkin does accept that rights can clash and may need to be balanced. But he believes that an appropriate balance will always exist, just as he contends that a given party must always have a right to win.[51] Again, this assumes commensurability at some level that may not exist.[52] For example, take the balance between privacy and freedom of speech. People holding different normative theories and priorities are likely to disagree not only about their relative weight – both with regard to each other and to other important values – but also over the nature of the two concepts. Thus, some may view the private sphere as one's immediate family circle, others include close friends, business associates (which may also involve family members and friends), or even everything that happens behind closed doors in a privately owned establishment, and so on. The same holds for 'speech', as disputes about the First Amendment testify. As a result, for some no clash between the two will have occurred, when for others it has. Because there is no commensurable scale on which privacy and speech can be weighed, and each is in any case defined and applied in ways that are subject to the 'burdens of judgement', then even if ideally there is an 'objective' balance between the two, any view of what that is will always be subject to reasonable disagreement.

Third, even though legal reasoning refers to rights, it does not follow there should be no reference to interests. Dworkin's division between 'policy' and 'principle' proves in this respect as contentious as Hayek's similar attempt to separate rules from any reference to specific ends. Rights certainly deserve to be regarded as weighty interests that any view of the public interest should take into account. But Dworkin accepts that not all rights are absolute – indeed, I argued in the last chapter that none are. Rights often derive their rationale not from their benefit to the rights holder *per se* but from the public goods they promote, as we saw was the case with freedom of speech. This broader context often comes into play when fixing the boundaries of rights, with courts being less inclined than Dworkin supposes to give any guarantee against offering an

---

[50] Sunstein, *Legal Reasoning*, pp. 48–50.
[51] Dworkin, 'Can Rights be Controversial?', in *Taking Rights Seriously*, pp. 286–7.
[52] Mackie, 'Third Theory of Law', p. 9.

expansive reading if that would not be conducive to the general welfare. Thus, Greenawalt reports the US Supreme Court as rejecting an official's claim not to produce an organisational record on the grounds it might incriminate him because such records offer the main source of evidence of wrongdoing and 'were the cloak of the privilege to be thrown around these impersonal records and documents, effective enforcement of many federal and state laws would be impossible'.[53] Likewise, when rights clash, interests and considerations of the general welfare may help determine which right is stronger in the particular circumstances. When comparing the rights of a property developer to build an airport on land legally purchased for the purpose, say, with the rights of nearby home-owners to enjoy their houses and gardens without suffering damaging noise pollution, then at least some view of where the public as well as private interests lie in this case seems a necessary part of any decision. Little would ever be done if collective benefits could never outweigh individual rights. Yet if this is true, then we appear to have a problem. Not only does Dworkin himself concede that weighing up the collective interest is best done by representative assemblies, he also notes that such considerations are likely to alter according to circumstances, making the prospective almost *a priori* account of law he seeks impossible.

Finally, Dworkin suggests that what the law is depends in certain instances on what is morally best. He believes this moral dimension gives a certain objectivity to judicial decisions. Certainly, moral judgements typically distinguish themselves from mere custom or convention by claiming to be objective. The difficulty lies in sustaining such claims in the face of the limitations of human reasoning which appear to allow for rival claims to be made. There is absolutely no reason to suppose the judiciary will concur on the morally best view of the law any more than the rest of the population if reasonable disagreements in this area are possible. Indeed, insisting that judges look for some comprehensive, objective theory of the law is more likely to generate such disagreements than a more modest approach. For a start, the judge or official will be invited to interrogate even law that appears to be settled to see if it 'fits' the preferred morally best view of law as a whole. That will have the potential effect of making all cases 'hard'. Moreover, if – as I have suggested – there are good grounds for assuming judges will disagree, consistency in the law will also be jeopardised. We have observed that applying rules to cases is far from

[53] *United States v White* 322 US 694, 700 (1944) (dissent) quoted in K. Greenawalt, 'Policy, Rights and Judicial Decision', in M. Cohen (ed.), *Ronald Dworkin and Contemporary Jurisprudence*, London: Duckworth, 1984, p. 107.

clear-cut. But the application of abstract principles of justice seems likely to be even more indeterminate.

In sum, Dworkin's principled approach fails to rule out judicial or official discretion and in many cases actively encourages it. By inviting judges to offer a view of 'good' law rather than law *per se*, Dworkin turns judges from third party arbiters into participants in many of the disagreements that it is politics' rather than the law's role to resolve. They become advocates like other citizens of a particular view of how society could best be organised. In the process, he undermines the distinction between law and legislation. Indeed, rights-based arguments more generally cannot avoid taking the consequences for policy into account and do not always offer a determinate 'right' answer. Far from promoting fidelity to law, the very ambition of Dworkin's approach risks undermining it by making law appear to be little more than the contentious opinion of a particular person. Rather than taking law out of politics, his theory serves to emphasise the degree to which law lies within the 'circumstances of politics'. It remains to see whether a more overtly political approach can address the worries that lie behind the desire of legal constitutionalists to exclude its influence on the law.

III Political rule

Both Hayek and Dworkin feared that because legislation was the product of the rule of persons it risked being arbitrary. The bogey figure in each case appears to be the Hobbesian sovereign – potentially as potent a force in the form of a sovereign parliament or people as it is in the guise of a monarch or dictator. Yet, ironically they fail to meet the Hobbes challenge and end up turning judges into sovereigns and potentially arbitrary legislators in their turn. Two problems emerge from the analysis thus far. First, is it possible to conceive of the process of legislation in what one might call a 'de-sovereigntised' way, so that the legislators make laws that evince equal concern and respect for the ideals and interests of those who are to live under them? Second, is it possible for judges and other officials to follow these rules without substituting their judgement for those of the legislature? Both questions are briefly addressed below. In each case, I argue the answer lies in so dividing power that politicians and courts alike are moved to make decisions in equitable and consistent ways that respect the reasonable disagreements that constitute the 'circumstances of politics'. This response draws inspiration from the republican tradition and will be most fully explored in Part II, especially chapter 5.

My aim here is simply to sketch its implications for how we understand the rule of law.

The politics of the rule of law

That a political system should constitute 'an empire of laws and not of men' is a prime tenet of the republican tradition,[54] at least in the neo-Roman variant of Cicero, Machiavelli and Harrington recently identified by Quentin Skinner and Philip Pettit.[55] Republicans contrast a law-governed polity with the domination of arbitrary rule. However, they believe the way to overcome the second and achieve the first lies in the form of government rather than the form of law. As we saw, the distinguishing features of arbitrary rule are the capacity to exercise discretionary power at whim and without consulting the interests of those affected. Republicanism's distinctiveness resides in noting how even an enlightened and benevolent ruler who possesses this power still dominates, even if he does not actually oppress, the ruled, for they are subjects of their ruler's will. Indeed, chapter 4 shall show how legal constitutions can become sources of domination in this latter sense. For the only alternative to the domination of personal rule is for the people to be citizens and rule themselves. Paradoxically, therefore, the rule of law depends on the democratic self-rule of persons. It can be secured only if all citizens, usually through their elected representatives, can command equal consideration in the making of collective rules, and everyone within the body politic – including those authorised to rule – is equally subject to whatever laws they impose upon themselves.[56] From this perspective, the rule of law arises from a particular civic condition – one where all citizens enjoy an equal political status and have no dominion over each other. To quote Harrington again, only when all are equal in the making of the laws will they be 'framed by every private man unto no other end (or they may thank themselves) than to protect the liberty of every man'.[57]

According to this way of thinking, rulers will only accept restrictions on their power and take account of the interests of others when obliged by

---

[54] E.g. J. Harrington, *The Commonwealth of Oceana*, ed. J. G. A. Pocock, Cambridge: Cambridge University Press, 1992, pp. 20–21

[55] Q. Skinner, *Liberty before Liberalism*, Cambridge: Cambridge University Press, 1998, pp. 44–5 and Pettit, *Republicanism*, pp. 172–83. See M. Viroli, *Machiavelli*, Oxford: Oxford University Press, 1998, pp. 121–5.

[56] Skinner, *Liberty before Liberalism*, p. 74.

[57] Harrington, *The Commonwealth of Oceana*, p. 20 and see Skinner, *Liberty before Liberalism* pp. 74–7.

necessity or because of the perceived benefits.[58] I noted above how rule by law is no guarantee of the rule of law in the sense of treating all as equals. Even tyrannical rulers can have an interest in making their rule reasonably predictable in order to create a regime – albeit of an authoritarian kind. Likewise, rich and influential groups can desire to have their privileges secured against both the rulers and the less well-off and powerful. Because rulers need their cooperation and support most of all, and they are best situated to get what they want by extra-legal means otherwise, the wealthy and well-organised will be the first to be provided with legal protection. Hence the primacy, both chronologically and, certainly in the past and in many respects today, substantively, of property over other rights. Legality in these cases helps stabilize the position of those concerned and incorporates potential rivals to the ruler's power and authority into the system. However, it also skews the law against the poor and less well-placed. If the law is to serve all citizens equally, then these groups must organise themselves in their turn and obtain some leverage on the powers that be. The paradigm example of modern politics in this regard has been the formation of trade unions and their subsequent use and legalisation of strike action and role in extending the franchise to the propertyless and organising political parties committed to the interests of labour.

Of course, the ideal would be a society without any factions or special interests, where all were committed to the common rather than their particular good. However, this scenario is unlikely in a society of any complexity and diversity. Therefore, the best chance for the rule of law prevailing is a pluralistic society in which many groups have roughly equal bargaining power. Any group will be tempted to employ the law to support their own interests. Consequently, asymmetries in power will lead to laws entrenching the privileges of the powerful at the expense of the weak. To overcome this imbalance, the weak must put themselves in a situation whereby rulers enable them to make and use laws to defend their concerns. Industrialists may get laws regulating ownership, trade, labour and capital in ways they find beneficial, but they will also have to accept health and safety and employment legislation that favours workers.

This picture may seem to sacrifice justice to power. But that view would be wrong; rather, it shows how justice emerges from a balance of power.

[58] See the detailed account of this tradition in relation to Machiavelli and Rousseau in S. Holmes, 'Lineages of the Rule of Law', in J. M. Maravall and A. Przeworski (eds.), *Democracy and the Rule of Law*, Cambridge: Cambridge University Press, 2003, ch. 1. See too R. Bellamy, 'The Rule of Law and the Rule of Persons', *Critical Review of International Social and Political Philosophy*, 4 (2001), especially, pp. 241–9, on which this section draws.

Every group may seek to employ the law for their own purposes, but when they are compelled to deal with each other they turn the law into a common asset. Thus, worker and industrialist, in the example given above, each have to accommodate the interests of the other. The result is that employment law, even if devised with the worker in mind, by being equally available to all will occasionally favour the industrialist. Similarly, workers may benefit from freedom of contract and trade laws designed with the industrialist in mind. Indeed, because the laws will be equally binding on all there will be an incentive to render them fair and make reciprocal concessions that recognise the special concerns and situation of each. In other words, laws will be framed in mutually acceptable ways and bear consistently and equally on all to whom they apply – whether they are common rules for all or special legislation that takes into account the peculiar circumstances of a few.

In sum, far from either being somehow at odds with, a basis for, or a necessary constraint upon democracy, the rule of law issues from democratic processes. As we shall see in chapters 5 and 6, these have the qualities of ensuring the public reason about their collective policies and arrangements on a fair and equal basis, confronting each other's views and concerns and weighing them in an impartial manner. Such democratic methods play both a negative and a positive role. Negatively, they provide a control mechanism. Governments can be held to account for neither taking people's interests seriously nor treating them with equal concern and respect. Positively, they inform governments and their fellow citizens about each other's interests and values, enabling them to give them due consideration and negotiate appropriate compromises when deliberating common rules and policies.

This democratic approach avoids a formulaic view that laws must be general, abstract and universalisable to preserve equality and freedom. For example, it enables special rules to be tested for their mutual acceptability by checking they are regarded as neither discriminatory by those to whom they apply nor unfair privileges by the rest. The central requirement is not that the law avoids any deviation from generality and abstractness but that any particular and specific provision should be justifiable in a mutually acceptable way and bear equally and consistently on all to whom it applies. Such public reasoning does not involve all adopting a common mode of reasoning, as some legal constitutionalists propose: merely the reciprocal giving and responding to the reasons of others that comes from using public procedures that treat all equally. It will not be possible to decide *a priori* what rules are likely to pass this test. Much will depend on the policy and the complexion of those involved. Thus, a call by Muslims for the education system to recognise their religion will play differently in a state that supports religious schools to one where it does not. In the former, a demand for equal treatment might support the establishment of Islamic schools, in the latter it might only lead to special provision within the national curriculum, such as the ability to take a state exam on Islam.

Thus, the rule of law simply is the democratic rule of persons. Only democracy overcomes the Hobbes challenge by obliging citizens to deal on equal terms with each other as rulers and ruled in turn, rather than being able arbitrarily to dominate them. It will be objected that democracy replaces the sovereign power with popular sovereignty, thereby raising the spectre of the tyranny of the majority. I discuss this objection fully in chapter 6, showing how it is a misleading characterisation of most democratic decision-making. By and large, democratic majorities have to be constructed between various often very different groups of people rather than reflecting the will of an undifferentiated people. As a result, democracy entails an evolving process of political negotiation as disparate and frequently competing groups devise laws that respond to their different values and interests – a process, which we shall see, encompasses the very rules of the game itself.

Democratising the judiciary

Democratic legislation still has to be interpreted and acted upon by judges and officials. How can we avoid arbitrariness here? Obviously, from a democratic point of view it is desirable that laws are sufficiently detailed and clear to yield a very strict application in most cases. However, an absolute application of even the best drafted laws is virtually impossible.[59] No matter how specific the rules and regulations passed by the legislature may be, these will still give rise to the problems of indeterminacy – the various 'gaps' in law – and the need for discretion that we have explored above.[60]

---

[59] This distinction between rules of 'absolute', 'strict' and 'discretionary' application comes from N. MacCormick, 'Norms, Institutions and Institutional Facts', *Law and Philosophy*, 17 (1998), pp. 311–18.

[60] This is the problem with approaches such as Antonin Scalia, 'The Rule of Law as a Law of Rules', *University of Chicago Law Review*, 56 (1989), pp. 1175–88 or T. Campbell, *Legal Theory of Ethical Positivism*, Aldershot: Dartmouth, 1996, pp. 129–48. For criticism see respectively C. Sunstein, 'Justice Scalia's Democratic Formalism', *Yale Law Journal*, 107 (1997), pp. 529–67 and N. MacCormick, 'Ethical Positivism and the Practical Force of Rules', in T. Campbell and J. Goldsworthy (eds.), *Judicial Power, Democracy and Legal Positivism*, Aldershot: Dartmouth, 2000, ch. 2.

Even the plainest language will not eradicate all 'linguistic' ambiguity. Nor can judges avoid interpretative arguments relating to the systemic properties of the law – as when they ponder under which rule a given case might fall. There will also be instances when the mechanical application of the law appears to produce unjust or dysfunctional outcomes.[61] Of course, the legislature can stipulate rules for the interpretation of rules, but these too will not be complete. Nor can appeals to legislative intent overcome the dilemma, for they likewise will be subject to interpretation. Not only is the history of any Act usually unclear and the imputing of intent to a collective agent notoriously difficult, but also the self-same linguistic ambiguities, problems of systemic coherence and unforeseen injustices and disutilities will reappear in a new guise as judges seek to ascribe to legislatures an intention to use words in given ways, to see the law as cohering with other laws in a given fashion and so on. Thus, the issue cannot be to outlaw judicial interpretation altogether, but to see if a form of judging exists that is consistent with the circumstances of politics and the primacy of democratic legislation. In fact, the solution among the judiciary turns out to parallel that of the legislature – namely, instituting a balance of power between different courts. This structure helps institutionalise a certain practice of judging that rests on analogy and allows incremental adaptation of the law to unforeseen contexts.

Cass Sunstein has provided a powerful argument for why analogical, case-by-case reasoning offers a better account of how judges can maintain fidelity to law than either Dworkinian judgement on principle or the view of Hayek and others that they should simply abide by the rules.[62] He identifies three advantages to this approach that are germane to our enquiry. First, focusing on the details of the case and looking for parallels with other cases in settled parts of the law in similar areas offers a means for overcoming 'reasonable disagreements' within the circumstances of politics. As we saw, a major problem with the Dworkinian approach is that it courts controversy. By contrast, the search for analogies offers a way of skirting around political conflict. People may have different views of why a previous case was settled correctly or why a given agreed outcome would be correct. By restricting their discussion to points of law, they can avoid raising their deeper, but in many cases only vaguely formulated,

---

[61] For these three broad categories of interpretative argument (linguistic, systemic and justice and utility), see N. MacCormick, 'Argumentation and Interpretation in Law', *Ratio Juris*, 6 (1993), pp. 16–29.
[62] Sunstein, *Legal Reasoning*, chs. 2 and 3.

conflicts of principle or rationale. As he puts it, their arguments can be 'incompletely theorised'.

Second, analogical reasoning overcomes the vagueness and obtuseness of rules and principles when it comes to the complexities of particular cases and the identification of relevant differences. It encourages an attention to the 'totality of circumstances' and peculiarities of the case at hand. It also allows multiple and diverse criteria to be taken into consideration. Many of these criteria may appeal to incommensurable moral views and factors. However, the casuistical approach does not require that all be measured or weighed according to some single metric. Instead, an attempt is made to appreciate their distinctive force in the context of the particular situation.

Finally, consistency in this approach comes not from the application of a rule or single principle, but through drawing parallels or contrasts with holdings in previous cases. Analogy invokes the doctrine of *stare decisis*, that we 'stand by things decided' to justify our decision by appealing to precedents in case law, while allowing incremental change to take account of new circumstances. Equality before the law dictates that we treat similar cases similarly. On this line of thinking, law does not consist of common rules or a consensus on principle. Rather, it provides a common resource of diverse considerations that defence and prosecution employ to debate the ways in which the current case is relevantly alike or unlike other cases. In other words, it becomes a means for expressing disagreements and differences within a common language.

Although analogical reasoning shares the Dworkinian concern with 'fit', it does not require a 'morally best reading' of the legal system. In many respects, the method can be compared to the way examiners in British universities classify borderline degree results as, say, a first or a 2:1. Generally, nobody re-marks the scripts so as to form a new substantive judgement on them. Instead, they compare the distribution of marks with those of other candidates and justify their views in relation to them. What makes one distribution 'like' or 'unlike' another does not depend on any deep view of the substantive merits of the candidates. They are anonymous and most of those making the judgement have not read the papers in question. Nevertheless, certain peculiarities of the particular case can be referred to – common statements are that the candidate 'improved in the final year', 'did outstandingly on two papers', 'has a high average' and so on. Of course, there can be reference to the ends the rule is supposed to serve – such as increasing firsts at one end and discouraging over-inflation of 2:1s at the other. There may also be reference to changing criteria – 'standards have relaxed and we have to reflect that'. In these ways, linguistic ambiguities in the rules, their place in the system as a whole and even issues of justice and utility get addressed, but without opening up what would be an endless and, for the case at hand, not very fruitful discussion over the point (or pointlessness) of exams themselves or even what ideal standards of marking or whatever consist in.

Cases that pose issues of injustice might seem to require more than these rather formal discussions. Yet they need not. Take the British case of *R v R* of July 1990, which led to a change in the law regarding rape in marriage.[63] In the original trial, CR pleaded guilty to the attempted rape of his wife and was sentenced to three years' imprisonment. He later appealed as far as the House of Lords and ultimately to the European Court of Human Rights on the 'rule of law' grounds that under English common law a husband had hitherto been immune from prosecution for rape of his wife because the marriage contract 'implied consent' to sexual relations.[64] Moreover, Section 1 (1) of the Sexual Offences (Amendment) Act of 1976 had specified that rape only arose when sexual intercourse was 'unlawful'. Given the case predated the Human Rights Act, which arguably provides judges with wide-ranging discretionary rules that might legitimate such a decision, then – from a positivist and democratic point of view – this judgement surely represented a breach of the rule of law and could only be reconciled with the doctrine by something like a Dworkinian approach. One response would be to grant this point but retort that when the law offends our moral judgements we should seek to change it through democratic channels rather than via creative judgements by the courts. However well-motivated, such creativity does undermine the rule of law and the various goods it serves, and could be exploited by those who do not share our moral views for purposes we would find objectionable.[65] Yet, this argument does not deal with the problem that courts will still find

---

[63] I am grateful to Sheldon Leader for drawing this case to my attention. I have taken the details from the judgement of the European Court of Human Rights in *CR v United Kingdom* (1996) 21 EHRR 363.

[64] The appeal to the European Court of Human Rights claimed there had been a violation of Article 7 (1) of the European Convention on Human Rights, whereby 'No one shall be held guilty of any criminal offence on account of any act or omission which did not constitute a criminal offence under national or international law at the time when it was committed.'

[65] These rule of law type objections to the discretionary effects of bills of rights are made by Jeffrey Goldsworthy, 'Legislative Sovereignty and the Rule of Law' and Tom Campbell, 'Incorporation through Interpretation', in T. Campbell, K. D. Ewing and A. Tomkins (eds.), *Sceptical Essays on Human Rights*, Oxford: Oxford University Press, 2001, chs. 4 and 5.

themselves having to take remedial action to avoid evils that come to light due to evolving circumstances – the legislature would be overwhelmed if they did not and decision-making by officials would be impossible. However, to fill such gaps judges need not articulate a complete moral philosophy or legal theory. They can simply engage in incremental adjustments that follow a general trend to be found in other cases.[66] In fact, this is precisely what the trial judge, Owen J, did in his judgement – as did Lord Lane in backing his decision in the Court of Appeal. They noted how the institution of marriage had altered considerably from when Sir Matthew Hale defended the notion that a man cannot rape his wife in 1736, that many exceptions had gradually been made to this view that reflected these changes and that this decision was in line with them. No reference was made, or had to be made, to any grand moral principles other than those that followed from the immediately related cases and what Lord Lane called 'the true position of a wife in present-day society'. In other words, their reasoning paralleled that over exam classification outlined above.

It may still be objected that analogical reasoning *per se* offers no genuine constraint on discretion. Every case is analogous to every other case in some ways and disanalogous in others. Consequently, you can find a precedent for pretty much any interpretation you might wish to offer. Logically this is true. However, we should not take the decisions and opinions of courts in isolation from those of other courts. Courts form part of a complex system of fairly autonomous units. They need to coordinate their activities, for the most part without relying on a centralised or hierarchical structure to do so. Judges do not derive their authority from being modern Solomons. Rather, they are expected to be experts on, and impartial appliers of, the law. So they have an interest in stressing that they are only saying what everyone else is saying. Lawyers share this interest. Their professional standing similarly rests on their legal expertise. Since they will appear before many courts, they want them to operate pretty much like one another. As a result, the likeliest way of winning a case is to stress that the court is acting like other courts rather than appealing to natural justice or some original, however brilliant, reading of the law. In other words, there is a strong systemic pressure towards *stare decisis*. Through an examination of tort law in the US and the UK, Martin Shapiro has shown that within this context analogical reasoning and reference to

[66] M. Shapiro, 'Stability and Change in Judicial Decision-Making: Incrementalism or *Stare Decisis*', *Law in Transition Quarterly*, 2 (1965), pp. 149–50.

precedent operates as a feedback mechanism.[67] The massive number and variety of cases dealt with by courts generate a lot of 'noise' in their communications with each other. Referring to an excessively large number of cases provides a mechanism for ensuring each court has moved in line with the others. It allows for feedback to correct errors or to note adaptations to meet new environments. The result is decision-making is small 'c' conservative, with change incremental and path-dependent.

In certain respects, this system allows law to rule for similar reasons to the way democratic legislators place themselves under the law. For the most part, there is no rational-hierarchical centralised decision-maker trying to run the system according to some common plan. Instead, there are a number of largely independent decision-makers that nevertheless wish to work harmoniously with each other. In other words, it is the balance of power among courts that renders them consistent – not the existence of a supreme court ensuring all decide according to constitutional principles or rules. In fact, such bodies are far more likely to overthrow precedent and be subject to disagreement precisely because they lack the same incentives as ordinary courts to coordinate with everyone else.

Conclusion

The rule of law has always seemed a paradoxical notion given that it relies on the rule of persons to uphold it. I have confronted this dilemma head on. No feature of law *per se* can secure its rule. Rather, it is precisely because persons in the plural rule that they place themselves equally under the law. Law operates within rather than above the 'circumstances of politics'. As such, it needs to be sensitive to difference and diversity. A balance of power between groups both within and competing to join the legislature encourages just that. Of course, there will always be asymmetries of power in certain areas. However, these weaknesses in the democratic system require democratic remedies. No other mechanism or metric exists for deciding fairly and legitimately what equal treatment requires. The role of courts is to uphold the resulting laws consistently and impartially. Since judges have the biases and prejudices of other persons, they cannot be expected to exercise discretion any more wisely or objectively than anyone else. Their partiality is constrained by the need to argue through

---

[67] M. Shapiro, 'Toward a Theory of *Stare Decisis*', *Journal of Legal Studies* I (1972), pp. 125–34. See too M. Shapiro and A. Stone Sweet, *On Law, Politics and Judicialization*, Oxford: Oxford University Press, 2002, ch. 2.

the law in a way that is comprehensible and acceptable to the rest of the legal community. The doctrine of *stare decisis* and the discipline of arguing analogically via cases curbs the temptation to engage in grander theorising, and allows those who disagree on many of these wider issues to agree on the particular merits of a given decision. In both politics and law, a concern for the public interest and equality before the law comes from the balancing of particular interests and views rather than the imposition of a general or universal perspective from outside the political or legal system. Yet, it will be argued, do we not need criteria for what the right or fair balance should be? Doesn't democracy itself imply rights that a constitution and its legal protectors ought to uphold? It is to these questions that we now turn.

3

Constitutionalism and democracy

The previous two chapters explored the alleged threat democracy poses to individual rights and the rule of law respectively. In both cases, we saw how far from endangering them, democracy provided much of their underlying rationale and their best defence. However, the very affinity between democracy and these values has prompted a third and, in many respects, the most powerful case for its constitutional limitation: namely, that entrenching certain rights and rules secures the preconditions of democracy itself. On this view, a 'constitutional democracy' is a tautology rather than an oxymoron. No tension exists between constitutionalism and democracy since the one merely codifies the underlying norms and procedures of the other. Not even a democratic government could abrogate or infringe such a constitution without abolishing or detracting from democracy itself. Consequently, it is an unconstitutional rather than a constitutional democracy that represents a contradiction in terms.

Though this resolution appears compelling, this chapter shall contend a continuing source of conflict remains. There are many different models of democracy, which define citizenship and the democratic game in a variety of, often incompatible, ways. For democracy to mean 'people rule', the demos should be free to redefine the nature of their democracy whenever they want and not be tied to any given definition. After all, we value democracy as giving effect to the status of individuals as autonomous rights-bearers. Therefore, a consistent democrat should believe individuals are entitled to determine both their rights as citizens and the political rules by which they have to play – a view explored in detail in Part II.[1] The need to keep open the possibility of democratic review seems particularly important when one remembers that the constitutions of many democracies have excluded significant categories of people from citizenship, notably women and those without property, and

---

[1] See R. Bellamy, 'Constitutive Citizenship versus Constitutional Rights: Republican Reflections on the EU Charter and the Human Rights Act', in T. Campbell, K. D. Ewing and A. Tomkins (eds.), *Sceptical Essays on Human Rights*, Oxford: Oxford University Press, 2001, pp. 15–39 and J. Waldron, *Law and Disagreement*, Oxford: Clarendon Press, 1999, ch. 11.

placed severe limits on the exercise of the popular will, such as the indirect election of representatives. Of course, some exclusions and limitations are inevitable – they are intrinsic to any rule-governed activity. That we are not lumbered with the exclusions and limitations of the eighteenth century, though, is in large part due to successive social and democratic movements and reforms.

However, a further source of potential complementarity or opposition arises at this point. Most constitutions have been democratically enacted and largely derive their legitimacy from that fact. The great constitutional moments, be they the British reform acts of the nineteenth and early twentieth centuries, the conventions of the French and American revolutions, or the constitutional assemblies of the post-1945 and post-colonial period, have been exercises of democratic politics that transformed earlier conceptions of democracy. As a result, we could see constitutions not as constraints imposed upon democracy but as the limits that a mature democracy places upon itself. Since constitutions have an actual as well as a logical relation to democratic practice, the earlier objection that they infringe the autonomy of individuals as citizens proves misplaced.

If constitutions are simply artefacts of democracy, though, it seems difficult to accord them any independent weight. All democratic regimes operate within a framework inherited from the past, but there seems no compelling reason to prevent them from updating and rejecting that inheritance. Indeed, the very possibility of a people binding not only themselves but future generations as well seems fraught with difficulties.[2] Yet, constitutionalists may retort that the notion of democracy pulling itself up by its own bootstraps or being able to abolish itself sounds similarly odd. Surely, they argue, democracy is constituted by values, such as autonomy and equality, and rules, such as one person one vote, that it does not itself create. If so, then their belief that the constitutional rules defining democracy cannot be curtailed even by the demos itself still holds. In which case, we appear to have come full circle, returning in the process to the objections raised against this argument above and in chapter 1.

This chapter reviews the four main arguments contemporary legal and political philosophers have employed to cut the Gordian knot of constitutional democracy. All four seek to redefine the terms of the opposition so as to render them compatible: the first by assimilating democracy into

[2] Even supporters of constitutionalism against democracy have regarded too rigid a constitution as problematic; see, for instance, A. de Tocqueville, who argued in favour of making the procedures for change easy, in *Recollections: The French Revolution of 1848*, quoted in J. Elster, *Argomentare e negoziare*, Milan: Anabasi, 1993, p. 23, n. 15.

constitutionalism and emphasizing the importance of a framework of rights and liberties as necessary conditions of citizenship; the second by insisting, more modestly, that certain rights and rules are simply inherent to, and so necessary for, democratic procedures; the third by attempting to synthesise these two and emphasising the implicit constitutional substance of democratic procedures; and the fourth by conceiving the constitution as the outcome of a democratic process. Two prominent versions of each of these arguments are examined below. All are found wanting, thereby paving the way for a full account in Part II of the constitutional and constitutive role of democracy itself.

As with the defences of other aspects of legal constitutionalism reviewed in chapters 1 and 2, the dominant versions of these four arguments have been inspired by different understandings of the US Constitution and the status of 'We the People' as its supposed authors. Yet, as we shall see, these idealisations of the American model prove not only disputable in their own terms, but also more often than not belied by the reality.[3] Moreover, focusing on the American case overlooks the existence of established democracies, such as the UK, which have functioned as well as, and in certain respects rather better than, the US without such constitutional supports.

I Constitutional democracy: substantive views

Theorists of judicial review have offered two main accounts of why democracy should be viewed as pre-constituted. The first claims democracy assumes certain moral values, notably that all citizens deserve equal concern and respect as autonomous rights-bearers, and that we need a constitution to ensure even democratically made laws adhere to them. The second merely observes that democracy involves certain rules and practices, such as majority vote and free speech, and that these alone deserve special protection. To use the terminology employed in chapter 1, the first account justifies constitutional judicial review to uphold democratic 'outputs', the second to ensure democratic 'inputs'. Accordingly, I shall begin by examining the merits and pitfalls of two substantive 'output' accounts of constitutional democracy, reserving to the next section an assessment

---

[3] Indeed, the US Constitution is somewhat anomalous among democratic constitutions. See R. A. Dahl, *How Democratic is the American Constitution?*, New Haven: Yale University Press, 2002, ch. 3 and S. Levinson, *Our Undemocratic Constitution: Where the Constitution Goes Wrong (And How We the People Can Correct It)*, New York: Oxford University Press, 2006.

of the various attempts to overcome their drawbacks within a procedural 'input' account that seeks simply to constitute democracy.

Dworkin and the substantive rights of citizenship

In recent writings, Ronald Dworkin has sought to reconcile his advocacy of judicial review based on the 'moral reading' of constitutions, explored in the last chapter, with what he calls the 'relational' conditions presupposed by democracy.[4] Dworkin contends the 'defining aim of democracy' to be 'that collective decisions be made by political institutions whose structure, composition, and practices treat all members of the community, as individuals, with equal concern and respect'.[5] He contrasts a constitutional democracy, where legislation is subject to rights-based judicial review, with a 'mechanical' or 'statistical' form of majoritarian democracy, where legislation need only to be endorsed by a majority or plurality of voters to pass. In his view, each type of democracy must be measured by its 'results' at promoting democratic rights. By this criterion 'the best institutional structure is the one best calculated to produce the best answers to the essentially moral question of what the democratic conditions actually are, and to secure stable compliance with these conditions'.[6]

To be applicable, there must be some generally acceptable view of the 'best answers' to this moral question. Yet, as we saw in chapter 1, there are a number of quite different and often conflicting answers that might reasonably be given. Indeed, it is this very conflict that majority voting seeks to overcome by offering an authoritative decision-making procedure. True, judicial review also offers an authoritative procedure for overcoming this dilemma. However, the test of its superiority cannot be that it is more likely to produce right answers and majoritarian democracy wrong ones if what counts as a right or wrong answer is precisely the issue in dispute. The appeal will have to be some intrinsic quality of the procedure that does not beg this particular question.

Dworkin hazards a number of arguments that might move in this direction. For a start, he suggests that even if the 'best' answer *sub specie aeternitatis* may be in dispute, those countries, like the United States, that have a written constitution could be said to have committed themselves to an answer – namely, that given in the constitution.[7] As we shall see in

---

[4] R. Dworkin, *Freedom's Law: The Moral Reading of the American Constitution*, Oxford: Oxford University Press, 1996, 'Introduction: The Moral Reading and the Majoritarian Premise', p. 24.

[5] Ibid., p. 17.   [6] Ibid., p. 34.   [7] Ibid., pp. 34–5.

section IV, its doubtful how far a people can be said to have committed themselves in this way, or what democratic authority it may claim. Worse, though, the problem simply reappears in the guise of conflicting interpretations of constitutional principles. Of course, constitutional law 'is anchored in history, practice and integrity' but, as Dworkin concedes and as we saw in chapter 2, 'we must not exaggerate the drag of that anchor. Very different, even contrary, conceptions of constitutional principle – of what treating men and women as equals really means, for example – will often fit language, precedent and practice well enough to pass these tests.'[8] As a result, we find ourselves back at square one and having to search for a reason why having judges decide these issues will be at least as democratic as leaving it to the demos. That can no longer be the result-based standard that they offer the 'best' answers. At most, it is the slightly different and more procedural argument that they are in some way better at, or more suited to, giving the answer.

Once it is conceded that 'personal moral conviction' proves more important than 'the ordinary craft of a judge' in deciding such issues,[9] then – even within an already established constitutional democracy – the reason for giving judges the power of substantive review cannot be that they are 'experts on the law'. Dworkin suggests an alternative reason is that majoritarian democracy is liable to flout – indeed, in many respects is logically at variance with – the basic values of democracy. Dworkin identifies these with the qualities needed for each citizen to count as 'a moral member' of the political community, that is as someone possessing 'equal status' within it. For moral membership to be secured an individual must be guaranteed 'a *part* in any collective decision, a *stake* in it, and *independence* from it'.[10] In other words, individuals have to be given equal and adequate opportunities to influence the political agenda and the decisions that get taken, be viewed as of equal worth and shown equal consideration in the decision itself, and finally, and most controversially, individuals must be able to take responsibility for certain features of their life by not being interfered with by collective decisions. How does majoritarianism fare with respect to each of these aspects of democratic morality?

Dworkin contends majority decision-making tends simply to aggregate interests, or arrange trade-offs between them, encouraging 'compromises that may subordinate important issues of principle'.[11] Yet, chapter 1 disputed this view of democracy as unprincipled bargaining, while noting that rights and interests are often intimately related. Moreover, it is

---

[8] Ibid., p. 11.   [9] Ibid.   [10] Ibid., p. 24, emphasis in the original.   [11] Ibid., p. 30.

arguably the very mechanical and statistical features of a majoritarian system based on one person, one vote that guarantee individuals play an equal 'part' and, because each counts for one and no more than one, ensures them an equal 'stake' in which their views are treated on a par with everyone else's. As for compromise, it too can often be a principled recognition of the equal stake each has in a decision and the need to make mutual concessions.

Of course, majoritarianism *per se* cannot guarantee that the electorate includes all relevant parties, that some voters will not be motivated by prejudice towards others, or that certain minorities might not be oppressed or individual rights curtailed by majority vote. However, neither can judicial review. As we noted in chapter 1, US legal history shows all too well how courts can interpret constitutional rules in ways that systematically prejudice the part, stake and independence of particular groups. Moreover, which interpretation prevails frequently turns on a majority vote among the Supreme Court Justices. In any case, Dworkin's apparent assumption that a crude American form of majoritarianism based on first past the post, on the one hand, and a Supreme Court practising rights-based judicial review, on the other, offer the only games in town is simply mistaken. Majority rule has more often than not been modified in various ways to reduce some of its potential tyrannical effects. Most majorities turn out to be shifting coalitions of minorities, which perforce must compromise with a wide range of groups to sustain a government, with consistent minorities often catered for by consociational or self-government arrangements that introduce a degree of proportionality into the system. The flawed majoritarianism of the US and British plurality systems, like US- and German-style substantive judicial review, are exceptions rather than the rule within mature democracies.

There is also little support for Dworkin's empirical assertion that substantive judicial review has rendered the United States more just (in the democratic sense of promoting equal concern and respect among citizens) than if rights had been left to majoritarian institutions.[12] In fact, judicial review has often blocked the very legislation that advanced rights protection in other democracies.[13] For example, if one takes women's parliamentary representation as an indicator of equal rights to play a 'part' in collective decisions, then as Dahl has shown, the US ranks eighteenth out of the twenty-two stable post-war democracies within advanced industrial

[12] R. Dworkin, *Law's Empire*, London: Fontana, 1986, p. 356.
[13] R. A. Dahl, *Democracy and its Critics*, New Haven: Yale University Press, 1989, pp. 189–90.

societies. It fares almost as badly on voter turnout, coming twenty-first.[14] These low levels cannot be attributed to satisfaction with the policies achieved by the judicial and other democratic delegates. If we take unemployment, family policy or the welfare state index as indicators of the 'stake' the poorest sections of the US have in the decisions made in their name, then the US scores eighth, twelfth and seventeenth respectively. In sum, it does no better, and on many counts substantially worse, than those democratic systems that have not adopted substantive judicial review.

Of course, this rough and ready empirical evaluation of these two models of democracy employs a 'results-based' test that adopts the largely social-democratic understanding of equal concern and respect that Dworkin favours (as do I). However, as we have seen, part of the problem is that no such agreement on results exists. After all, the assessment might be rather different from a libertarian's point of view. For example, they might be inclined to think that only property-owners (or taxpayers) should rightfully play either a part or be accorded a stake, since they foot the bill for government action. Suppose, though, that we were agreed on the best understanding and the Supreme Court was made up of clones of Ronald Dworkin who could be guaranteed to make the 'right' decisions when democratic values were at stake. Would a democrat not be entitled to feel there had been a diminution of democracy? On non-democratic issues, Dworkin accepts there would be a loss of self-government, but not in the case of a decision about democracy.[15] In his view, if the legislation struck down by the Court had violated the 'best' understanding of democratic conditions, then the judiciary's 'decision is not anti-democratic, but, on the contrary, improves democracy'.[16] This conflation of democratic ends and means seems somewhat curious. Surely we would designate a regime where a paternalistic dictator treated all his subjects with equal concern and respect a dictatorship rather than a democracy?

Dworkin offers two responses to this objection. He identifies one reason for criticising a purely results-based conception of democracy in the 'civic republican' argument for the morally improving character of political participation and deliberation. Dworkin suggests that civic republicans overlook that Supreme Court decisions can also spark 'a widespread public discussion' within the media, classrooms and around dinner tables that, because it's focused on matters of principle rather than political horse-trading, 'better matches [the] conception of republican

---

[14] Dahl, *How Democratic is the American Constitution?*, Appendix B, Table 5, pp. 168–9.
[15] Dworkin, 'The Moral Reading', p. 32.   [16] Ibid.

government than almost anything the legislative process on its own is likely to produce'.[17] This thesis seems doubly flawed. For a start, whatever the failings of debates within the legislature, they clearly provoke just as lively and principled debates outside the chamber as anything achieved by the courts. As Jeremy Waldron has noted, one has only to think of the discussion surrounding the legalisation of homosexuality sparked by the 1957 Wolfenden Report in Britain, which precipitated the extended exchange between Hart and Devlin over the law's role in enforcing public morals.[18] It might be suggested that the advantage of judicial review is that it focuses attention on the interpretation of constitutional rights. But neither Hart and Devlin, nor the many others who entered the debate, were inhibited from considering the principles involved by the absence of this dimension. Indeed, one could say they were better able to engage directly with the philosophical questions thrown up by the issue through *not* having to couch their arguments in terms of a particular reading of a loosely worded eighteenth-century document and the ways one ought to interpret it. It is also misleading to view the debates sparked by Court decisions as Platonic dialogues, untouched by interest group pressures, prejudice or ideology. As we saw in chapter 1, when the Court becomes the maker of important policy decisions then campaigning groups simply turn their attention to capturing the court and pressurising judges. Indeed, the court generally follows public opinion on key moral issues.[19]

Most importantly, though, Dworkin's counter-argument simply misses the point that it is not just debating but also deciding that matters. Certainly, participation in a public debate can be educationally and no doubt morally improving – as experiments with purely advisory citizens' juries reveal. However, these studies also show that it is the sense that one has played a part in a collective decision that generates a sense of moral responsibility on the part of citizens, obliging them both to respect the views of their fellows and to abide by the majority view. If the decision is effectively taken out of their hands, then why should they feel any need to moderate their views to accommodate others or view it as in any sense 'theirs'?[20] The importance of deciding as well as debating becomes

---

[17] Dworkin, 'The Moral Reading', pp. 30–31, *Freedom's Law*, ch. 17, pp. 345–6.

[18] Waldron, *Law and Disagreement*, p. 290.

[19] R. J. McKeever, *Raw Judicial Power? The Supreme Court and American Society*, second edition, Manchester: Manchester University Press, 1995.

[20] See G. Smith and C. Wales, 'Citizen Juries and Deliberative Democracy', *Political Studies*, 48 (2000), pp. 51–65, who note, p. 60, the importance of political efficacy in promoting the beneficial effects associated with deliberation, such as attitudinal change.

even more heightened once we acknowledge that courts can get it wrong. Dworkin remarks that since politicians may also be mistaken, the potential damage done to democracy by courts and legislatures making an error is 'symmetrical'. Yet, in the latter case, citizens may either blame themselves or the politicians they elected. In particular, they can rectify the error by threatening to withdraw their support from the incumbent government unless the decision is altered.

Dworkin's second argument comes in here. He argues that the appeal of democracy cannot be that it gives citizens an equal impact or influence over issues. These goals are not only unrealistic, since those in positions of power or with greater wealth will inevitably exert greater sway over any decision, but also undesirable, given that 'we want those with better views, or who can argue more cogently, to have more influence'.[21] What counts is equality of status. That merely requires that the rules for selecting decision-makers, be they judges or politicians, do not formally discriminate against any group, and that the decisions themselves treat all equally.[22]

Now, wealth and privilege may be even more of an advantage for those pursuing a political career, at least in the United States, than they are in aiding access to a top-flight law school and ascending to the bench. However, you do not have to become a politician or fund a political campaign to have your vote count the same as everyone else's. Certainly, the weight of any single vote is very small. But the need to woo ordinary voters should not be discounted either. As the women and workers who struggled for the vote appreciated all to well, periodic elections provide politicians with a crucial incentive to respect the interests of citizens – those without the franchise tend to get overlooked. Even so, do we really wish to accord equal weight to the ignorant, stupid and bigoted as we do to the well-educated, intelligent and fair-minded? Unfortunately, prejudice, self-interest, short-sightedness and indifference are not exclusive to the ill-educated or unintelligent. The rich, powerful and even the clever are all too often ill-informed about, and uninterested in, the experiences of those less fortunate than themselves. If we have no agreed metric for deciding the best way of according each individual equal concern and respect, then we have no reason not to give everyone an equal weight in determining how this principle will be deployed in their community. Not to do so would be to deny them equal status as rights holders to play an equal part in defining and defending their rights on an equal basis with others.

---

[21] Dworkin, 'The Moral Reading', p. 27.   [22] Ibid., p. 28.

Moreover, as we have seen, on Dworkin's own account of what equality involves, all the evidence suggests it is the most reliable (if not an infallible) way to ensure all citizens have an equal stake in that decision too.

It will be countered that this conclusion raises the issue of how we determine whether the process is itself equal for all. Before turning to this procedural argument in the next section, we need to deal with two final arguments for the substantive view – one raised by Dworkin, the other developed by Rawls in his later writings. As we saw, Dworkin defines the relational conditions of democracy as involving 'independence' from a collective decision as well as a 'part' and a 'stake' in it. At first blush, this criterion appears more as a right against democracy than one entailed by democratic values. However, Dworkin insists he is not invoking the 'rights as trumps' argument here. Rather, he maintains that if collective decision-making is to preserve self-respect, then those involved in it must be free to make up their own minds about certain issues and have a realm of personal responsibility.

The first element is certainly an intrinsic part of democracy, and can be stated even more strongly as a right to dissent. We shall look at the case for constitutionalising such procedural rights in the next section. The second is trickier, though, because that realm will itself have to be a matter of collective agreement and concern. Indeed, it may even be made possible by collective measures. Moreover, as critics of J. S. Mill's self-regarding/other-regarding distinction have observed, there are relatively few (if any) personal acts that do not have implications for the public good. For example, we see marriage and the family as 'private', 'personal' matters. However, both are largely defined by law and relations within them are publicly regulated – we no longer think a man's home is his impregnable castle where he is free to batter his wife and abuse his children. Dworkin clearly has issues such as abortion and euthanasia in mind, both of which have been treated by the Supreme Court as personal matters protected by the individual's right to privacy.[23] Yet, these cases reveal the weaknesses of this individualistic approach more than its strengths. Democrats have always been suspicious of rights against the collective process because they see them as attempts by individuals to escape their collective responsibilities and retain their unmerited or indefensible privileges. Making something a private matter, though, can also be a way of removing a collective responsibility for it and ignoring the effects of personal choices on others. As Mary Anne Glendon has shown, this is

---

[23] The origins of this line of argument go back to *Griswold v Connecticut*, 381 US 113 (1973).

precisely what has happened in the United States with regard to abortion. Meagre social support for maternity and child raising, and the absence of public funding for abortions in many jurisdictions, leave poor, pregnant woman 'largely isolated in their privacy'.[24] By contrast, in Europe, where abortion has been largely tackled by legislatures, there has been much more social support and flexibility, both to facilitate continuation or overcome the trauma of termination.[25] In other words, we should see 'independence' as a democratic right, but, like other such rights, one that, through being subject to democratic approval, we have a collective responsibility to uphold.

Rawls and the citizens' contract

Dworkin infers democratic morality from a given account of democracy. He defines democracy in a certain way and then contends that all calling themselves democrats must agree with the reading of democratic principles that is most consistent with this model. That seems too neat – it builds one's conclusions into a particular and rather contentious premise. Rawls can be interpreted as trying to reach rather similar conclusions from the other end. Instead of deriving democratic principles from a given view of democracy, he argues that democracy presupposes certain principles. He contends that citizens would only be willing to adopt and abide by democratic decision-making if there was a consensus on certain political principles. To illustrate this argument, he models the substantive rights of citizenship as the product of a democratic contract. Unfortunately, this approach merely serves to underscore the circularity of the constitutionalist case, since his conception of the democratic contractors is derived from his account of what he believes them to have consented to.

Rawls's theory appears particularly promising for this book's argument because he takes as his starting point the 'burdens of judgement'.[26] Chapter 1 argued that these largely define the 'circumstances of politics'. However, Rawls draws diametrically opposed conclusions from this situation to those offered here. He contends that the difficulties of reaching any agreement between opposed ideological and cultural views make such disagreements the prime source of tension and instability within modern

[24] M. A. Glendon, *Rights Talk: The Impoverishment of Political Discourse*, New York: Free Press, 1991, p. 65.

[25] Ibid., pp. 61–6.

[26] J. Rawls, *Political Liberalism*, New York: Columbia University Press, 1993, pp. 54–8.

societies.[27] Consequently, politics must be isolated as far as possible from these disputes.

A constitution achieves this isolation in three distinct ways. First, the constitution itself has to be based on a strictly 'political' conception of justice that is 'freestanding' with regard to any given metaphysical position.[28] Rawls maintains that persons who are inclined to work together as democratic citizens are able to abstract from their distinctive ethical, epistemological and ontological allegiances to arrive at an 'overlapping consensus' on purely political values – the basic liberties that supposedly must be respected for democracy to exist.[29] Such a consensus is possible because, although people often disagree about the nature of the good, they can agree on the principles of justice that govern their behaviour towards others when pursuing whatever good they may value. Thus, although he argues this consensus is based on a liberal reading of political values, he does not believe it is premised on a commitment to liberal ideals of autonomy and equality.

Second, constitutions apply to, and both constrain and defend, a narrowly defined political sphere, consisting of the basic social and political institutions. As a result, there is a clear separation of the public and the private. On the one hand, the Rawlsian constitution protects the realm of what Dworkin called 'independence', where people may choose to act on their deep personal commitments on matters such as abortion. On the other hand, these same commitments are excluded from political debate when constitutional essentials are at stake. He thinks both the limited scope of the political sphere and its insulation from non-political considerations are vital to the success of his project.

Finally, to ensure this is the case, the legislative process has to be subject to judicial review by an independent court that can guarantee political values are upheld. Like Dworkin, Rawls portrays the resulting system as an idealisation of American constitutional arrangements and the role of the Supreme Court. Indeed, he explicitly endorses the Court's deliberations as offering a model of his account of public reasoning.[30]

The upshot of Rawls's threefold set of exclusions is for the constitution to effectively de-politicise basic political rights and liberties. It not only 'takes those guarantees off the political agenda' it also 'removes from the political agenda the most divisive issues', the various other values and

---

[27] Ibid., p. xxv.   [28] Ibid., pp. 10, 12.   [29] Ibid., pp. 140–42.

[30] This aspect is particularly evident in Lectures 6 and 8 of *Political Liberalism*, for example pp. 231–40 and 340–63, where Rawls gives detailed accounts of the Supreme Court's function and discusses certain test cases with regard to free speech and equal opportunities.

commitments that might lead us to interpret the political values in conflicting ways – or even dispute their importance in the first place.[31] The
result, he claims, will be a stable political settlement based on mutual tolerance. By contrast, I shall argue this proposed insulation of the political
sphere from people's prime concerns is not only impossible but also undesirable. It prevents politics from performing its crucial function of recon-
ciling differences through negotiation and debate. It also risks excluding
important minority issues from the political agenda and thereby dele-
gitimizing the public sphere – the very problem Rawls seeks to avoid.
Moreover, it assumes what it purports to show – namely, that a functioning democracy requires that citizens adopt a certain view of democratic
values.

Rawls's theory of an 'overlapping consensus' on political values rests
on claims of both a socio-historical nature and of a more philosophical
kind. Sometimes, Rawls argues he is only articulating the ethos of the liberal democratic tradition as it has developed since the wars of religion of
the sixteenth and seventeenth centuries.[32] Originating as a *modus vivendi*
thanks to a fortuitous equitable balance of power between competing
religious groups, liberal democratic values have gradually become part
of the unconscious convictions of most citizens within Western societies.
The philosopher's task is to bring these principles and their underlying
rationale to light so that they may be adequately protected. The 'original
position' should not be interpreted as an objective point of view for judging the justice of all possible societies and moralities, as he appeared to
argue in *A Theory of Justice*. Instead, it serves as a 'device of representation'
that 'models' the basic intuitive ideas at the heart of the liberal democratic
tradition and brings them into some degree of 'reflective equilibrium'.[33]

There are several oddities in this argument. For a start, it potentially
undermines much of his case for constitutional democracy. If citizens
already act on liberal democratic principles, then articulating the theoretical basis of this practice seems not only redundant but also, as conservative and communitarian critics of liberalism point out, risks producing
a rationalistic and limited abridgement that fails to do justice to its true
complexity and so potentially undermines it.[34] However, matters are not
quite so neat, because the cunning of reason through history has not cul-
minated so clearly in the Rawlsian state. On the contrary, the political

---

[31] Rawls, *Political Liberalism*, pp. 161, 157.   [32] Ibid., 'Introduction'.
[33] Ibid., pp. 22–8, clarifying J. Rawls, *A Theory of Justice*, Oxford: Clarendon Press, 1971.
[34] The *locus classicus* for this argument is probably E. Burke, *Reflections on the Revolution in
France*, Oxford: Oxford University Press, 1993, for example, pp. 33–5.

arrangements of the world's most stable democracies vary considerably. They have very different electoral systems, forms of judicial review, types of executive and divisions and levels of governmental power. These differences seem to go against Rawls's contention that stability can only be obtained if the political system takes a certain canonical form. Granted, because these countries are all democracies, they acknowledge more or less the same set of political and civil rights. However, their ways of doing so often diverge considerably, both in terms of the mechanisms employed to secure them and the precise meanings they are given. Rawls does accept that even within an agreed account of political justice there will be arguments over the details. Yet, there are quite a few detailed variations, such as the public funding of religious schools, that he rules out but many mature democracies rule in. In particular, those countries where cultural and other cleavages are greatest have tended to secure consensus not by removing these differences from politics but by giving them explicit political recognition through consociational and other types of power sharing. In fact, there are ongoing disagreements about political justice within all democracies – indeed, these disputes animate much political debate. Certainly, there is no agreement on the peculiarly American liberal reading that Rawls gives of the basic liberties. Rawls has invented, and then idealised, a historical consensus that does not, and probably could not, exist.

To see why Rawls overlooks such dissent (and is wrong to do so), we need to turn to the philosophical assumptions of his theory. Rawls contends democracy rests on a distinctive conception of the citizen as possessing two moral powers: a capacity to form, revise and pursue a conception of the good, and a sense of justice.[35] However, the key issue for him is how far these two powers are separable, so that the former can be exercised in the private sphere subject to the public constraints determined by the latter. It is certainly true that claims for political justice can be distinguished to some degree from conceptions of the good. Few Catholics, for example, would advocate political rule by the Pope. Yet, there are liberal, socialist and conservative Catholics, amongst others – in other words, disagreement about political justice in this case cuts across their agreement on the nature of the good. Meanwhile, in many cases their different views of political justice will at least partly reflect conflicting interpretations of Christian morality. So what sort of person could adopt the Rawlsian model? Probably, only liberals who do not just conceive

---

[35] Rawls, *Political Liberalism*, p. 19.

society in terms of a collection of free and equal individuals pursuing autonomously chosen goals, but also share Rawls's particular reading of what autonomy and equality involve.

Rawls argues the 'basic liberties', which on his view underpin democracy and provide the language of political argument, must themselves be 'no longer regarded as appropriate subjects for political decision by majority or other plurality voting . . . They are part of the public charter of a constitutional regime and not a suitable topic for ongoing public debate and legislation.'[36] Nevertheless, Rawls accepts that conflicts between the different liberties occasionally arise. However, he believes that a given liberty can only be restricted by a different liberty, and the general intention must always be to promote to the full the overall scheme.[37] Moreover, he thinks that such balancing should only be done by judges in a constitutional court. The 'basic liberties', though, may prove not only non-compossible but also incommensurable. As I noted in chapter 1, the way we characterize any given liberty and identify the constraints that determine its presence or absence depends on normative and empirical judgements that he admits the 'burdens of judgement' make subject to reasonable disagreement. Such factors not only undermine the neutral balancing of liberties, they may even result in a failure to agree whether a conflict of liberties exists or not. Needless to say, the problem of on-balance judgements becomes even more intractable when liberty has to be weighed against other values because the exercise of freedom itself causes harm or suffering. These sorts of difficulties lie at the heart of some of the most heated contemporary American constitutional debates – from disagreements over the legitimacy of affirmative action or welfare, to debates about the character and range of free speech raised by issues such as pornography and official secrets. In such cases, it will be impossible to weigh up the basic liberties involved, and in some cases balance them against other values, without referring to our comprehensive moral commitments.[38]

These considerations substantially weaken the case for restricting the debate of constitutional and other principled matters to the Supreme Court. Rawls's reasons for so doing appear to be largely pragmatic. Judges' legal training and life tenure supposedly render them relatively immune to 'non-political' influences compared with politicians, and so they are more inclined to reason solely in terms of public values when constitutional

---

[36] Ibid., p. 151, n. 16.   [37] Ibid., Lecture 8.
[38] This criticism is developed more fully in R. Bellamy, *Liberalism and Pluralism: Towards a Politics of Compromise*, London: Routledge, 1999, pp. 52–60.

fundamentals are at stake.[39] However, I have questioned the theoretical possibility of isolating these values in this way. If this criticism is correct, then it will be impossible for judges to resolve conflicts between the basic liberties under discussion in a 'pure' manner simply on the basis of an interpretation of 'higher' constitutional law. Rather, they will end up drawing on their own more 'comprehensive', and often partial, background values, opinions, prejudices and interests.[40]

As a result, the practical consequences of such judicial foreclosure may be quite other than those anticipated by Rawls. If people can reasonably dissent from the Court's view, they cannot be expected not to do so, especially in cases where an unrepresentative position gets foisted upon them. If they cannot voice their opposition via regular political channels, they will be tempted to employ unreasonable methods – such as violent attacks on doctors in abortion clinics. I would not wish to deny that on rare occasions it might be advisable either to take certain things off the agenda or hand them to a third party, and that this decision could be the only stable solution where disagreement risks turning into armed conflict. The mistake is to turn what may be an occasional necessity in exceptional circumstances into a matter of general policy.

In *A Theory of Justice* Rawls observed how the principle of participation is intimately related to the contractarian argument, directly following from the notion that the social compact should be capable of gaining the assent of free and equal individuals. As he put it, 'the principle of participation transfers [the notion of equality] from the original position to the constitutional process'. In this context, it 'requires that all citizens are to have an equal right to take part in, and to determine the outcome of, the constitutional process that establishes the laws with which they are to comply'. Indeed, 'if the state is to exercise a final and coercive authority over a certain territory, and . . . affect permanently men's prospects in life, then the constitutional process should preserve the equal representation of the original position to the degree that this is feasible'.[41] Unfortunately, Rawls failed to draw the radical conclusions to which his contractual argument points.[42]

---

[39] Rawls, *Political Liberalism*, p. 240.

[40] For a path-breaking, if occasionally overstated, analysis of this phenomenon among British judges, see J. G. A. Griffith, *The Politics of the Judiciary*, Glasgow: Fontana, 1981. Parallel observations so far as American courts are concerned have fuelled the Critical Legal Studies movement; for example, M. Tushnet, *Red, White and Blue: A Critical Analysis of Constitutional Law*, Cambridge, MA: Harvard University Press, 1988.

[41] Rawls, *A Theory of Justice*, pp. 221–2.   [42] Waldron, *Law and Disagreement*, pp. 156–7.

Rawls's contractarian thesis suggests that citizens must always have the ability to contest and reconstitute the rules of the democratic game and ensure that they treat them as equals – including making adjustments for relevant differences. Given that people's disagreements over political justice are both intractable and constantly evolving as their ideals and concerns alter in response to changing circumstances, constitution-making needs to be seen as an ongoing political process.[43] Think of the ways the successive demands for equal treatment by workers, women, minority ethnic groups and environmentalists, to name just some of the more obvious examples, have altered our understanding of how politics should be framed. Consider, too, how each of these demands has been contested in their turn, often with some success.[44] Rawls overlooks these processes of political contestation because he assumes that the only possible choice in the original position would be in favour of his principles of justice and that these provide the necessary basis for our disagreements to play out.[45] Within a 'well-ordered', stable democracy, disagreement must be not between different conceptions of political justice but only different understandings of his own two principles. That contention is demonstrably false in both theory and practice. Not only has the derivation of the two principles been widely disputed (as has the chosen starting point), but also it is plain that opposed views of justice inform political debate in all mature democracies without threatening their very existence.

What Rawls ignores is the 'civilising activity' of politics itself, the moralising role played by citizenship I explored in the discussion of Dworkin. He fears that political solutions may be unjust and unstable, the product of a temporary *modus vivendi* between groups motivated by interest and prejudice rather than fairness. That can be true. But, as the historical aspect of his theory clearly assumes, successive compromises and negotiations can also bind people to doing things in a certain way and gradually produce a consensus. Moreover, such agreements come not from people dropping their interests and values but through them seeing them recognised and respecting those of others through the political process. After all, when workers struggled for the vote they did so in order to advance the cause of labour. Likewise, as Rawls himself notes, civil rights activists

[43] See Bellamy, 'Constitutive Citizenship versus Constitutional Rights'.
[44] J. Tully, 'The Agonic Freedom of Citizens', *Economy and Society*, 28 (1999), pp. 161–82.
[45] Rawls, *A Theory of Justice*, p. 198 and *Political Liberalism*, p. 227.

such as Martin Luther King frequently referred to their conception of the good, in his case his Christian beliefs. That does not mean people can make no distinction between political justice and their conception of the good. Clearly, committed democrats do distinguish their acceptance of the political process from their agreement with the outcome. At least part of that acceptance, though, comes from the process allowing the expression of their deep commitments and concerns rather than excluding them. The problem with both Rawls and Dworkin is that they blur that distinction by trying to skew the process so as to yield their preferred result.

II Constituting democracy: procedural views

A number of theorists have accepted this criticism of the sort of substantive constitutional judicial review advocated by Dworkin and Rawls, but have argued that a role remains for courts to police democratic procedures. The claim here is that although we should allow the democratic process to decide such issues as abortion, capital punishment and privacy, we need judicial review to oversee that the process by which these decisions are made is fair – that minorities are appropriately represented and so on. How far is this possible? Can this position really be distinguished from the arguments from democracy that Dworkin and Rawls present themselves?

Policing the democratic process: J. H. Ely

John Hart Ely has been the most influential exponent of the procedural view – not least because he challenges the interpretation of the US Constitution and the activism of the Warren Court that provides the backdrop to much of Dworkin's and Rawls's arguments. Ely starts by criticising what he calls the 'fundamental values' thesis, according to which the Supreme Court is empowered to strike down legislation that infringes the key principles enshrined within or underlying the US Constitution.[46] He argues that no clear enumeration of such values can be found in it, nor is there any unambiguous source for them outside it. Judges invariably disagree about what these values and sources may be, and even when they agree dispute their implications for a given case – that's why the decisions of

---

[46] J. H. Ely, *Democracy and Distrust: A Theory of Judicial Review*, Cambridge, MA: Harvard University Press, 1980, especially chs. 2 and 3.

the Supreme Court (like other constitutional courts) are so rarely unanimous. Summarising his survey of the various failed attempts to find a non-personal, objective method for interpreting the values lying within or behind the constitution, he concludes 'what [the judge or commentator in question] is really likely to be "discovering", whether or not he is fully aware of it, are his own values'.[47]

Drawing inspiration from Justice Stone's famous footnote in *United States v. Carolene Products Co.* of 1938, Ely proposes an alternative approach.[48] What constitutional courts should really do is 'to ensure the political process – which is where such values *are* properly identified, weighed, and accommodated – [is] open to all view points on something approaching an equal basis'.[49] Like Dworkin, he regards majority tyranny as the chief problem with democracy.[50] However, he proposes combating it not by asking whether the decision itself conforms to a given understanding of rights or equality of concern and respect, but by seeing that the procedures by which it has been made are equitable. In other words, the aim of both a constitution and its judicial guardians should be to realise the ideal of equal participation enunciated by Rawls in the quote towards the end of the last section. Of course, as Ely concedes, participation itself is a value, which (somewhat controversially) he is asserting to be fundamental to the US Constitution. Nevertheless, he disputes that his view thereby collapses into the position he is criticising. For 'value imposition refers to the designation of certain goods (rights or whatever) as so important that they must be insulated from whatever inhibition the political process might impose, whereas a participational orientation denotes a form of review that concerns itself with how decisions effecting value choices and distributing the resultant costs and benefits are made'.[51] The crux is whether this distinction does actually hold.

According to Ely, 'the original [US] Constitution was principally, indeed I would say overwhelmingly, dedicated to concerns of process and structure and not to the identification and preservation of specific substantive values'.[52] As he notes, the body of the text 'is devoted almost entirely to structure'.[53] However, he also claims that we should pursue a processual reading of the Bill of Rights. These rights focus on either 'procedural fairness in the resolution of individual disputes (process writ small)' or 'ensuring broad participation in the processes and distributions of government' – what 'might be capaciously designated as process

---

[47] Ibid., p. 44.   [48] Ibid., pp. 75–7.   [49] Ibid., p. 74.   [50] Ibid., pp. 81–2.
[51] Ibid., p. 75.   [52] Ibid., p. 92.   [53] Ibid., p. 90.

writ large'.[54] Above all, the Constitution seeks to guard against majority tyranny. However, he maintains this defence is achieved not by setting up a body independent of the majority that can itself represent the will of the community but, as Madison put it in *Federalist* 51, 'by comprehending in the society so many separate descriptions of citizens as will render an unjust combination of a majority of the whole very improbable, if not impracticable'. Indeed, as Madison noted, this second method is much more certain than the first – which seems more appropriate to a hereditary system and 'at best is but a precarious security; because a power independent of the society may as well espouse the unjust views of the major, as the rightful interests of the minor party, and may possibly be turned against both parties'.[55]

I find this approach highly congenial, and will defend it at length in Part II. Yet, Ely believes it insufficient in itself. This political constitutionalism needs reinforcing by a limited form of legal constitutionalism. Why does he think so? As I have remarked in earlier chapters, the basis for democracy lies in a pluralist society in which rulers require the collaboration of the ruled to govern. Political institutions, which constitute the way politics works within any polity, facilitate and partly mould the social competition required for democracy. However, they also reflect and are shaped and sustained by these social forces. Unfortunately, Ely has little faith in these social processes lying behind democratic institutions. The pluralist model may work 'sometimes', but, as he (rightly) notes, it is not an absolute guarantee. 'No matter how open the process, those with the most votes are in a position to vote themselves advantages at the expense of others, or otherwise refuse to take their interests into account.'[56] Of course, overturning the unjust privileges of a minority would be an entirely

---

[54] Ibid., p. 87. A number of commentators have disputed this reading of the Bill of Rights, arguing that seeing the criminal justice provisions or rights to property as rights to political participation is far-fetched (e.g. M. Tushnet, 'Darkness on the Edge of Town: The Contribution of John Hart Ely to Constitutional Theory', *Yale Law Journal*, 89 (1980), p. 1046 and L. Tribe, 'The Puzzling Persistence of Process-Based Constitutional Theories', *Yale Law Journal*, 89 (1980), pp. 1066–7). I think they probably can be seen in these terms. After all, the possession of property was often a precondition of the vote and the rationale for that criterion – namely, that it gave the voter a stake in the country and also a certain independence in making judgements – might be said to still operate in defending the institution of private property as an important factor in maintaining democracy and a stake being a good reason to deny the franchise to transient residents. Such arguments might also buttress seeing social and economic rights as linked to democratic citizenship. Whether this is all there is to such rights, or offers the best characterisation of them, is a different matter.

[55] *Federalist* 51 cited in Ely, *Democracy and Distrust*, p. 80.

[56] Ely, *Democracy and Distrust*, p. 135.

legitimate reaction of a hitherto oppressed majority – indeed, democracy has played this crucial role throughout its history. Nevertheless, as Ely appositely remarks with regard to the black minority within the US, minority oppression can be compatible with that minority having gained every official attribute of access to the democratic process. So it turns out that it will not be sufficient just to check that participation 'in the political process by which values are appropriately identified and accommodated' has not been 'unduly constricted'. It will also be necessary to ensure 'the accommodation those processes have reached' also admits an equal opportunity to participate so as to protect 'even minority interests that are not voteless'.[57] In particular, it may be necessary to prevent a majority motivated by pure prejudice from consistently ignoring the interests of what Justice Stone in his famous footnote called 'discrete and insular minorities'.[58] The danger for such groups is that, for one reason or another, their votes never count enough, if at all, to give them any bargaining power with the main competing parties. Each can obtain power without them, so may safely overlook or even actively discriminate against them.

Ely has undoubtedly identified a real worry for pluralist politics, even convincing the premier theorist of contemporary political pluralism, Robert Dahl, of the need for procedural judicial review to guard against such pitfalls.[59] However, I think his solution proves incoherent. The problem for Ely and those who follow him, and one Dworkin has not hesitated to jump on,[60] is that you cannot judge whether the process is fair without a view of what counts as a fair outcome, and one cannot judge a fair outcome without referring to some account of fundamental values. Put succinctly, the only coherent way to adjudicate on the justice of democratic 'inputs'

---

[57] Ibid., pp. 77, 86.
[58] *United States v Carolene Products Co.* 304 US 144 at 152 n. 4 (1938), Ely, *Democracy and Distrust*, pp. 75–7.
[59] R. A. Dahl's *A Preface to Democratic Theory*, Chicago: Chicago University Press, 1956 was criticised by Ely for overlooking the limits of pluralist politics, e.g. *Democracy and Distrust*, pp. 80, 135. Dahl seems to have taken these criticisms to heart and in *Democracy and its Critics*, pp. 191 and 359, n. 9 concurs with Ely's view that 'a court whose authority to declare laws unconstitutional was restricted to rights and interests integral to the democratic process would be fully compatible with the democratic process'. See too Dahl, *How Democratic is the American Constitution?*, pp. 152–4 and 189, n. 4. Others who generally privilege democracy over judges likewise endorse his approach, e.g. Cass R. Sunstein, *Legal Reasoning and Political Conflict*, Oxford: Oxford University Press, 1996, pp. 179 and 209, n. 11, who approvingly cites Ely for his view that 'the most promising approaches to constitutional interpretation call for an aggressive judicial role when there are defects in purportedly democratic processes'.
[60] R. Dworkin, *A Matter of Principle*, Oxford: Clarendon Press, 1986, pp. 57–69.

is to have some notion of what counts as a just 'result'. As a result, the distinction between substantive and proceduralist approaches to judicial review collapses.

The difficulty arises from there being different models of democracy, each of which rests on divergent and often incompatible normative assumptions. Choosing between them is just as contentious and often intimately related to, substantive disagreements over policy. Different models of democracy offer contrasting accounts of the virtues and vices of alternative electoral systems, from first past the post to the many versions of PR; the design of constituencies – such as whether territorial units should be supplemented or even supplanted by functional ones; the advantages and disadvantages of unicameralism as opposed to bicameralism; the pros and cons of presidential and parliamentary systems; the democratic merits of different kinds of judicial review; and so on. These disagreements relate to the very two issues Ely wants judges to settle – namely, who gets included, and the ways their voice gets heard. Moreover, though they relate to process, which procedure you prefer will largely depend on your view of the purpose of democracy and the type of outcomes you hope to promote. For example, if you see the main aim of democracy as choosing effective leaders, then you are likely to hold a different view of the most appropriate procedures to someone who prioritises the aggregation of preferences. These differences, in their turn, involve divergent views of the substantive value of participation, and hence of what equal participation entails. Those who believe participation involves direct involvement in deliberative processes will have rather more exacting views of what equal treatment requires to those who contend that popular involvement should be limited to casting a periodic vote for a credible leader. As a result, any decision over the appropriate representation of minorities is likely to be as contested and spark as much disagreement as decisions on non-procedural policy questions.

These disagreements over the democratic process will frequently be motivated by the self-same reasons underlying divisions on substantive policies. On many issues, people's policy preferences either reflect their view of democratic morality, and in particular their understanding of equality, or *vice versa*. For example, libertarians wanting to restrict the role of the state and promote the market, tend to have a narrow view of participation. As I mentioned earlier, some even favour only enfranchising those who pay taxes in order to guard against the poor engaging in what they regard as rent-seeking behaviour by voting to increase welfare spending. By the same token, social democrats have both a broader view

of the state and usually a similarly enlarged view of participation as well –
advocating corporatism, say, or forms of industrial democracy.[61]

These problems clearly emerge from Ely's own discussion of his
approach. He takes freedom of speech as a key instance of a 'processual
right' that is vital to a well-functioning democratic system.[62] However,
there are many different rationales for why that is so – be it that free
competition and criticism is the best way for truth to emerge, or that free
discussion is of fundamental importance to individual development and
so on. These various rationales may in their turn yield rather different
policy recommendations when it comes to limiting speech. Even among
those who hold similar views, there may be a divergence of opinion on a
given case. Though Ely takes a largely libertarian view of the matter, the
record of the Supreme Court has been somewhat mixed. As he remarks,
the cases that introduced the 'clear and present danger' test following the
First World War saw the defendants going to prison for ten years 'for quite
tame and ineffectual expression'.[63] The difficulty is that it is practically
impossible for the Court not to get involved in contestable substantive
judgements over whether speech is related to the political process or not,
and so has a *prima facie* case for being protected on his view, or the degree
to which certain instances of it may or may not damage that process. As
he acknowledges, even an absolutist, no restrictions ever, stance would
be substantively contentious and raise difficulties as to its application.[64]
Think of the way the US Supreme Court has employed this position to
prevent limitations on campaign finance.[65]

Matters get even more complicated when we turn to those areas where
he expects the Court to ensure not just that the process is formally open but
also gives minorities a fair hearing. This has been a key issue in the United
States, where a number of devices – from the inconvenient location of
polling booths, to the imaginative drawing of constituency boundaries –
have been employed in southern states in particular to weaken the impact
of black votes. In fact, creative redistricting to favour incumbents has
become the norm.[66] Moreover, most states lack a tradition of independent public service, making electoral commissions heavily biased towards
the prevailing administration of which they often form a part, either as

---

[61] E.g. R. A. Dahl, *A Preface to Economic Democracy*, Cambridge: Polity Press, 1985.
[62] Ely, *Democracy and Distrust*, pp. 105–16.   [63] Ibid., p. 107.
[64] Ibid., p. 109.   [65] *Buckley v Valeo*, 424 US 1 (1976).
[66] For example, in 2002, out of 435 contested Congressional seats, only four incumbents
     lost to challengers. See report BBC News 8 October 2004 http://news.bbc.co.uk/1/hi/
     world/americas/3724372.stm.

appointees or as members of the same electoral ticket. Yet, it has been an area where the Court has usually been reluctant to intervene. This reticence is unsurprising, for it is a political minefield. Take the familiar arguments about the various merits of different electoral systems. In the US, as in the UK, there has been a broad popular debate about the relative virtues and vices of both the plurality, first past the post, system and of the various systems of proportional representation. As with freedom of speech, all these arguments involve substantive judgements about outputs, not just a view on the fairness of inputs.[67] Who or what should be represented is intimately linked to the ends you see the process as serving – the trade-offs one makes between representativeness and accountability, say, or whether one wants a politics of ideas or of presence, or the degree one sees representatives as being mandated delegates or free to exercise their own judgement and so on. Related issues emerge in debates about districting. Here too one can give different rationales for drawing the lines of constituencies in particular ways, depending on what you are trying to achieve. Some seek to represent a territorial community, for example, others given groups of people as identified by religion, occupation, gender and so on.

Ely tries to get around this problem by not judging the outcome *per se* but rather focusing on the motivations of those proposing the policy. If the intention of a policy was to discriminate, then on his reading we are only objecting to a distortion in the process – not the substance of the policy as such. Of course, he admits that motives are always difficult to uncover and will usually have to be inferred from outcomes. However, he maintains that some policies involve such egregious distortions that their aim cannot but have been discriminatory. He takes as an example, the redrawing of the City of Tuskegee boundary by the Alabama legislature in 1957, that changed it from a square shape to an 'uncouth twenty-eight-sided figure' that just happened to exclude all but a handful of the city's previous 400 black voters – an action the Supreme Court did in fact invalidate.[68] Once again, though, the difficulty is that in certain circumstances just such discrimination might be thought by some to be justified. For instance, it can be a way of securing a 'presence' for

---

[67] See, for example, D. J. Amy, *Real Choices/New Voices: The Case for Proportional Representation Elections in the United States*, New York: Columbia University Press, 1993 and Lani Guinier, *The Tyranny of the Majority: Fundamental Fairness in Representative Democracy*, New York: Free Press, 1994. Guinier failed to be confirmed as assistant attorney general for civil rights because of her views.

[68] Ely, *Democracy and Distrust*, pp. 139–40. See *Gomillion v Lightfoot* 364 US 339, 347 (1960) for the Court's decision.

particular disadvantaged groups by increasing the likelihood they will be represented by a member of their minority group. This rationale has been used to justify majority/minority districts, for example.[69] Here, too, what does the work will be not the uncovering of a discriminatory input but one's evaluation of the discriminatory character of the output.

The difficulties with this approach become even more evident when Ely applies it to cases that are not directly related to process but nevertheless seem intended to discriminate against minorities, such as the racial segregation of schooling in the US south. As we saw in chapter 2, it is possible to devise general laws that apply equally to all and yet adversely discriminate against particular groups. Consequently, the legal formalities of equity and fairness can be preserved, yet a particular group explicitly or implicitly get picked out for special treatment in ways that adversely affect them. Yet, I also noted that all law discriminates to some degree, and special treatment can often be legitimate when there are relevant differences that call for people being treated differently to others. How, then, can we have a non-substantive, processual way of deciding when such discrimination is unjustified?

Ely relies once more on seeking out discriminatory motivations, seeing the doctrine of 'suspicious classifications' as a key tool for identifying them.[70] This doctrine involves determining whether the policy goal, or the means employed to pursue it, could only have been chosen if there was some malign intent to discriminate. There has to be a reasonable fit between the ostensible goal and the classification, with neither the burdens nor the benefits disproportionately impacting on any group. The supposed paradigm case is a 'self-serving generalisation' when a dominant 'we' devises a rule that will only impact adversely against a certain minority 'them'.[71] However, there are a number of problems with applying this criterion.

---

[69] See the discussion in R. J. McKeever, 'Race and Representation in the United States: The Constitutional Validity of Majority-Minority Congressional Districts', *Journal of American Studies*, 33 (1999), pp. 491–507.

[70] Ely, *Democracy and Distrust*, p. 145.

[71] Ibid., pp. 157–61. NB Ely (pp. 170–72) does not want to rule out 'positive' 'we–they' discrimination, such as affirmative action programmes, even if he acknowledges such polices may be unfair to particular individuals. He argues these are allowable because there is no danger of a white majority, say, discriminating against whites because of racial prejudice. However, many of those excluded by such programmes claim this is precisely what has happened. Ely has here elided means and ends. The point is not that a white majority cannot make what many of them believe to be an unjustifiably discriminatory policy even with regard to its own, but that those who feel aggrieved have a better chance than certain minorities of overturning that decision through the political process.

First, discriminatory 'we–they' legislation is often inevitable and arguably justified. Consequently, as Ely himself acknowledges, such scrutiny can be problematic because the ostensible goal may appear harmless or be given a *prima facie* acceptable justification, yet in reality hide a more sinister purpose. For example, a headmaster may justify black and white children sitting on different sides of the school stage at a graduation ceremony for aesthetic reasons, even if the real reason is segregation.[72] How can we uncover such spurious rationalisations without judging the purposes to which they have been put? After all, progressive taxation has a negatively discriminatory 'we–they' character. As Riker and Weingast ask, 'why is the abridgement of some minority's economic rights less troubling than an abridgement of the political rights of minorities?'[73] True, this particular 'they' can influence the political process in other ways than sheer numbers of votes. Yet, a participational approach might want to close off such informal channels. In which case, such measures do appear procedurally unacceptable on Ely grounds – a conclusion that many, Ely included, would find counter-intuitive. If 'we–they' legislation *per se* is not illegitimate, though, then the problem of finding procedural grounds for distinguishing acceptable from unacceptable policies remains.

Second, in any case, not all 'we–they' legislation need be presented as such.[74] It can be formally dressed up as 'we–we' by being framed in very general terms, or 'they–they' by specifying certain features of the legislation rather than others. Criminal legislation, for example, is formally 'we–we', since all of us might commit a crime. Yet, most legislators probably assume that neither they nor their constituents will become members of the criminal class, peddling rather softer in those areas – such as driving offences – where that assumption does not hold, and in this case unfairly discriminating against victims in the process. It might be argued that the tendency of legislators to be too severe in the former cases and too lenient in the latter makes this a rather good area for Elyish judicial review to protect the rights of certain kinds of criminal. However, as I've noted, this is a grey area – we are potential criminals in a way a white person is not potentially black. Moreover, with regard to many crimes most voters and

---

[72] Ibid., p. 148.
[73] W. H. Riker and B. W. Weingast, 'Constitutional Regulation of Legislative Choice: The Political Consequences of Judicial Deference to Legislatures', *Virginia Law Review*, 74 (1988), pp. 378–9, cited in I. Shapiro, *The State of Democratic Theory*, Princeton: Princeton University Press, 2003, p. 65.
[74] Tushnet, 'Darkness on the Edge of Town', pp. 1052–3.

legislators will be neither criminal nor victim, so much criminal legislation is really 'they–they' (or, with ingenuity, could be portrayed as such).
Victims' rights also need to be factored in and arguably should count for
more – and 'we' are more likely to fall into that category. Meanwhile,
judges are no less members of the dominant 'we' than legislators – a point
to which I shall return below.

Third, Ely's thesis will only really apply to consistent minorities. Yet,
these are fairly rare in national politics. Within pluralist democracies, most
majorities are coalitions of minorities which shift from issue to issue. As
priorities alter, so parties tend to alternate in power. There is no settled
'we' oppressing a given 'they' – the 'we' prevailing today may well be the
'they' that gets outvoted tomorrow. At the local level, a given 'they' may
consistently lose. But if they can form part of a national 'we' that could
override that local legislation, or could move to another locality, then
'participational' avenues arguably exist and court intervention would be
inappropriate.[75] Ely's support for the Warren Court suggests he would
still want judicial review in such circumstances. However, we noted in
chapter 1 that such judicial intervention may not only be illegitimate in
his own terms, but may also be less efficacious, and potentially detract
from, action by a national legislature and government.

Fourth, 'we–they' stereotyping may not be the main source of discrimination. Ely grants that his approach will offer little succour to the
poor. Though many laws actively (or more commonly perhaps, passively
through government inaction) discriminate in favour of the wealthy, they
rarely do so 'by drawing on some comparative generalization about the
relative characteristics of the poor on the one hand, and those who more
nearly resemble the legislators on the other'.[76] Of course, as with criminals, some very diffuse and unarticulated prejudices may underlie many
policies – people tend not to ascribe their good fortune to luck alone.
However, sorting out which of these assumptions, if any, might be justified or not will be highly contentious. The problem for the poor lies not
in the blocking of formal channels or deliberate discrimination but in
their social powerlessness leading them to fail to exploit fully the political
power formally open to them: they find it hard to organise and a high
proportion do not vote. As a result, they cannot make people aware of the
often mistaken views they may hold about their plight. Notwithstanding
Ely's participational approach, though, he fails to address such problems.

---

[75] Ibid., pp. 1048–51.   [76] Ely, *Democracy and Distrust*, p. 162.

In fact, it's hard to see how judicial review could be employed to do so without giving courts the very sort of broad brief to address substantive issues he wishes to exclude from their authority.

The main trouble for Ely's approach is that one person's 'suspicious classification' may often be another person's valid interpretation of 'equality of concern and respect'. None of the criteria he offers seems able to distinguish unreasonable bias from an acceptable difference of opinion. Take a decision to segregate schools on the basis of gender, subject to a proviso that the facilities will be 'separate but equal'. The policy might be defended on the basis that some evidence exists that on average girls perform better in single-sex schools. Though boys do marginally worse, that result could be seen as justifiable given that on the whole social structures still favour men more than women, with males generally enjoying higher pay, better employment prospects and so on. The policy merely evens out women's chances by giving them a better start. By contrast, opponents might argue that a mixed environment is better for the socialisation of both sexes and may work against those structural disadvantages that still adversely affect women and perhaps long term tackle the conditions that at present lead girls to perform worse in co-educational compared to all-girl schools. Some might worry a separate system would never be equal – that one or other sex will suffer.

Here we have two views of education policy, each of which could charge the other with having discriminatory effects. Ely would be unable to say which would have been chosen had there be no discriminatory intent in the process without taking sides on the issue of substance. Even if there was very good reason in the 1950s and 60s US debates about racially segregated schools to doubt the good intentions of those concerned, one can certainly imagine an argument being made about how such segregation might actually counteract discrimination by allowing black children to be educated in an environment where nobody is intimidating them or setting inappropriate standards. Indeed, this is just the sort of case that has been used to justify all-girl schools, and that some have employed in Britain to defend separate schools for pupils of different religious faiths.

The fact is, good or bad intentions are not really what count here, but a judgement call on outputs. Given that there are many imponderables in what might happen, and a range of non-discriminatory values that might be invoked to evaluate such a policy, a decision by a constitutional court in this area will involve precisely what Ely has been seeking to avoid – namely, judges rather than elected legislators deciding the issue of substance and weighing the various principled and other considerations involved.

Nemo iudex in sua causa: *breaking the monopoly of democracy's winners over the means of their success*

Although Ely has been most associated with trying to decouple procedural from substantive views of democracy, his argument does not necessarily turn on this distinction – or at least a strong version of it. Indeed, much of the time he accepts that our understanding of the democratic process may well be conditioned by substantive policy considerations. However, precisely for that reason he argues that decisions about democracy itself ought not to be left to those involved in that process. Ely suggests that his approach might be likened to 'an "antitrust" as opposed to a "regulatory" orientation to economic affairs'. Because input into the process and policy outcomes are so related, those in power often have an incentive to 'choke off the channels of effective change' or, if their majority is secure, can afford to discriminate against a minority without fear of any effective opposition. Now, if they are the main culprits, it seems 'obvious' that 'our elected representatives are the last persons we should trust with identification of either of these situations'. Though 'no one could suppose' that any evaluation of how far the representative system is doing its job of representing interests 'won't be full of judgement calls', as 'comparative outsiders' the courts are appropriate third-party arbitrators.[77]

How convincing is this argument? Let's take an example that illustrates both the strengths and weaknesses of this proposal: the Supreme Court's ruling in *Bush v. Gore* in the aftermath of the 2000 United States Presidential election.[78] On the one hand, the dispute over the Florida electoral count was one that clearly was hard for the partisans themselves to resolve in a way most would accept as fair. The election in both the country and Florida was too close for a decision not to matter or be easy to call as obviously favouring one of the parties regardless of the disputed chads. The administration of the election was also open to suspicion of self-serving bias given that, as is common practice in the US, many of the officials involved were political appointees, while the state governor was a brother and fellow party member of one of the candidates. In this sort of situation, deference to a respected third party applying the acknowledged rules of the game seems a reasonable, if not uncontested, solution.

---

[77] Ibid., pp. 102–3.   [78] *Bush v Gore*, 531 US 98 (2000).

On the other hand, however, though the losing litigant, Al Gore, stayed true to his pledge to accept the Court's ruling without criticism, the decision attracted widespread condemnation for alleged partisan bias by the judges. Over 500 US law professors signed a public statement declaring 'the U.S. Court used its power to act as political partisans, not judges of a court of law'.[79] Indeed, in an unprecedented move, a minority on the Court itself condemned the ruling for eroding 'the Nation's confidence in the judge as an impartial guardian of the Rule of Law'.[80]

The Florida case seems to offer as good an example as one could find for Ely's argument.[81] It had the policing of the democratic process at its heart, with the politicians and the electorate not only obvious partisans but evenly split, making third-party arbitration an obvious way to resolve the impasse. However, it quickly emerged that the judges were themselves a party to the more general political disagreement. Like every other US citizen, they were affected by the outcome of the Presidential election and held opinions on the merits of the candidates. On the issue of the rules of the democratic game, there can be no group that has to live under those rules that is not a judge in their own case. Indeed, the judges are doubly so – both as citizens and as adjudicators of their own place within the system. Because they are at the apex of the system, they are judges over their own constitutional competence in the matter too. Yet, that issue was as contentious as the decision itself. As Jeremy Waldron has observed,[82] disagreement over the Court's decision was not just over whether it had interpreted this or that provision of Florida electoral law correctly. Rather, there was a far broader debate, related to differing interpretations of the rule of law, over whether the Court should be involved at all and,[83] in the event of a recount, if there were either clear rules officials could follow or any truly independent electoral officials to administer them.

Of course, it might be argued that judges have fewer incentives to distort the process or accumulate power in self-serving ways than politicians.

---

[79] Statement of Law Professors for the Rule of Law, *New York Times*, 13 January 2001.

[80] 531 US 98 (2000), at 128–9 (Stevens J.).

[81] E.g. Shapiro, *The State of Democratic Theory*, p. 64 sees it in these terms.

[82] J. Waldron, 'Is the Rule of Law an Essentially Contested Concept (In Florida)?', *Law and Philosophy*, 21 (2002), pp. 137–64.

[83] As Larry Kramer has shown, deference to the Court on this issue indicates a shift in attitudes towards it over the past fifty years or so. In the past its decision would almost certainly have provoked far more political and popular opposition than it did. See L. Kramer, *The People Themselves: Popular Constitutionalism and Judicial Review*, New York: Oxford University Press, 2004, pp. 231–2.

Perhaps. To ensure that is so, though, the procedures employed to select judges and the balance of opinion among them will become of as much interest as those surrounding the choice of democratic representatives. In fact, this has already happened to a large extent. Despite Gore's personal demurral, the Court has become so politically controversial within the United States that any decision was likely to attract accusations of bias from some quarter. As a result, the self-same procedural issues surrounding the legislature arise with regard to the Court – and who is going to rule on them? We seem faced with an infinite regress.

III Constitutionalist democracy: a middle way between substance and procedures?

A number of theorists have acknowledged the difficulties of both substantive and procedural accounts and searched for a middle way. Two attempts at such ecumenical solutions will be explored. The first distinguishes striking down a law on substantive grounds related to the morality of democracy from a constitutional court's putting forward its own substantive solution to a given issue. The second goes further and sees substantive values as issuing from the theoretical and practical attempt to design perfect democratic procedures.

The substance of procedures: the Burt–Ginsburg view

Theorists who attempt the first approach accept that courts inevitably employ substantive judgements in ruling on process, but contend that they can still avoid imposing their own substantive view of what the policy should be. They argue that courts can legitimately suspect legislation that appears to involve a majority employing its power to dominate another by not affording them equal protection of the laws. Moreover, such domination can be identified by procedural criteria – namely, that the policy fails to provide the same opportunities for the equal consideration of relevant interests one expects from an open democratic procedure. However, the role of a court should not be to offer its own solution to the policy in question but rather to send it back to the legislature for it to devise an alternative.[84]

---

[84] E.g. R. A. Burt, *The Constitution in Conflict*, Cambridge, MA: Harvard University Press, 1992 and Shapiro, *The State of Democratic Theory*, pp. 66–77.

In developing this middle way, Robert Burt compares the decision in *Dred Scott v Sandford*[85] with that of *Brown v Board of Education*.[86] These cases have become the benchmarks of the US Supreme Court's authority. No acceptable theory of constitutional adjudication can fail to declare *Dred Scott* wrong or *Brown* right. Yet, Burt argues that the reasons for doing so are often unconvincing.[87] These cases might be thought to confirm the straightforwardly substantive approach. After all, most people now would want to condemn *Dred Scott* for supporting slavery and praise *Brown* for defending racial equality. However, placed in the context of the times, the 'outcome' approach yields the embarrassing result of endorsing certain questionable aspects of *Dred Scott*.[88]

In Burt's view, the fault in the *Dred Scott* decision lay less in the Justices' substantive interpretation of the Constitution, morally repugnant and arguably wrong though it was, than in the Court's view that its role was to decide the policy issues the case raised rather than simply determining the parameters within which any such decision could be made.[89] He argues the real question posed by the case was how this deeply divisive issue could be resolved in ways that enabled the antagonistic parties to remain equal members of the same Union. In finding the ongoing political process of seeking compromises unconstitutional, Burt contends the Court implicitly suggested that the Union should be dissolved. The reasons the Supreme Court chose to act in this way were ones that proponents of

---

[85] 60 US (19 How.) 393 (1857). Dred Scott was a slave who had travelled with his owner to both a free state and a free territory that prohibited slavery. On his owner's death following his return to the slave state of Missouri, he brought a suit against his owner's widow claiming he had effectively been emancipated by his previous residence in free regions of the Union. Though the state court held for him, the Missouri Supreme Court overruled the decision. He then brought a new proceeding before the federal court following the transfer of control over him to his owner's widow's brother, John Sanford. The court ruled he was still a slave and he appealed to the Supreme Court which found in Sandford's [*sic*] favour, ruling slaves were not citizens under the Constitution and could not sue before federal courts, that the relevant state courts had jurisdiction on the substantive issue in their jurisdiction and that Congress had lacked the authority to prohibit slavery in the territories.

[86] *Brown v Board of Education I*, 247 US 483 (1954) and *Brown v Board of Education II*, 349 US 294 (1955). This landmark decision overturned the Court's previous holding that racially segregated public education could be 'separate but equal' and hence compatible with the Fourteenth Amendment to the Constitution.

[87] As he rightly notes, the least convincing in this respect are the contortions of the 'originalists', such as Bork, to square *Brown* with their view – an exercise that, in so far as it requires an 'up-dating' of the Founders' views to meet problems they did not anticipate, effectively undermines their position. See Burt, *The Constitution in Conflict*, pp. 12–13.

[88] Ibid., pp. 13–15.

[89] R. A. Burt, 'What was Wrong with *Dred Scott*, What's Right about *Brown*', *Washington and Lee Law Review*, 42 (1985), pp. 16–17.

'outcome' or 'result-based' judicial reasoning typically advocate.[90] Congress and the territorial legislatures were denied authority on the question on the grounds that public institutions were bound simply to uphold the 'private rights' of masters in their slave property. Issues of 'private right' were to be decided by those courts with the appropriate jurisdiction. No doubt, the Court also hoped that taking the issue off the political agenda might avert civil war. Far from being viewed as an impartial and neutral arbitrator, though, the Court itself became an object of criticism for having usurped the democratic role of the people.

This critique was made most famously and forcefully by Lincoln in his first inaugural address. As he put it:

> If the policy of the Government upon vital questions, affecting the whole people, is to be irrevocably fixed by decisions of the Supreme Court, the instant they are made, in ordinary litigation between parties in personal actions, the people will have ceased to be their own rulers, having to that extent practically resigned their government into the hands of that eminent tribunal.[91]

Lincoln's point – delivered at a time when he still hoped to avert war, and powerfully reiterated in the Gettysburg Address – was that a political community can only subsist if all participants remain committed to finding solutions to common problems as a collectivity. That commitment is subverted when one party is prevented from putting forward its case and negotiating with others.

To say, as most contemporary substantive theorists would, that the Court's mistake lay in getting it wrong by deciding for the slave holders rather than slaves misses the point. The Court would have been 'wrong' in Burt's sense even had they decided the case for the other side. Judgement on the basis of 'good' or 'bad' outcomes is fine in retrospect but, as Burt remarks, 'it gives no guidance for action in confronting an uncertain future'.[92] For a start, this argument ignores the fact that the substantive outcome was a matter of such deep dispute at the time that the Court could (and did) adopt a view we now would all reject. Given that the Justices belong to the same political culture as ordinary citizens, one can not expect them to get it right at a time when everyone else – or a large proportion of them – is getting it wrong. Even more important than these pragmatic considerations, though, is the normative point that a

---

[90] Burt, 'What was Wrong with *Dred Scott*', p. 11.
[91] Cited in Burt, *The Constitution in Conflict*, pp. 1–2.
[92] Burt, 'What was Wrong with *Dred Scott*', p. 19.

democratic community cannot subsist if one group's views in a deep dispute are simply ruled out of consideration. If we deem the prime purpose of a constitution within a democracy to be upholding its core values, then the role of judicial review ought not to be to decide outcomes in ways that effectively exclude one group in a dispute from making its case. That can only alienate that group from the political community. Instead, Burt contends their aim should be to uphold the process as an ongoing search for solutions that treat the parties equitably.

On this account, a constitution serves as a framework for ongoing dispute resolution within a political community, not a resource of right answers to those disputes. Burt's claim is that what *Brown* got right was precisely to see its task as 'facilitating a process of public conversation, of mutually respectful dialogic engagement, between the adversaries' rather than as cutting off that conversation by placing the issue out of bounds of politics and putting forward a resolution of its own supposedly derived from constitutional principles.[93] He observes how *Brown* presented much the same dilemma as *Dred Scott*. In both cases, the Court was faced with a profoundly divided nation, in which the parties were putting forward apparently irreconcilable claims. In each case, victory for one party would be interpreted as a crushing defeat for the other and lead them to challenge the legitimacy of existing political arrangements. Yet, whereas *Dred Scott* effectively declared victory on one side, thereby consigning the other to perpetual defeat, *Brown* studiously avoided offering a settlement of the case. All it did was insist that any resolution had to be on the basis of the mutually acknowledged equality intrinsic to the democratic process.

Of course, there are matters of substance in such procedural decisions. *Brown*, after all, did 'unsettle a legislative resolution that one disputant found intolerable'.[94] And it did so on the substantive grounds that the segregation laws 'violated the democratic principle of equality by inflicting a permanently subordinate status on blacks (marking them, in effect, as "permanent losers" in any disputes with whites)'.[95] The key aspect, though, was that 'this unsettling was all the Court in fact did in *Brown*'.[96] In *Brown II* the Court steadfastly 'refused to specify what would constitute an ultimately appropriate resolution . . . and instead remanded this issue for further proceedings in the various federal district courts'.[97] In effect, it acknowledged the difficulties of blacks getting an equal hearing in the state and other more local democratic forums, but tried nonetheless to create forums where black and white disputants could face each other

[93] Ibid., p. 21.   [94] Ibid.   [95] Ibid., pp. 21–2.   [96] Ibid., p. 21.   [97] Ibid., p. 22.

and try and seek a solution for themselves. The Court only took a more proactive role in the wake of the more substantive civic equality called for by the Civil Rights Acts of 1964, 1965 and 1968.

Does Burt's argument square the circle between process and substance? Ian Shapiro claims this approach avoids the problems found in Ely and Dworkin respectively by being 'more than process, less than substance'.[98] The problem is its view of process is so substantial that it effectively decides the very issues it claims to leave open. As Burt concedes, *Brown* aroused huge opposition because it had clearly required desegregation, even if it had not determined how it was to be implemented or when. The distinction between disallowing and deciding has a tendency to get blurred once its clear that only a small range of policies of a certain kind will be allowed. Even Burt admits the Court arguably overstated its case in contending that separate could never be equal as a matter of principle grounded in 'objective' social scientific fact.[99] As I noted in discussing Ely above, however right the decision may have been in the context of the American south, in other conflicts separate provision has been seen as a guarantee or sign of equality – for example, in Northern Ireland where Catholics and Protestants are educated in separate religious schools and in the desire of British Muslims for publicly funded faith-based schools alongside those of Jews, Catholics and the Church of England on the mainland. True, the Court pragmatically waited for the political process to decide. But it's unclear that it did so for quite the principled, process-related reasons Burt attributes to it.[100]

Perhaps *Brown* is a bad example. More recently, Burt – and following him, Ruth Bader Ginsburg, now a Supreme Court Justice, and Ian Shapiro, have made parallel points in comparing *Brown* with Justice Black-mun's 1973 judgement in *Roe v Wade*.[101] Once again, we have a deeply contentious issue, with current American debates over abortion being spoken of as the source of a second civil war. In Dworkin's words: 'Abortion is tearing America apart . . . distorting its politics, and confounding

[98] Shapiro, *The State of Democratic Theory*, p. 66.
[99] Burt, *The Constitution in Conflict*, pp. 14–16.
[100] But this was no less imposed, with an unprecedented two-thirds Senate majority being used to squash an overwhelmingly southern filibuster in the Senate to pass the 1964 Civil Rights Act. Such a one-sided democratic majority ought on Burt's reading to be as tyrannous as a Court majority.
[101] *Roe v Wade*, 410 US 113 (1973) and commentary by Burt, *The Constitution in Conflict*, pp. 344–52 and Shapiro (who also cites Ginsburg) *The State of Democratic Theory*, pp. 67–73.

its constitutional law.'[102] Burt *et al.* argue *Roe* resembles *Dred Scott* in misguidedly trying to decide the case. Rather than just striking down the offending Texas abortion statute, the Court essentially authored a statute of its own by laying out a detailed test specifying the conditions under which abortion would be acceptable.[103] But arguably Shapiro does much the same in laying down procedural criteria for an acceptable decision. It's not just that these criteria for 'a non-dominating policy' are themselves subject to different interpretations, but also that applying these considerations rather than others is itself controversial. He suggests that abortion policy should be guided not by considerations of any 'metaphysically imponderable' 'right to life' but by whether a policy places an undue burden on a woman's democratic procedural rights.[104] However, a woman's 'democratic procedural rights' are as 'metaphysically imponderable' as the right to life and subject to just as much disagreement.[105] Choosing these criteria is also to effectively take sides in the debate and suggest that the 'right to choose' of the mother takes precedence.

Burt and his followers see his substantive process approach as less confrontational than the substantive outcome view of Dworkin. Yet, there is no real evidence that it is in practice, or that it can avoid it in theory, effectively shading into an outcome view in much the same way as Ely's did. Many analysts argue *Brown* added to southern resentment, producing a sharp shift to the right of southern politicians, without advancing the black cause. All agree the crucial changes came from the civil rights movement and the resulting democratic decisions of the Civil Rights Acts. There is some support for Burt's view in the fact that *Brown* did provide a symbol that helped mobilise civil rights action. For example, the first Freedom Ride of 1961 was planned to arrive at its destination on the anniversary of *Brown*. However, it seems pretty likely that some civil rights movement was inevitable and that this would have engaged the sympathy of a national political majority that had increasingly found southern segregation and political discrimination an embarrassment – even

---

[102] R. Dworkin, *Life's Dominion: An Argument about Abortion and Euthanasia*, London: HarperCollins, 1995, p. 3

[103] Shapiro, *The State of Democratic Theory*, p. 67.

[104] Ibid., pp. 70–73, commenting on *Planned Parenthood of Southeastern Pennsylvania v Casey*, 505 US 833 (1992).

[105] As Shapiro, *The State of Democratic Theory*, pp. 71–2 notes, Justice Scalia in his dissent pointed out 'that the idea of undue burden involves philosophical choices about which justices will continue to differ'. E.g. see *Stenberg v Carhart*, 530 US 914 (2000).

in 1954.[106] Meanwhile, the Civil Rights Act, which allowed federal funds to be denied to schools that continued to discriminate, was arguably also an 'imposed' decision. After all, only seven Senators outside the south voted against the southern filibuster that sought to derail it, as similar measures had been in the past. Yet there is a difference in a defeat by, at the time, an unprecedented two-thirds majority of the representatives of millions of fellow citizens making common cause with a black minority and a vote by nine judges representing nobody. The former is much harder to portray as an elite affair. Rather, it signified the entry of blacks into a condition of political equality in which they could demand a say in how the affairs of the south were run – a point reinforced dramatically by the Voting Rights Act that was to transform southern politics. It also shows that legislative majorities need not be tyrannous (just as *Dred Scott* indicates how courts do not necessarily uphold the rights of minorities). In other words, the substantive procedural claims of democracy were far more effectively made through struggles within the democratic process itself than they ever could have been made via the courts.

Substantive procedures: Habermas and the preconditions of democratic discourse

Jürgen Habermas also seeks a way out of Ely's dilemma. Like Ely, Habermas maintains that 'the *democratic process* bears the entire burden of legitimation'.[107] In a 'postmetaphysical' age, an uncoerced, rational consensus between autonomous individuals offers the only acceptable basis for law.[108] However, he also believes this approach presupposes a substantive theory of the preconditions of democracy and criticises Ely for assuming, but failing to develop, such a position.[109] He contends this gap can be filled by an account of the 'system of rights that makes citizens' private and public autonomy equally possible'.[110] Habermas claims that the resulting conception of democracy is a procedural one. It looks at 'on the one hand, the communicative presuppositions that allow the better arguments to come into play in various forms of deliberation and, on the other, procedures that secure fair bargaining conditions'.[111]

---

[106] For a detailed analysis, see M. Klarman, '*Brown*, Racial Change and the Civil Rights Movement', *Virginia Law Review*, 80 (1994), pp. 7–150.

[107] J. Habermas, *Between Facts and Norms: Contributions to a Discourse Theory of Law and Democracy*, trans. W. Rehg, Cambridge: Polity Press, 1996, p. 450.

[108] Ibid., p. 448.   [109] Ibid., p. 266.   [110] Ibid., p. 263.   [111] Ibid., pp. 278–9.

Habermas sees his argument as a synthesis and critique of 'communitarian' or 'civic republican' accounts of democracy and judicial review, on the one hand, and 'liberal' positions, on the other. The first treat democracy as a process premised upon, and aimed at, the discovery of common values.[112] Habermas criticises these views for seeing citizenship in ethical terms, as membership of a community possessing shared values, rather than in legal–political terms, as simply involvement in a set of common discursive practices. In today's complex and pluralist societies, a convergence on values is unlikely. Judicial review premised on this understanding of citizenship will necessarily fall foul of Ely's strictures regarding a substantive values approach, with the judge ending up imposing his or her own views in the name of society as a whole.[113] The second, liberal positions, though, go too far in the opposite direction. They see democracy simply as the pushing and shoving of interests between self-owning rights-bearers.[114] These approaches treat rights as 'natural' and so pre-discursive and pre-social. Rights thereby become endorsements of self-interest, legitimising the ways those with most power skew or subvert the process of bargaining in self-serving ways within both the public and private spheres.[115] Liberal models also ignore the fact, recognised by communitarians, that democracy concerns arguments and not just interests.[116] Theorists who view democracy in these terms either demand too little of judicial review, simply looking to see if formal rights to vote are granted to all, or are tempted to correct its potential injustices by demanding too much, asking the courts to pronounce on the policy implications of defending pre-political individual rights.[117]

His own position aspires to overcome the respective problems of these two approaches by seeing courts as defending the norms of democratic discourse.[118] Habermas contends that, unlike either communal values or individual natural rights and interests, these norms are not relative to the society or persons concerned. Rather, they are universal preconditions of rational communication oriented towards a consensus. As a result, he argues 'a constitutional court guided by a proceduralist understanding of the constitution does not have to overdraw on its legitimation credit' – it

---

[112] Ibid., pp. 269–79. His main example of this position is F. Michelman, 'Conceptions of Democracy in American Constitutional Argument: Voting Rights', *Florida Law Review*, 41 (1989), pp. 291–319.

[113] Habermas, *Between Facts and Norms*, p. 279.

[114] Ibid., pp. 268–70.   [115] Ibid., pp. 271–2, 282–3, 293–4.

[116] Ibid., pp. 273–4.   [117] Ibid., pp. 297–8.   [118] Ibid., pp. 296–7.

can merely stay within its authority to maintain the law as given by the
'logic of argumentation'.[119]

I doubt this. As we have seen, people may reasonably disagree about
the right as well as the good. They can differ in their views of private and
public autonomy, and so propose different accounts of democracy and
the procedural rights it entails. Indeed, communitarian and liberal views
offer two such different accounts. Both involve democratic communication – they simply entail different conceptions of political communication
to his. Habermas argues that 'a consistent proceduralist understanding of
the constitution relies on the intrinsically rational character of a democratic process that grounds the presumption of rational outcomes'.[120] That
sounds like a pure proceduralist argument, but turns out to be a form of
perfect proceduralism. Because a 'rational outcome' for Habermas proves
to be a decision that respects what he regards as the criteria for a rational process: namely, one that respects a certain reading of civil, political
and social rights that derive from his understanding of autonomy.[121] This
argument brings us full circle back to Dworkin, as well as being circular
in itself.[122] For the conditions of communication can be as much at issue
as what is communicated – the two are frequently intimately related.

Habermas does partly acknowledge this dilemma. In a critique of
Rawls's *Political Liberalism* he has complained that the American's idea of
a democratic contract places the foundations of democracy outside the
democratic process, so that 'the act of founding the democratic constitution cannot be repeated under the institutional conditions of an already
constituted just society'. As a result, 'it is not possible for the citizens . . .
to reignite the radical democratic embers of the original position . . . for
. . . they find the results of the theory already sedimented in the constitution'.[123] However, despite this criticism, Habermas himself can only find
a space for the remaining elements of radical constitutive democracy outside the formal channels of already constitutionalised politics. The pressure for constitutional change comes from a diffuse public opinion, operating through the media, unions, social movements, churches and other
institutions of civil society.[124] The supposed dangers of majoritarianism

---

[119] Ibid., p. 279.   [120] Ibid., p. 285.   [121] Ibid., pp. 241–2, 269.
[122] For a comparison of the two thinkers, which notes how Habermas himself to a degree
'savours' this very circularity, see F. Michelman, 'Democracy and Positive Liberty', *Boston
Review: A Political and Literary Forum*, 21:5 (1996), pp. 3–15.
[123] J. Habermas, 'Reconciliation Through the Public Use of Reason: Remarks on John Rawls's
Political Liberalism', *Journal of Philosophy*, 92 (1995), p. 128.
[124] Habermas, *Between Facts and Norms*, pp. 358–9, 369–70.

are to be avoided by divorcing a populist and allegedly 'subjectless' constitutional politics from a constitutionally constrained normal politics.[125] It is to the coherence of such populist appeals to the constitutive power of 'the people', and the division between 'normal' and 'constitutional' politics on which it rests, that we now turn.

IV Constitutive democracy: populist constitutionalism

The problem with both the substantive and procedural accounts of how democracy should be constituted is that they simply end up advocating those policies the theorist in question believes an ideal democracy *ought* to come up with. They overlook the substantive and procedural virtues of democratic decision-making as a mechanism for legitimately handling our disagreements – including those about the very constitution of democracy. However, a third group of theorists have sought to overcome this objection by seeing the constitution as the product of a special kind of democratic politics. On this account, democracy binds itself. Such self-binding is not of the idealized kind that I discussed in chapter 1, and that could be said to emerge from a Rawlsean or some other democratic contract. Rather, it involves real politics. Nevertheless, it implies a qualitative difference between 'constitutional' and 'normal' politics that only makes sense if the first can be treated as somehow more ideal than the second. In other words, here too the ordinary processes of 'actually existing' democracy are to be regulated by the norms of some version of 'true', populist democracy.

Constitutional politics: Bruce Ackerman's We the People

Bruce Ackerman's *We the People* provides one of the most elaborate theories of how a people employ a democratic constitutional consensus to bind the process of democracy.[126] Though offered as an account of US constitutional history, it has been taken up by others as a more general democratic justification for a constitution. Ackerman argues that we must distinguish between 'normal' politics, which occurs under settled constitutional systems, and 'constitutional' politics, which arises in exceptional times and places the whole system of government in discussion. By

---

[125] Ibid., pp. 304, 486.
[126] B. Ackerman, *We the People: Foundations*, Cambridge, MA: Harvard University Press, 1991.

virtue of this 'dualist' scheme,[127] he aims to cut through the vicious circularity that surrounds the relationship between constitutionalism and democracy.

Ackerman contends that the constitutionalists' objections to simple majoritarianism are valid with respect to 'normal' politics but do not hold for 'constitutional' politics. During 'normal' politics, people do not speak with a single voice but are divided into different ideological factions and interest groups. At such times, the democratic process is best captured by an 'economic' model which characterizes voters as instrumental agents bent on maximizing their own preferences. Consequently, fear of a tyrannous majority during such periods is fully justified: judicial review, divided representation and Madisonian checks and balances are needed to curb such tendencies as much as possible.[128] 'Constitutional' politics, by contrast, only takes place when some national crisis manages to unite the people and leads them to transcend their own particular interests and consider the common good. On such occasions, political decision-making is deliberative rather than economic in nature. The aggregating and trading-off of group interests gives way to debate on the basis of publicly justifiable reasons. The aim is no longer the will of all, so much as the general will. As a result, objections to the will of the majority lose much of their force. Instead of representing the aggregate of the largest number of personal preferences, which then gets imposed on others who wanted something quite different, a deliberative majority reflects a general opinion on the rules and principles necessary to benefit everyone. In this latter case, voters should already have taken the rights of other individuals into account when making their decision and, when necessary, weighed them as best they could.[129]

Ackerman identifies three instances of constitutional politics in the United States – the Founding, Reconstruction and the New Deal. These constitutional moments established a framework for normal politics that the Supreme Court could then defend from populist incursions until such time as 'we the people' reconvened to reform it.[130] This thesis aims to synthesise three different views of constitutionalism.[131] The concerns of 'rights foundationalists', such as Dworkin, can be catered for because dualist democracy gives rights special protection by making them only reformable in the context of constitutional politics. Between times they can be upheld by judicial review. Ackerman also hopes to accommodate

---

[127] Ibid., pp. 3–33.   [128] Ibid., pp. 181–3, 186–95.
[129] Ibid., pp. 266–94.   [130] Ibid., pp. 58–104.   [131] Ibid., pp. 7–24.

the views of 'monist' democrats, who believe that the will of the people should always prevail. These theorists make the mistake of believing that the popular will is expressed in the ordinary law-making of 'normal' politics. In fact, at such times personal interests tend to supervene over the national interest, so that the everyday legislation of governments reflects at best majority preferences rather than the common good. However, the constraints imposed on majorities by the Constitution and its judicial guardians result from constitutional politics and so do genuinely mirror the collective voice of the people. In bowing to them, therefore, governments submit not to certain elites or imposed norms but to the considered will of the demos. Finally, Ackerman also tries to take the approach of historicist interpreters of the Constitution on board. This group divides into roughly two camps: those who argue that judicial interpretation should concentrate on divining the original intent of the Founders, and those who regard the Constitution as an evolving document that judges need to update to reflect current conditions. Ackerman merges the two within his dualist perspective. The role of Supreme Court judges must be to uphold the intentions of the people as expressed at the last relevant moment of constitutional politics. Since the Constitution has never been entirely rewritten, this will almost always involve them in a complex process of integrating various elements from each of the three moments. The Founders' intentions remain important, but have been modified by later new beginnings. The Constitution does evolve, but not as a result of judicial interpretation. It would be quite illegitimate for judges to take on the responsibility of updating it. Rather, the judges' role is to force the people to deliberate on whether they think change is necessary or not by upholding the *status quo* until they are sufficiently minded to do so.

Allowing a constitutional role for politics appears to be diametrically opposed to the contractual argument of Rawls or the results-based view of Dworkin. In Rawls's words, for these theorists 'the idea of right and just constitutions and basic laws is always ascertained by the most reasonable political conception of justice and not by the result of an actual political process'.[132] Constitutions are inevitably framed by fallible human beings, but their legitimacy will always derive not so much from the act of framing itself as their meeting certain substantive criteria that judges are fully justified in seeking to read into them. However, Ackerman's view of constitutional politics turns out to incorporate many of the conditions

---

[132] Rawls, *Political Liberalism*, p. 233.

that are supposed to give rise to an 'overlapping consensus' on a reasonable conception of political justice and orientate judicial decision-making about its implications. The added advantages are supposed to be twofold. Greater democratic legitimacy is said to arise from its being an act of self-commitment, while periodic review allows for the correction of errors and its adaptation to changing circumstances.

Let's take each of these points in turn. Like others,[133] Ackerman portrays 'constitutional' politics as a form of deliberative democracy. According to its proponents 'deliberation aims to arrive at a rationally motivated *consensus* – to find reasons that are persuasive to all who are committed to acting on the results of a free and reasoned assessment of alternatives by equals'.[134] This account is plausible enough as a characterisation of the best rationale for democratic argument – namely, the desire to win one's opponents round by appealing to the fairness and correctness of one's position. However, we all know that real democracy often falls short of this ideal. Deliberative democrats standardly attribute such shortcomings to group interest or ideology leading politicians or citizens trying simply to get their own way and abandoning reasoning for rhetoric and bargaining. Undeniably, much political debate eschews argument from the very beginning. However, often arguments simply run out – there is a reasonable difference of opinion or a clash of legitimate interests, with no convergence of views on a single position all regard as right in sight. As we saw in chapter 1, in these circumstances argument has to be re-orientated towards the search for mutually acceptable compromises – that is, solutions all can live with, even if all the participants personally regard other solutions as superior.

Deliberation is frequently associated with communitarian theories that stress the need for shared goals and mores for democracy. Here, discussion serves merely as a means of discovering what those common understandings and ends are. But, as I noted above, in modern pluralist societies, such commonality is unlikely. It may be that in the periods of crisis Ackerman associates with constitutional politics, a shared fear of some military or economic threat brings people closer together in ways that make convergence more likely. Certainly, a crisis may promote a willingness to make greater sacrifices and cooperate more for the common good. However, the

---

[133] E.g. D. Gauthier, 'Constituting Democracy', in D. Copp, J. Hampton and J. Roemer (eds.), *The Idea of Democracy*, Cambridge: Cambridge University Press, 1993, p. 322.

[134] J. Cohen, 'Deliberation and Democratic Legitimacy', in S. Benhabib (ed.), *Democracy and Difference: Contesting the Boundaries of the Political*, Princeton: Princeton University Press, 1996, p. 23.

evidence of constitutional conventions reveals political divisions remain – of both a bad, narrowly self-interested kind, and a good or legitimate nature. Each sort was plainly in evidence at Philadelphia. As Dahl recounts: 'The delegates had to confront . . . the need to engage in fundamental compromises in order to secure agreement on any constitution at all . . . Compromises were necessary because, like the country at large, members of the convention held different views on some very basic issues.'[135] If slavery is the notorious example of a bad compromise, others, such as the Presidency and the mechanisms employed for his election, evolved out of genuine disagreements about the nature of a republic, the dangers of popular rule, and so on. A very similar mix surfaces in other conventions.[136] Indeed, they provide a vivid illustration of how the very constitution of politics itself always lies within 'the circumstances of politics'.

Constitutional politics, therefore, turns out to be remarkably similar to normal politics – the one is less high-flown and consensual than its advocates imagine, the second more principled – even in the negotiation of compromises, than its critics contend. As a result, it becomes hard to accord it any special weight. Many of the agreements will simply reflect the concerns and beliefs of people at a given time, and these can be expected to change. For example, the US Constitution was drafted prior to the era of mass party politics and before parliamentary systems had properly emerged. There is evidence that as these began to develop, Madison for one changed his views regarding the anti-majoritarian biases of the Constitution.[137] Had the Constitution been drafted in 1820, it would have had a very different shape to that of 1787.

As I noted in chapter 1, some commentators view a constitution as a form of popular pre-commitment. Yet, as Jefferson noted, it is not the same people binding themselves. Why, he asked, should the living be bound by the dead? Surely, the collective autonomy of the demos required that 'each generation is as independent of the one preceding, as that was of all which had gone before', possessing 'like them, a right to choose for itself the

---

[135] Dahl, *How Democratic Is the American Constitution?*, pp. 12–13.
[136] See, for example, my analyses of the Conventions that drew up the EU Charter of Rights and Draft Constitution in R. Bellamy and J. Schönlau, 'The Normality of Constitutional Politics: An Analysis of the Drafting of the EU Charter of Fundamental Rights', *Constellations*, 11:3 (2004), pp. 412–33 and Bellamy and Schönlau, 'The Good, the Bad and the Ugly: The Need for Constitutional Compromise and the Drafting of the EU Constitution', in Lynn Dobson and Andreas Føllesdal (eds.), *Political Theory and the European Constitution*, London: Routledge, 2004, pp. 57–71.
[137] Dahl, *How Democratic Is the American Constitution?*, pp. 31–7.

form of government it believes most promotive of its happiness'.[138] That
certainly is a powerful case if we see pre-commitment as a set of discrete
individual acts. Of course, we usually see such binding as a collective act
of the people as a whole. As such, it is more plausible to imagine a people
thinking about future generations as well as its own concerns. Still, how
far-sighted can any people be? Moreover, the notion of self-binding works
if one regards the danger as periodic weakness of will, myopia or madness,
as with Ulysses tying himself to the mast to be able to resist the allures of
the sirens.[139] But what a constitution effectively binds people to is a view of
the nature of democracy and its workings about which they may well have
disagreed even at the time. The analogy here would not be with a drunk
being bound by his sober self, but with someone, in more secular times,
being bound by a long, if by some members disputed, family tradition of
the eldest son entering the priesthood even if he had lost his faith or had
never believed.

It is sometimes argued that because democracy would not even exist
without certain constitutive rules securing the conditions of vigorous
debate, democrats should surely want to bind themselves to some rules.[140]
As we have seen, though, there are no views of democratic procedures that
all can agree best produce majority rule, guarantee free discussion or protect minorities – even if democrats of all persuasions would sign up to
these goals in the abstract. Issues such as the televising of parliament,
public funding for parties, term limits and proportional representation
have always been controversial. Moreover, the balance of opinion about
them has often shifted over time. As new information comes to light and
societies change, it is perfectly possible for people's opinions to alter. For
example, when the Philadelphia convention chose to submit members
of Congress to two-yearly elections they followed a fairly common contemporary view about the desirability of having a frequent turnover of
representatives and holding them very regularly to account. With experience, most people now regard these terms as too short, more or less
forcing US politicians to continually campaign and raise funds, responding to short-term demands rather than tackling long-term problems.[141]

---

[138] T. Jefferson, Letter to Samuel Kercheval, 12 July 1816, in M. D. Peterson (ed.), *The
Portable Thomas Jefferson*, New York: Viking Press, 1975, p. 560. See the discussion in
S. Holmes, 'Precommitment and the Paradox of Democracy' in J. Elster and R. Slagstad
(eds.), *Constitutionalism and Democracy*, Cambridge: Cambridge University Press, 1988,
pp. 202–5.
[139] J. Elster, *Ulysses and the Sirens*, Cambridge: Cambridge University Press, 1984, p. 36.
[140] Holmes, 'Precommitment', pp. 227–8, 232–5.
[141] A. King, *Running Scared*, New York: The Free Press, 1997.

True, it is possible that reforms may be motivated by the desire of a dominant group to entrench its power even more. However, that cannot be regarded as the norm. If one thinks of the successive constitutional changes in Britain throughout the nineteenth and twentieth centuries, these have been invariably motivated to give greater numbers of people more of a say, either by enfranchising previously excluded groups or through the devolution of power to sub-units. The amendments to the US Constitution have largely operated in a similar direction.[142] Even so, there is never likely to be total agreement. After all, referenda on constitutional amendments are rarely unanimous and, where supermajorities are not required, often get through with a bare majority. So though we do need procedural rules to hold elections, conduct debates and so on, we cannot fix which set is the most constitutive of democracy. That always remains open.

Naturally, it would be unwise to alter the rules of the democratic game too often. Madison objected to Jefferson's proposal of periodic conventions to allow each generation a chance to bind itself on just these grounds, fearing it would produce a highly unstable system.[143] To some degree, Ackerman's argument for periodic 'constitutional moments' offers a more restrained and plausible version of that thesis. Yet, it still begs the question of whether change can only be justified in exceptional circumstances and through a special kind of politics. If the debates of constitutional politics cannot result in a rational consensus that transcends the disagreements and compromises of normal politics – and we have seen they cannot because the burdens of judgement render such agreement unachievable – then the rationale of a Rawlsean-style democratic contract cannot be invoked for this limitation. Nor does the mere possibility of formal amendment overcome this problem. Unless the amendment process is as easy as ordinary legislation, it simply reflects and entrenches the now discredited pre-commitment thesis. A purely pragmatic case for constraining change might be made if subsuming constitutional reform within normal politics produced regular root and branch alterations of the potentially destabilising kind Madison feared from Jefferson's scheme. However, in countries such as Britain and New Zealand, where hitherto parliament has had

---

[142] Alan Grimes, *Democracy and the Amendments to the Constitution*, Lexington, MA: Lexington Books, 1978, p. 166.

[143] Jefferson, Letter to James Madison, 6 September 1789, *The Portable Thomas Jefferson*, pp. 444–51 and J. Madison, Letter to T. Jefferson, 4 February 1790, in M. Meyers (ed.), *The Mind of the Founder: Sources of the Political Thought of James Madison*, Hanover, PA: Brandeis University Press, 1981, pp. 176–9.

the power to make sweeping changes, reforms have been incremental and piecemeal. Instead of a Jeffersonian new beginning, there has been a more or less ongoing constitutional debate as part of the normal legislative process. For, as we saw in chapter 1, most policy decisions have constitutional implications for how the scope, sphere, style and subjects of politics are defined. As a result, explicit and major constitutional reforms are rare, and invariably partial. Precisely for this reason, though, it is implausible to justify constitutions as the products of a special 'moment' of popular pre-commitment. Instead, a people continuously reconstitute themselves and democracy through normal politics.

Popular constitutionalism

This view of constitutional politics as normal politics needs to be distinguished from popular constitutionalism. Recent commentators on the US Constitution have revealed the assumption that the Supreme Court is the authoritative interpreter of the Constitution to be relatively new.[144] Though conservative federalists promoted the Court's primacy from early on as a means for defending the rights of property and implementing a Union-wide free-trade zone, democrats from Jefferson onwards had challenged this view – often successfully. They argued that at best the judiciary had equal status with the legislature and the executive, with each department having the right to decide its prerogatives and powers under the Constitution for itself. When they clashed, then the ultimate arbiter was not the Court but (in Madison's words) 'the people themselves'.[145] Such popular control was exercised not simply in exceptional moments and via special expedients, such as the amendment process. Elections, petitions and non-violent protest were all seen as proper mechanisms for the people to express their view – either forcing the President or Congress to back down in any confrontation with the Court, or empowering them to instigate measures to force them to give way by imposing new responsibilities designed to make their lives miserable (as Jefferson did), ignoring or frustrating the Court's judgement (as Jackson and Lincoln did), threatening to slash its budget or strip it of jurisdiction (as the Reconstruction Congress did), or pack it with new members (as the Reconstruction Congress did and Roosevelt threatened).[146] This argument, which largely prevailed for

---

[144] See, in particular, M. Tushnet, *Taking the Constitution Away from the Courts*, Princeton: Princeton University Press, 1999, especially ch. 8, and Kramer, *The People Themselves*.
[145] Kramer, *The People Themselves*, pp. 105–14.   [146] Ibid., p. 231.

the first 150 years of US history, was succinctly summed up by Roosevelt in 1937:

> . . . for one hundred and fifty years we have had an unending struggle between those who would preserve this original broad concept of the Constitution as a layman's instrument of government and those who would shrivel the Constitution into a lawyer's contract . . . Unlike some lawyers, [the lay rank and file] have respected as sacred *all* branches of their government. They have seen nothing as *more* sacred about one branch than about either of the others. They have considered as *most* sacred the concrete welfare of the generation of the day . . . [They] can take cheer from the historic fact that every effort to construe the Constitution as a lawyer's contract rather than a layman's charter has ultimately failed. Whenever legalistic interpretation has clashed with contemporary sense on broad national policy, ultimately the people and Congress have had their way.[147]

Roosevelt was right. By and large, as I noted in chapter 1, the Court has followed the polls when it comes to decisions supported by sustained, national majorities.[148] Nevertheless, having found only two federal laws unconstitutional pre-Civil War, it struck down twenty between 1865 and 1900, a process that had steadily grown by the 1990s to thirty laws in that decade alone.[149] Given that judicial activism had been mainly aimed against the labour movement up to the 1930s, the main opponents had been the progressives. That changed following Roosevelt's successful challenge to judicial opposition to the New Deal. As a liberal Court supported the civil rights movement, it was the conservatives' turn to fulminate against judicial legislation. However, the debate had subtly changed. By the 1980s, few questioned the Court's standing as the final arbiter on the Constitution.[150] Conservatives merely argued that the role of judges should be restricted to the 'intentions' of the framers or a strict interpretation of the Constitution – notions I questioned in chapter 2. One person's legitimate interpretation is another's illegitimate judicial legislation. Focus moved from opposing the people's view to that of the Court to simply packing the Court.

There are two difficulties with populist constitutionalism. The first difficulty is illustrated by its gradual marginalisation within the US: it simply

---

[147] F. D. Roosevelt, Address on Constitution Day, Washington, DC, 17 September 1937, cited in Kramer, *The People Themselves*, p. 217.

[148] See R. A. Dahl, 'Decision-Making in a Democracy: The Supreme Court as a National Policy-Maker', *Journal of Public Law*, 6 (1957), pp. 279–95.

[149] Kramer, *The People Themselves*, p. 213.   [150] Ibid., pp. 221, 233.

faces an unequal battle with any constitutional court. Particularly within a federal system, there is a natural trend towards a gradual accretion of power by a central court.[151] The reason is simple – such a court offers an obvious mechanism for resolving boundary disputes and ensuring that all abide by a relatively standard interpretation of the rules. While each state may prefer to interpret them for themselves, they accept that for all to do so would be worse for everyone. Though closely associated with the federal system, and so likely to support the government in any jurisdictional battle, the court is independent from it and can maintain the fiction that its authority comes simply from applying 'the law'. Judicial discretion is conveniently passed over. A written constitution gives this court an especial advantage. Unlike statutes, constitutions tend to be very general and flexible. And whereas a legislature can overcome a judicial interpretation of a statute it does not like by rewriting the law, constitutions are usually much harder to amend. Likewise, taking on the court proves equally hazardous, if not unknown, without overwhelming popular support. Being in office for comparatively smaller periods, governments have to pick their fights well and only enter those likely to have an immediate electoral pay-off. Very often large policy implications lurk in decisions of low political salience, that are then absorbed into the court's case law only resurfacing much later as a precedent. To this extent, Ackerman is right – democratic stand-offs with the court over constitutional interpretation are rare because exceptionally difficult. Only extreme judicial provocation, such as Roosevelt encountered with the New Deal, is likely to promote governments to risk it. As a result, courts slowly turn the constitution into a body of constitutional case law and incrementally extend their sway over ever more areas. Legislatures also happily allow the court to take electorally difficult decisions for them. All these factors favour judicial review over popular constitutionalism.

The second difficulty follows on from this last issue and concerns the relationship between populism and democracy. As I noted earlier, the US Constitution predates the era of mass, party politics. Populism tends to denote an appeal to a 'public opinion' that has been somehow ignored by formal political channels or established politicians, with populist leaders typically claiming to articulate the concerns of a 'silent majority'. It is undoubtedly true that the prevailing channels of political communication

---

[151] For a good summary, see M. Shapiro, 'The European Court of Justice', in P. Craig and G. de Búrca, *The Evolution of EU Law*, Oxford: Oxford University Press, 1999, especially pp. 321–7.

often do block – either directly or indirectly – particular voices. However, there's a significant difference between political movements, such as those seeking reform of the suffrage to include workers and women, and populist movements. The former seek inclusion within the normal political process. Such inclusion alters the constitution of politics thereafter – by recognising the voice of women, for example, the view of the public/private divide with regard to the family, say, and notions of equality and discrimination have also been changed in important ways. However, women's perspectives also become an aspect of more general political programmes, supplementing but also at times in competition with and giving way to other concerns. In sum, they become part of the general system of politics and are orientated towards improving its overall effectiveness and fairness.[152] By contrast, populism tends to be anti-system – a straight appeal against it. As such, it frequently proves anti-political and produces either ephemeral or radical, and anti-democratic, change. These qualities make populism a crude and ambiguous source of constitutional control, far inferior to popular control via the ongoing system of democratic politics, the constitutional properties of which are defended in Part II.

It should be noted that similar difficulties beset Habermas's aforementioned reliance on social movements as the source of democratic input into the constitutional system.[153] These tend to focus on single issues and like populism have little incentive to relate their demands to those of others within the political community or even to have much of an interest in ensuring the fairness and equity of the system as such. Their overriding concern is with attaining certain specific ends. Once again, this placing of constitutional politics outside the normal political realm fails to see how it is precisely through viewing one's political claims as part of a normal political process that gives them a genuinely constitutional colour. It is only then that people begin to place their concerns in the context of a system that seeks to give adequate consideration to the concerns of all.

If the 'people themselves' are to be the final arbiters of the constitution, therefore, ordinary legislation within the legislature has to be the sphere of constitutional politics. After all, as we have noted, this was how workers and women obtained the vote during the nineteenth and early twentieth century in most Western countries. More recently, New Zealand has introduced a form of PR as has Britain for certain local and European elections.

---

[152] Bellamy, 'Constitutive Citizenship versus Constitutional Rights', pp. 19–20.
[153] E.g. Habermas, *Between Facts and Norms*, pp. 304, 486.

What of the danger of being judge in one's own case? Against this worry there is the equally important epistemic principle that decisions are best made by those with a sufficient stake in the matter to decide responsibly.[154] Since all citizens are affected by any change in the rules, they should all have a say in how they are changed. The judicial obstruction of the labour movement throughout the so-called *Lochner* era arguably originated not so much, or only, from the ideological convictions of the judiciary, as their lack of appreciation of the conditions under which ordinary men and women lived and worked. They simply lacked sufficient interest in the legislation to appreciate the stakes involved.

It might be objected that this solution risks being viciously circular.[155] If the democratic system is imperfect, then surely any decision will be tainted by this imperfection. To a degree, it will be – though flawed democracies can and do improve themselves. Indeed, in such circumstances the judiciary will share this taint – for it too belongs to that system. If minorities are under-represented in the legislature, they almost certainly will be in the judiciary too. More importantly, though, will those who want reform have to appeal to a results-based view to justify their argument? Yes and no. As with any democratic decision, people can distinguish acceptance of the legitimacy of the democratic procedure from agreement with the policy that emerges from that procedure. Just as I can prefer politician A to politician B, but still regard a majority vote as the legitimate way of choosing between them even if I know most people will opt for B, so I can believe that PR is better than the current plurality system yet acknowledge that the only legitimate way of instituting PR would be by the prevailing system. My preference for PR will be a substantive, results-based view, but I can still acknowledge there are valid arguments against such a system. As a matter of practical politics, therefore, it will be necessary to defer to some procedure to decide the issue, and as a democrat an imperfect democratic procedure through which citizens have some chance of having their say can be reasonably preferred to one that has fewer democratic credentials. Meanwhile, since citizens could use a PR system to opt for a plurality system as well as *vice versa*, there is no necessary circularity in using a democratic procedure to reform democratic procedures. Whatever the inevitable flaws of any system, it retains an authority and legitimacy that is independent from the right or wrongness of the policies it is employed

---

[154] Waldron, *Law and Disagreement*, pp. 296–8.
[155] I deal with the related criticism (e.g. T. Christiano, 'Waldron on Law and Disagreement', *Law and Philosophy*, 19 (2000), p. 521), that seeing democracy as both constitutive and constitutional involves an infinite regress, in the next chapter.

to decide – including those about democracy itself. Thus, democracy proves self-constituting, with the only effective and valid constitution being the ongoing and continually constitutive processes of democratic politics itself.

Conclusion

Even in their own terms, none of the four arguments surveyed above works. Throughout this critique of legal constitutionalism, I have maintained that the true protection of rights, the rule of law and even democracy comes from democracy – the power of individual citizens to claim and frame their rights and demand they be treated on equal terms with others. In fact, as I observed Ely noted, the bulk of most constitutions deal with the operations of the political system. This forms the political constitution of the body politic. Popular constitutionalism and constitutional politics apart, the constitutional role of democratic politics has been largely ignored or dismissed in the recent legal literature. The emphasis is always on constraining or regulating political power. In Part II, therefore, I turn to this unduly neglected topic and show how the normal democratic process involves far more legitimate and effective constitutional protections than a legal constitution can hope to provide.

PART II

Political constitutionalism

4

The norms of political constitutionalism: non-domination and political equality

The argument of Part I has been largely negative, criticising the claims and aspirations of legal constitutionalism. I now want to explore how these criticisms coalesce around the positive case for a political constitutionalism. Part II seeks to explain why the legal constitutionalist's fears about democracy prove misguided, with democratic decision-making actively promoting, rather than threatening, constitutional values. Moreover, unlike constitutional judicial review, democracy performs this constitutional role in ways that are congruent with these values being subject to the 'circumstances of politics'. As we have seen, defenders of legal constitutionalism tend to focus on the capacity of a judicially protected and entrenched constitution to secure appropriate substantive results or outputs – notably, the defence of a given theorist's favoured view of individual rights, legality and democracy. While far from indifferent to these concerns, a political constitutionalism also looks at inputs. As such, it focuses on the legitimacy of the processes whereby we define and promote or restrict rights through legislation and administrative action. From this perspective, a failure to acknowledge the disagreements that surround constitutional values, and the resulting need for political mechanisms to resolve them, can itself be a source of domination and arbitrary rule that impacts negatively on rights and the rule of law.

Chapter 1 identified the core impetus of legal constitutionalism in the emphasis on rights and the need to protect them from political encroachments, not least by supposedly tyrannous democratic majorities. This chapter now reverses the legal constitutionalist perspective by noting how removing rights from democratic politics produces domination, the overcoming of which motivates political constitutionalism. Legal constitutionalism takes the prime task of constitutional government to be the placing and policing of various boundaries to politics. However, it overlooks the ways such limitations incorporate and risk generating injustices in their turn. A political constitutionalism tackles this dilemma by concentrating on who exercises power and how, rather than trying *a priori* to circumscribe where it can be used and for what purposes.

Accordingly, the key tasks of this chapter are threefold: to show first, how depoliticising constitutional values in the manner of legal constitutionalism creates domination; second, that such domination undermines the underlying values of constitutionalism – namely, the defence of individual autonomy and the need to treat human beings with equal concern and respect; and third, that domination of this kind can be avoided only through a self-governing political system that recognises our fellow citizens as autonomous reasoners who are entitled to an equal status as potential sources of argument and reasonable information.[1] The first task duly occupies section I. Here I discuss how strategies for depoliticising rights, either on the grounds that they are pre-political or justified as products of an ideal political process, not only risk oppressing individuals but are inherently dominating forms of 'arbitrary rule' because of rights being within the 'circumstances of politics'. Section II then tackles the second and third tasks by investigating the notion of domination and its avoidance further. The republican ideal of freedom as non-domination is compared to the classical liberal notion of freedom from interference. The latter has often inspired legal constitutionalism, not least because it makes a political constitutionalism seem a contradiction in terms. However, it proves to be itself contradictory and incoherent, resting as it does on the first depoliticising strategy that tries to place rights beyond politics. By contrast, the notion of non-domination explicitly sees freedom as the achievement of certain sorts of egalitarian political relations. Nevertheless, it remains consistent with the liberal constitutional values of autonomy and equal respect and concern that stand behind notions of rights. I then take issue with certain republican thinkers who have thought non-domination could be secured all the same by either substantive or procedural forms of legal constitutionalism. They adopt the second depoliticising strategy of seeing rights as products of an idealised apolitical politics. Since this strategy fails, non-domination is only available under some kind of self-rule that embodies political equality. That sets the scene for examining in chapter 5 the political forms such a non-dominating kind of rule would have to take, and for illustrating in chapter 6 how actually existing democracy satisfies both the norms and forms of political constitutionalism by providing appropriate guarantees against the use of arbitrary power.

---

[1] This sentence adapts Albert Weale's characterisation of political equality as the underlying rationale of democracy. See A. Weale, *Democracy*, Basingstoke: Macmillan, 1999, p. 57.

I Depoliticising the constitution as a source of domination

Legal constitutionalism attempts to take certain fundamental constitutional principles outside of politics, viewing them as constraints upon, goals of and preconditions for the political system.[2] It employs two main strategies for depoliticising issues.[3] The first consists of seeking to establish boundaries to the political sphere, designating certain values and areas of life as beyond the realm of politics. The second applies a form of apolitical politics to discuss and settle particular issues. Neither works. Instead, both offer a potential source of arbitrary rule and domination, risking oppression as a consequence.

The first depoliticising strategy can take a number of forms. Historically, it has been mainly associated with the liberal belief – expressed most powerfully, perhaps, by Locke – that political power exists to protect (or preserve) certain pre-political rights, a position we saw lies at the heart of legal constitutionalism.[4] Politics is limited by such rights in two senses. On the one hand, political bodies and their agents ought not to interfere with individuals in ways that might infringe these rights; on the other hand, they have an obligation to positively promote them. After all, even 'negative' liberty rights, such as the freedom not to be physically assaulted by others, require positive state action in the form of a police force and a regular system of criminal justice in order to be secured. As a result, though, an ambiguity as to how far any given sphere is truly beyond politics enters into this argument from the beginning. For all but anarchists, the preservation of any 'natural' or 'private' area of liberty will be a political act – a matter of government action or deliberate inaction.

This ambiguity resurfaces even more damagingly in the very attempt to determine how such rights are to be identified. If rights are to be placed outside politics, then they need to meet two fairly demanding

---

[2] R. Dworkin, 'Constitutionalism and Democracy', *European Journal of Philosophy*, 3 (1995), p. 2.

[3] My account of these two strategies adapts and modifies Ian Shapiro's description of what he calls the two 'narrow' conceptions of politics found in the Western tradition of political theory – the one which seeks to set boundaries, which he associates with liberal tradition post-Locke, the second that focuses on a supposed, and curiously apolitical, 'essence' of politics, which he links with the communitarian tradition and theories of deliberative democracy. See I. Shapiro, *Democratic Justice*, New Haven and London: Yale University Press, 1999, pp. 5–10.

[4] E.g. J. Locke, *Two Treatises of Government*, ed. P. Laslett, Cambridge: Cambridge University Press, 1990, II sec 23, p. 284, sec. 135, pp. 357–8 and secs. 203–7, pp. 401–4.

conditions.[5] First, to achieve widespread support, human rights must be capable of appealing to a plurality of different people and types of institution motivated by often diverse principles and goals. In particular, they must be able to sustain in a plausible manner their claim to be fundamental and universal conditions of a just social order, which are capable of applying equally to all individuals. To meet this condition, a distinction needs to be drawn between the 'right' and the 'good', between the framework of basic rights and the conceptions of the good people may pursue within that framework. Human rights cannot themselves be based on any particular ethos or conception of the good, therefore. Second, whilst being sufficiently general and abstract to meet the first condition, rights must also be precise enough for us to be able to apply them to concrete circumstances, and the criteria defining what counts as a right stringent enough to prevent each and every goal or preference we have becoming the subject of a human right. Those who doubt the usefulness of rights language have usually been particularly critical of the tendency for the class of human rights to expand seemingly indefinitely to include each and every person's favoured cause.

Most philosophers now accept that the natural rights tradition, with its appeals to either a divinely ordered natural law or to human nature, fails to meet these two conditions.[6] The difficulty of identifying and interpreting natural law has bedevilled the tradition from the start. Given that the world contains not only wide differences of religious belief but also a large proportion of atheists as well, God has become even more contentious a starting point for a theory of rights aiming at near universal acceptability and applicability. The secularism of modern science has also rendered human nature a similarly problematic basis for rights. Those theorists who begin from here argue that our rights should protect, and possibly promote, the conditions necessary for human beings to flourish. We establish these rights by identifying the distinctive characteristics of the human species and the circumstances necessary for them to develop. However, numerous difficulties arise with this procedure. In the first place, one immediately comes up against the 'is'–'ought' problem. That something happens to be a fact about human beings tells us nothing in itself about its moral significance. After all, there are many human traits that mark us out from other animals, such as cruelty and killing for reasons

---

[5] The following couple of paragraphs draws on R. Bellamy, *Rethinking Liberalism*, London and New York: Pinter, 2000, pp. 165–6.

[6] E.g. B. Williams, *Morality: Introduction to Ethics*, Cambridge: Cambridge University Press, 1972.

other than food, which most people would find morally repugnant. More-over, even those traits that appear to be rather more attractive, such as rationality or creativity, may be put to morally ambiguous or positively immoral uses, such as devising sophisticated and subtle forms of torture. Indeed, the empirical evidence tends to suggest quite a variety of often conflicting forms of human flourishing even within the range that most people would find acceptable. Thus, the selection of the distinguishing marks inevitably presupposes certain moral judgements about the nature of the good life, so that it is our views about morality rather than any empirical facts about human beings *per se* that actually do the work in our selection of human rights. As a result, the appeal to human nature will not get us very far. It will generate as many conceptions of rights as there are moral views and hence fail to pass the two conditions.

This dilemma has led many contemporary philosophers to follow Kant and opt for a 'transcendental' argument for human rights. In other words, they have tried to associate rights with the preconditions necessary for us all to make moral judgements and choose to flourish in any recognis-able form at all. But this strategy also proves contentious. The categorical imperative proves as indeterminate as natural law as a basis for rights, with different authors drawing conclusions ranging from libertarian anarchism to state welfarism.[7] Similar difficulties disturb alternative approaches, such as Mill's 'harm' principle, that seek to avoid basing their arguments on rights altogether.[8] Thus, what counts as harm – only physical interfer-ence, or also degrees of mental offence or cruelty – and how far harm has to be directly or indirectly caused, intended or merely foreseeable, in order for the person responsible for it to merit sanctioning, these and other issues relating to Mill's 'simple' principle are all notoriously complex and contested. As with neo-Kantian appeals to autonomy, if some formula-tions appear impossibly stringent, suggesting no allowable interferences, others appear far too lax, allowing almost indiscriminate interference.

The indeterminacy and contestability of rights means their, or indeed any other criterion's, use to demarcate the limits of politics is, as we saw in chapter 1, itself inextricably political. In other words, there will be disagreements about their character and implications that in turn reflect the usual divisions of normal politics. The second form of depoliticising

---

[7] Compare, say, the Kantianism of J. Rawls, *A Theory of Justice*, Oxford: Clarendon Press, 1971, pp. 251–8 with that of R. Nozick, *Anarchy, State and Utopia*, Oxford: Blackwell, pp. 84–117.

[8] J. S. Mill, *On Liberty*, in *Utilitarianism, On Liberty and Representative Government*, London: Everyman, 1971, p. 72.

politics – namely, recourse to an apolitical form of politics to overcome such disagreements, arises in part to overcome this dilemma. Such apolitical forms of politics standardly appeal to particular modes of public reasoning and deliberation that are said to remove the sources of partiality and self-interest, and so lead to convergence on the public interest. On this account, if all persons are obliged to argue on a basis of equality with others, so that they can only pursue their own good in ways that show equal concern and respect for the good of everyone else, then it should be possible to arrive at a reasonable consensus on the rules that are to govern their existence and, on some accounts, even collective policies too.[9]

The aspiration is to make political deliberation on matters of public policy more equitable, appreciative of the range of concerns in play, and focused on the common good. It's certainly a laudable ambition and one, as we shall see below and more especially in chapter 5, that political constitutionalism shares. Where this style of argument goes wrong is in assuming this goal can be generally (if ever) achieved to everyone's reasonable satisfaction. That assumption leads certain advocates of deliberative democracy to consider any failure to reach a consensual agreement as a sign of malign intent, ignorance or stupidity on the part of those concerned – especially when matters of principle, such as constitutional issues, are at stake. As a result, they are tempted to restrict politics to particular non-political forums – such as courts or other kinds of expert bodies – where they believe that removal from public pressures will, somewhat paradoxically perhaps, lead those concerned to a more disinterested and reasoned consideration of the public good.

Though supposedly process-based arguments, such purified versions of deliberative democracy and public reasoning in fact rest on the 'output' approach criticised in Part I – particularly in chapter 3. We observed how this approach suffers from two main failings – one theoretical, the other more practical. Theoretically, the only way to show certain procedures will lead to a rational consensus is to have some idea of what that consensus should be and then devise the procedures accordingly. However, this can make the procedures too stipulative and the argument largely circular – a weakness to which I argued Habermas's theory was prone. Relaxing the procedural constraints, though, risks the opposite hazard of rendering them too indeterminate to actually produce the desired consensus.

---

[9] E.g. J. Cohen, 'Procedure and Substance in Deliberative Democracy', in S. Benhabib (ed.), *Democracy and Difference: Contesting the Boundaries of the Political*, Princeton: Princeton University Press, 1996, ch. 5.

In other words, the self-same theoretical problems associated with defining pre-political rights resurface in creating ideal procedures whereby they might be identified and interpreted. The adequacy of the procedures depends on the acceptability of the consensus they are intended to produce and which guides their design. Yet this consensus is subject to the burdens of judgement and so likely to be contested – as is the degree to which any set of procedural constraints really does produce the results desired by its creators.[10] These theoretical problems lead to a broader practical quandary. For no real-world procedures are ever likely to produce the sorts of outcomes their proponents imagine. Thus, we have noted in earlier chapters how courts – often singled out as exemplars of public reasoning – can be as prone to the usual human failings, and have similarly limited powers of reason, as political bodies, while, as we saw in chapter 1, judicial argumentation involves peculiar distortions of its own.

If we have no good reasons for believing that any given view of rights or set of constitutional or other rules are incontestably in the public interest, then the attempt to take such matters out of the political domain risks being arbitrary. In other words, far from being the true or even the consensual view of rights or the public interest, they may be little more than the view held by the hegemonic group or officials with the power to decide. Such arbitrariness, as I noted in chapter 2, produces domination and may lead to oppression. Both the distinction between domination and oppression, and the links between them, need emphasising. For a major lacuna of legal compared to political constitutionalism lies in ignoring this linkage and neglecting domination more generally.

Oppression involves harming an individual's interests through such forms of direct or indirect interference as exploitation and violence or marginalisation. Domination issues from an individual or body possessing the power wilfully to exercise such interference over others, or in other ways to ignore or override their opinions and interests.[11] Typically, oppression and domination go hand in hand. Each can be the source of the other, with oppression both generating and being a product of domination. However, as I noted in chapter 2, they may also exist separately.[12]

---

[10] The same difficulty has bedevilled Rawls's 'original position', for example, that critics complain either fails to generate his two principles of justice (or, at least, not exclusively these principles), or does so only by building his conclusions into his idealised premises. E.g. B. Barry, *The Liberal Theory of Justice*, Oxford: Oxford University Press, 1973.

[11] I adapt these definitions from I. M. Young, *Justice and the Politics of Difference*, Princeton: Princeton University Press, 1990, p. 38.

[12] This is a key insight of P. Pettit's republican account of domination in *Republicanism: A Theory of Freedom and Government*, Oxford: Clarendon Press, 1997, pp. 63–6.

An enlightened despot might strive to avoid oppressing his or her subjects but would still dominate them, while individuals may come unwittingly to be oppressed by rules or regulations they had been in a position to freely debate and decide upon, but the full implications of which were impossible, or very difficult, to foresee at the time.

Distinguishing domination from oppression in this way highlights that being dominated constitutes a form of injustice in its own right. Those who are dominated are treated as subjects – they lack one of the basic sources of being treated as an equal, that of having an equal say with their fellows in how their collective arrangements are to be organised. Most legal constitutionalists place great weight on promoting equality of concern and respect. Yet, they all too often ignore their intrinsic, as opposed to merely instrumental, links with the ability to participate on an equal basis to others in decisions concerning the very foundations of their political and social life. It is this aspect of equality that the political constitutionalist's emphasis on process as well as output seeks to capture. Even if the enlightened despot is infallibly right, therefore, something is lost. His or her subjects are diminished relative to the citizens of a free state. Of course, no human institution will always be right – including a democracy of free citizens. However, the presence of domination adds to the resulting oppression.

There are also good reasons for thinking domination makes oppression more likely.[13] The danger of oppression is increased not only because domination renders it easier to inflict and harder to rectify, but also, and most importantly, because in such circumstances oppression may simply go unacknowledged as such. If the dominant group define what counts as oppression, then they will be able to delegitimise all attempts to question prevailing definitions – especially if these have been taken outside the realm of politics. Classic cases of the way depoliticisation can fuel domination and with it oppression are the treatment of women within the 'private' sphere of the family and of workers within similarly 'private' enterprises. Though paternalist legislation in both cases had some impact in alleviating the plight of these two groups, change only began to come when they gained a political voice of their own and it became more accepted that the home and the workplace were legitimate spheres of political intervention.

That politics goes all the way down does not mean that everything is politics, or that politics is the main thing in life, or even that no withdrawal

---

[13] Shapiro, *Democratic Justice*, pp. 9, 18–21, 29–45.

from political life is possible or acceptable.[14] Most of us most of the time want to do other things than participate in politics – watch football, play music, read novels, write poetry, make love or whatever. Likewise, our dealings with many of the people we regularly interact with – possibly the majority – are governed by norms of love, affection, friendship, neighbourliness, collegiality and so on, rather than politically defined considerations. In these interactions we regularly go beyond what could reasonably be expected of us as citizens. However, it is politics that creates and protects the space for these non-political activities and relationships, providing a safety net when they break down. For example, it is often said that politics should keep out of sport. In certain senses, no doubt it should – political affiliations, say, like race and religion, should not be criteria for membership of a normal league team. Yet, it will be politics, in the form of equal opportunities employment practices in this case, that guarantees such openness. It may even be used to ensure the rules of play get changed in ways that are fair to all clubs and players – not just the big teams with large chequebooks. Even on the field, the rules of play may be insufficient in certain cases. A player who employs excessive physical aggression against opponents or spectators, not only breaks the rules of football but also potentially the law. Likewise, we know that, sadly, even loving parents are capable of abuse, that marriages can collapse and divorces be messy, and that former friends can become the bitterest of enemies. In these circumstances, we need a political framework to regulate conduct – send social workers into homes to check on children, guide the fair division of a divorced couple's property and so on. Indeed, without political institutions and regulations, many otherwise private social relations – such as marriage – simply would not exist. However, because we will often disagree about how given practices and relations ought to be best managed to protect the vulnerable and guarantee fairness, the only way to ensure our concerns get taken into account is through having some say in, and exercising an element of control through, the political process that decides such matters.

Thus, politics permeates everywhere, even if it is far from being everything we care about and do. There being no sphere outside politics, the attempt to depoliticise certain areas of social life proves impossible. Trying to do so is itself arbitrary and produces arbitrary rule that is dominating and potentially oppressive. Legal constitutionalism accepts the need to guard against the latter, but the circumstances of politics, combined

---

[14] Ibid., pp. 10, 21–4.

with the fact that politics proves omnipresent, make protecting against the former equally – if not more – compelling. For, not only is domination pernicious in itself, but also, as we have seen, all too often oppression has its origin in domination.

II Repoliticising the constitution: from non-domination to democracy

Quentin Skinner and Philip Pettit have recently shown how the avoidance of domination, or freedom as non-domination, offers the hallmark of a particular neo-Roman strand of the republican tradition.[15] As its name implies, the shift from subject to citizen also lies at the heart of the repub-lican project. Indeed, in certain salient respects republicanism holds that the arbitrary rule of monarchs and their modern successors can only be avoided by some form of self-rule. This section traces the argument from non-domination to a political constitutionalism in which the political process plays a central role.

Republicanism, liberalism and constitutionalism

Republicanism has been both contrasted with and seen as a complement to liberalism and hence, by a not entirely clear-cut extension, legal con-stitutionalism as well.[16] The contrast has been drawn most commonly in terms of republicanism resting on a form of positive liberty, whereby human self-realisation requires political participation. Certain liberals criticise this view for involving an unhealthy and mistaken identifica-tion between individual liberty and the state. Adopting a negative theory of liberty as 'freedom from interference', they argue that the key issue is not who holds power but how much power or political authority is placed in any one person's, group's or institution's hands. On this account, limited government simply means less government. It has no necessary

---

[15] Q. Skinner, *Liberty before Liberalism*, Cambridge: Cambridge University Press, 1998 and Pettit, *Republicanism*.

[16] I add this rider because both historically and, as shall see, substantively, there has been a considerable overlap between liberalism and republicanism. Moreover, some republicans, such as Pettit, *Republicanism*, pp. 181–3 and H. Richardson, *Democratic Autonomy: Public Reasoning about the Ends of Policy*, Oxford: Oxford University Press, 2002, pp. 9, 16, have argued that it can accommodate a liberal orientated legal constitutionalism, while certain liberals, such as J. Waldron, 'Judicial Review and Republican Government', in C. Wolfe (ed.), *That Eminent Tribunal: Judicial Supremacy and the Constitution*, Princeton: Prince-ton University Press, 2004, pp. 159–80, have advocated a more political constitutionalism.

connection with democracy and may even be compatible with certain limited forms of autocracy, such as a constitutional monarchy.[17] Instead, those who stress the complementarity of republicanism with at least certain elements of liberalism take a different tack. In the manner of the theorists examined in chapter 3, they see a legal constitution as establishing the preconditions for republican self-rule. They also argue that a legal constitution satisfies one of the prime goals of republicanism, that of forcing political and other kinds of power to be exercised according to the rules rather than at the whim of its possessor.[18]

In linking the republican account of non-domination with a distinctively political view of constitutionalism, I want to rebut both these arguments. With regard to the first, freedom as non-domination can be seen as occupying a distinctive space between the views of freedom as non-interference and as self-mastery characteristic of nineteenth-century liberalism. A negative view, it focuses on freedom from mastery rather than interference *per se*.[19] As I shall show below, in itself freedom as non-interference proves a confused notion. It relies on the first depoliticising strategy criticised in the last section, and as such begs the issue of political domination that the republican thesis addresses. However, tackling that issue through the democratic exercise of popular control need not imply a more positive view of freedom. The negative desire to avoid domination is sufficient to motivate a concern with self-rule.

Nevertheless, proponents of the second argument are right to see an affinity between certain liberal ideals and republicanism. Indeed, an ongoing liberal preoccupation with the republican notion of non-domination animates the Kantian concern with 'independence' and the later liberal support for equality and autonomy more generally: for example, in Mill's critique of the subjection of women. Yet, or so I shall show, for many of the reasons rehearsed in chapter 3, taking the claims of equality and autonomy seriously ultimately proves incompatible with legal constitutionalism. For, as we shall see, these arguments turn out to rest on the second depoliticising strategy criticised above, and so also fail to overcome domination.

In the case of both arguments, the republican view of non-domination does not imply an outright rejection of either constitutionalism or

---

[17] For the canonical formulation of this thesis, see I. Berlin, *Two Concepts of Liberty*, Oxford: Oxford University Press, 1969, pp. 129–31.

[18] E.g. F. Michelman, 'Law's Republic', *Yale Law Journal*, 97 (1988), pp. 1493–537; Pettit, *Republicanism*, pp. 172–83 and Richardson, *Democratic Autonomy*, pp. 11, 67–72.

[19] Pettit, *Republicanism*, p. 22; Richardson, *Democratic Autonomy*, p. 29.

liberalism. The need to limit the power of government, on the one hand, and the constitutive role of considerations of equality and autonomy, on the other, all receive their due. However, each of these notions is placed in a broader political context that entails the prioritising of democratic self-rule as the legitimate means to realise these ends. Indeed, as I have observed elsewhere, republicanism can be characterised best as a form of democratic liberalism.[20] The point is important because republican critics of legal constitutionalism are sometimes castigated as anti-liberal and sceptical of rights, accused of pitting democracy against constitutionalism, of being opposed to judicial review and so on. None of these criticisms is true – or, at least, not of the argument I put forward here. A political constitutionalism takes rights, equality and the rule of law extremely seriously. However, in perceiving how each of these considerations is animated by the need to avoid domination, it seeks to prevent their instantiation in ways that render them dominating in their turn. To see why, let's explore each of these liberal constitutionalist arguments further and examine how they relate to, and are modified by, freedom as non-domination.

Negative liberty

Freedom as non-interference

I have already remarked that the prevention of interference with fundamental rights provides the standard legal constitutionalist rationale for constitutional government. However, I have also observed how rights cannot be taken as given. They have to be politically constructed. So, the political legitimacy of their construction necessarily takes precedence over the issue of their being interfered with. Yet, that concern with political legitimacy has at its heart many of the preoccupations motivating arguments for freedom from non-interference – in particular, the view of individuals as autonomous agents who should be allowed to choose and think for themselves, even when that involves making mistakes. Seeing liberty as freedom from mastery rather than from interference brings out this common rationale, while revealing why we should see limited government in terms of popular controls rather than a *priori* restrictions on certain kinds of governmental intervention.

---

[20] R. Bellamy, *Liberalism and Pluralism: Towards a Politics of Compromise*, London: Routledge, 1999, ch. 5.

In itself, freedom as non-interference proves incoherent. It assumes the realm of 'natural', pre-political liberty criticised above. Take the description of the market as an example of 'natural liberty' employed by certain liberal thinkers from Adam Smith on. In order to view sellers and buyers as engaging in 'free exchanges' a certain framework of legitimate entitlements must first be established. After all, even many libertarians acknowledge certain limits to what sellers can do with their property – accepting, say, that the monopolist of a vital resource, such as a waterhole in a desert, cannot use this power to coerce others by forcing them to sell themselves into slavery, or refuse access altogether.[21] To argue government ought not to interfere with the freedom of the market ignores the fact that this liberty is structured by the establishment, through governmental action, of property rights and contract law – including an account of duress, a system for policing and settling property and contractual disputes (and another for financing it) – and so on.

In other words, quite a lot of governmental interfering, including preventing the oppressive ways that private individuals and organisations can interfere with each other, has to go on to establish a realm where talk of non-interference would be appropriate. Of course, there have been social liberals who have appreciated this circumstance yet simply taken a broader view of interference than libertarians to include social and structural factors.[22] Yet, such attempts to further 'hinder the hindrances' on individual freedom run into an additional difficulty. For once it is appreciated that interference can come not just from the state but also from other people and a whole range of non-state institutions, then trying to use the minimising of interference itself as a yardstick for judging the degree of freedom becomes computationally well-nigh impossible.[23] Worse, what metric do we use to judge whether we have reduced or enhanced freedom overall through interfering with a potential interference?[24] If I restrict freedom of speech, say, to enhance freedom of privacy, how can I tell if my interference is greater or less than those I was seeking to prevent? Such judgements will always turn on contentious normative evaluations that will differ according to the moral and social theories held by those making them.[25]

[21] E.g. F. A. Hayek, *The Constitution of Liberty*, London: Routledge, 1960, p. 136.
[22] E.g. L. T. Hobhouse, *Liberalism*, Oxford: Oxford University Press, 1964, p. 71.
[23] Richardson, *Democratic Autonomy*, p. 32.
[24] O. O'Neill, 'The Most Extensive Liberty', *Proceedings of the Aristotelian Society*, 80 (1979/80), pp. 45–59.
[25] J. Gray, *Liberalisms: Essays in Political Philosophy*, London: Routledge, 1989, ch. 9.

Meanwhile, governments often have to interfere with the freedom of individuals to promote certain public goods and cement or even create various valuable social options and relationships.[26] Far from being spontaneous products of voluntary human interaction, as certain libertarians contend, a great deal of social life has to be directly or indirectly coordinated to resolve collective action problems, settle matters that convention leaves indeterminate, or achieve desirable ends that are unlikely, due to inadequate incentives, to be undertaken privately. In fact, many social activities would not exist unless governments interfered to give them a certain institutional or legal form. A view of freedom simply as non-interference has problems grasping the freedom-enhancing aspects of such government action, seeking merely a reduction of the public sector. Certain past liberals have wanted to accommodate these kinds of state activity under the framework of positive liberty.[27] Yet, the sorts of ethical naturalist arguments required for such perfectionist doctrines are likely to prove even more controversial than theories of basic rights, and as such more subject to the circumstances of politics. Indeed, proponents of freedom as non-interference have with some justification regarded the pursuit of positive liberty as posing a particular danger to individual rights through the imposition of spurious duties on citizens.[28]

Freedom as non-interference makes a political constitutionalism seem a contradiction in terms. The truly free condition will be the putative unfettered liberty of the state of nature. Legal restraints offer a second best that seek to keep the mutual interferences of private individuals to a minimum. A state may be required to keep all in awe, but as a potential interferer in its turn needs to be similarly restrained. However, this picture now seems fatally flawed. In various ways, free exchanges turn out to be the products of law and hence of the political arrangements that enact and uphold them. How far these necessary legal and political interventions have themselves diminished or increased interference overall proves hard – if not impossible – to say. Positive liberty offers a potential solution, but generates the very risks of political social engineering that advocates of liberty as non-interference most fear. By contrast, seeing interference

[26] Richardson, *Democratic Autonomy*, p. 26.
[27] E.g. T. H. Green, 'Lecture on "Liberal Legislation and Freedom of Contract"', reprinted in his *Lectures on the Principles of Political Obligation and Other Writings*, ed. P. Harris and J. Morrow, Cambridge: Cambridge University Press, 1986.
[28] See the analysis of Green in this regard in R. Bellamy, *Liberalism and Modern Society: A Historical Argument*, Cambridge: Polity, 1992, pp. 35–47.

through the normative prism of domination overcomes these various dilemmas – or, rather, grasps the nettles they present.

Freedom as non-domination

Domination sets interference within the context of a particular kind of social and political relationship, while remaining a negative view of liberty which neither treats political participation as necessary to self-realisation nor empowers the state to compel political obedience as the path to 'true' freedom. This context not only adds a new dimension to the issue of freedom that concentration on interference *per se* neglects, but also allows a distinction to be drawn between legitimate and illegitimate interference. This distinction turns on the degree to which interferences result from and promote or produce mastery over others. As Philip Pettit has observed, the paradigm case of domination is that of master and slave.[29] Slaves may be directed to do anything their masters bid – they are subject simply to their master's *arbitrium*, and must act according to whatever judgement or decision he or she chooses to give. We saw earlier that the key feature here is not whether masters actually interfere with their slaves, but their broad capacity to be able to do so at their pleasure: as, when and for whatever purposes they will, without reference to the opinions or interests of those affected. Though usually subject to some limitations, albeit of an often nominal kind, domination still persists within the allowed sphere. Consequently, domination can be present in the absence of any interference. It arises from the very nature of the master–slave relationship and the servile behaviour it wittingly or unwittingly encourages, even when the master proves kindly and non-interfering. Meanwhile, interference may occur in a non-dominating manner. For example, we may employ others as agents of our self-mastery – though without the metaphysical or ethical naturalist connotations this notion has in accounts of positive liberty. Thus, in acceding to his request that they bind him to the mast, Ulysses' sailors interfered with him but did not exercise mastery over him. Many of the interferences required to solve collective action problems and secure public goods take this non-dominating form.

By contrast to freedom as non-interference, no latent contradiction exists between freedom as non-domination and political society. It is not just that political initiatives can foster mutually beneficial collective goals, as in the last example. Non-domination is a creature of certain

---

[29] Pettit, *Republicanism*, pp. 22–3.

sorts of political and legal arrangements. Both domination and non-domination are products of the social condition. They reflect certain kinds of social relations. A single shipwrecked mariner possesses dominion over his desert island yet neither dominates nor is dominated by anyone. Domination arises not only from a person or group possessing superior power of various kinds, and hence the potential to interfere, but also from social, legal and political hierarchies of formal and informal kinds – which may not be linked to greater resources and power, though they usually are – through which certain individuals acquire the assumed or actual right to lord it over others. In either case, it operates less through actual interference than deference and the acceptance by the dominated of the dominator's entitlement to impose duties upon them. Thus, non-domination issues from a condition of political and legal equality in which such deference no longer obtains.

To the extent government action emanates from arrangements that are consistent with this condition of equality, it will not dominate. As we saw, freedom as non-interference suggests all government damages liberty to a degree, so that it should be kept to a minimum. However, freedom as non-domination allows that law, and hence interference, can be productive of liberty. The crucial factor is that government power not be exercised in a dominating way – that is, in a way consistent with the absence of deference and without producing it. I shall argue below that the intrinsic political egalitarianism of freedom as non-domination cannot be captured by a legal constitution aiming to secure equality of concern and respect but ultimately requires democratic decision-making even on constitutional essentials. In other words, it is the democratic form of government that offers the most appropriate mechanism for constraining political power, not a legal framework. However, before exploring the specific link between non-domination and democracy in the next subsection, I want to close this comparison between freedom as non-interference and as non-domination by examining their relationship to equality a bit further.

It is often assumed that freedom as non-interference will at least require conditions of formal equality, such as might be provided by constitutional rules and arrangements, in order to ensure each individual has the greatest degree of liberty compatible with a like liberty for all.[30] Indeed, one of

---

[30] Probably the most sophisticated defence of this argument and the points, reported in the rest of this paragraph, associated with it is Hayek, *The Constitution of Liberty*. But though Rawls, also a devotee of freedom as non-interference, does not draw quite the same conclusions with regard to social rights, he likewise advocates 'equal liberty' rather than liberty *per se*, *A Theory of Justice*, pp. 201–5, a claim that we shall see proves suspect.

the main advantages of this view of negative liberty is supposedly that it makes possible such a formal egalitarianism while still preserving freedom of individual choice and responsibility. Instead, arguments for more substantive equality are criticised for requiring almost constant interferences with individual freedom of action in order to ensure all stay at the same level. These incursions are viewed as both inefficient and highly coercive, requiring the state to aspire to a literally totalitarian degree of power in a vain attempt to organise the whole of social life in a putatively just, that is egalitarian, way.

Does freedom as non-domination fall foul of these charges? Note first that freedom as non-interference generates problems of its own in this regard. We have already seen that an uncontentious metric of the 'greatest equal freedom from interference' is not available to ground such a legal and political order.[31] Worse, though, maximising freedom as non-interference may not even have the formal egalitarian implications advocates claim for it. Potentially, one could maximise freedom as non-interference in an inegalitarian manner by only constraining those most likely to interfere with others. Yet, that would produce precisely the concentration of power theorists of freedom as non-interference claim to fear. The trouble is they fail to address the problem fully by not considering a given person's or body's latent and dominating capacity for interference. By contrast, the same strategy would be inconsistent with freedom as non-domination. For the power amassed to subdue certain prime dominators would similarly dominate, albeit latently, the rest.[32] Domination depends on the relative standing and power of citizens, so attempts to maximise non-domination for some will impose parallel costs on others. So, the avoidance of domination will tend to the equalisation of the degree to which any agent or agency, government included, can dominate others.

Is it necessarily just *political* equality that matters for freedom as non-domination, though? Clearly all sorts of resources other than governmental authority can produce domination – Pettit lists 'financial clout, social connections, communal standing, informational access, ideological position, cultural legitimation, and the like' as potential candidates.[33] The determining factor in these cases is when differential possession or access to these resources renders them marks of unequal status, allowing those who hold them to dictate terms to those who do not. For example, money, connections, privileged access and professional standing can all

---

[31] See too the critique of Hayek's account of the rule of law in chapter 2.
[32] Pettit, *Republicanism*, p. 111.   [33] Ibid., p. 59.

become attributes of a class or caste that produce unmerited deference in others. However, as Pettit notes, overcoming the dominating effect of such resources need not require a radical form of material equality.[34] Wealth extends the domain in which a rich person can exercise his freedom, allowing him to indulge a taste for classic cars or old masters denied to most of us, but such activities in themselves need not dominate others. Money only dominates when the wealthy man is able to influence public affairs more than the poor simply on account of his wealth, or is able to employ it to impose harsh contractual terms on his employees.

Of course, as earlier republicans well appreciated, conspicuous consumption can have political effects even when not directly targeted at political purposes – hence their advocacy of anti-sumptuary laws and distrust of the corrupting effects of luxury more generally. Nevertheless, while non-domination is intrinsically linked to equality of political resources, a similarly intimate tie does not pertain between non-domination and material equality. As a result, the promotion of non-domination need not require the constant interferences with the extent of undominated choice wealth brings in the ways certain liberals fear necessarily arise with more substantive theories of equality. At the same time, non-domination creates an even stronger bond than liberty as non-interference between freedom and the need for structures that ensure all are equal before the law and count as one and only one in political decision-making. The issue now to be addressed is whether such political equality requires a legal constitution or is best met through some form of democracy.

Equal concern and respect

The second liberal argument noted above comes in here. Obvious similarities exist between the republican argument for political equality to avoid domination and the liberal desire to provide equal concern and respect for autonomous individuals through a suitable constitutional settlement. We can imagine such rules as imposing appropriate constraints that ensure politicians and others cannot act in wilful or whimsical ways that do not treat others as equals. Not surprisingly, perhaps, a number of republicans have embraced legal constitutionalism as a mechanism for preventing arbitrary rule and promoting non-domination.

As we saw in chapter 3, there are two ways such constitutional rules might be said to constrain political action. On the one hand, they can

---

[34] Ibid., pp. 117–19.

be aimed at ensuring the policies themselves show equal concern and respect – the substantive, results-based or outcome view of constitutionalism adopted by Dworkin and Rawls. On the other hand, they may be viewed as defending the process and making sure all views are given equal consideration in determining the policy – the tack taken by Ely and others. I have already criticised the coherence of both these arguments. Now I want to underline that critique by showing how neither is compatible with the republican concern with non-domination. Though a number of prominent republican theorists have thought otherwise, I believe they are mistaken. With regard to both constitutional substance and process, domination can only be avoided if all have an equal right to decide these issues. Such an equal right is only likely to be realised, albeit indirectly, through normal democratic procedures. Indeed, this right is tied in an intrinsic, and not merely an instrumental, manner to the republican tenet that we only achieve an equal status and an end to deference when we are all considered as citizens, entitled to be rulers and ruled in turn.

Republicanism and substantive legal constitutionalism

Philip Pettit offers a prominent example of a republican argument for the substantive view of legal constitutionalism. He maintains that arbitrary rule, and hence domination, arises when there are no guarantees in place that would ensure that governmental and other power holders 'track the common recognisable interests' of those affected.[35] For only the pursuit of such genuine public interests can treat all with equal concern and respect. He suggests that a process of rights-based judicial review, supplemented by various contestatory democratic mechanisms, offers the most appropriate means to achieve this goal. If we see rights as protecting the basic common interests of all individuals, judges as the impartial arbitrators of this structural framework able to ensure all power holders abide by these standards, and popular contestatory mechanisms as a final safeguard to make sure all follow the rules of the game, then we would seem secure from arbitrary government.[36]

The success of this argument involves us being able to come up with an objective account of 'common recognisable interests' and our accepting the legitimacy of a constitutional court as their best guardian. Yet both these elements are doubtful. Pettit attempts to get round the worry

---

[35] Pettit, *Republicanism*, pp. 56, 184 and his 'Democracy: Electoral and Contestatory', in I. Shapiro and S. Macedo (eds.), *Designing Democratic Institutions*, New York: New York University Press, 2000, p. 107.
[36] Pettit, *Republicanism*, ch. 6.

that one might be deferring simply to some individual's or group's view of common interests by imagining they have emerged from a hypothetical democratic process, similar in kind to the contractarian reasoning employed by Rawls and examined in chapter 3. A 'common interest', he writes, is one supported by 'cooperatively avowable considerations' – that is 'considerations such that were the population holding discussions about what it ought to cooperate in collectively providing, then they could not be dismissed as irrelevant'.[37] If autonomy is regarded as being able to choose on the basis of reasons, then – so the argument goes – we can surely model a description of the public interest that is non-arbitrary if it is based on reasons none could reject, and so treats all equally as autonomous agents.

This thesis adopts the second depoliticising strategy criticised earlier – that of substituting an idealised apolitical process for real politics. No doubt, hypothetical reasoners who are suitably abstracted from their core commitments in some way might be able to reach such a consensual agreement. However, that begs the question of the legitimacy and uncontroversial character of these abstractions. As Henry Richardson has remarked, in real politics the reasons none can reject is likely to be an empty set.[38] Within pluralist societies, the range of core values held by individuals is so wide that almost any proposed reason is likely to conflict with that of someone else.

Pettit's idealised political process assumes a hypothetically possible convergence on substance. But the dilemma confronting real politics is that no such convergence is likely. The role of the political process in these circumstances is as much about authorising the decision-maker to take decisions that at least some will disagree with as with informing the decision itself. In other words, the test of a political process is not so much that it generates outcomes we agree *with* as that it produces outcomes that all can agree *to*, on the grounds they are legitimate. A non-dominating process operating within the 'circumstances of politics' will have to meet two criteria in this respect. First, citizens will need to feel that no difference of status exists between them and the decision-makers. The decision-makers cannot be chosen because for some reason they are deemed to be 'superior' sorts of people. Second, the reason the views of some citizens may count for less than those of others in the actual decision cannot be because some people hold the 'right' view and others the 'wrong' one.

---

[37] Pettit, 'Democracy, Electoral and Contestatory', p. 108.
[38] Richardson, *Democratic Autonomy*, p. 53.

A standard democratic process meets these criteria in a fairly straight-forward way. A defining characteristic of a democratic vote is that each person counts for one and none for more than one. In elections for local or national legislatures, all citizens are treated equally in this respect – including members of the currently incumbent government. The reason that the legislature favours certain people's views more than others is because more people have voted for a given party's representatives than for those of other parties. Such aggregative accounts of democratic voting are sometimes criticised as mechanical or 'statistical'.[39] These critiques are more fully addressed in chapter 6. But whatever the supposed failings of democratic decision-making, this very mechanical aspect of democracy has a decided advantage in the context of disagreement. It allows every-one to be counted equally and to accept the legitimacy of the view that prevails – even if they disagree with it. That position has been regarded as paradoxical.[40] Yet, any decision-making procedure involves accepting some distinction between the legitimacy of the process and one's view of the result.[41] After all, a court may also produce results litigants or observers disagree with, but will be accepted nonetheless because it satis-fies procedural norms of due process. However, the distinctiveness of the democratic process lies in its non-dominating character. For it involves accepting one's own view as just one among others – even if one feels passionately about it, because others feel just as passionately on the other side. Democratic citizens must step back from their own preferred views and acknowledge that equal concern and respect are owed to their fellows as bearers of alternative views. It is only if we possess some such detach-ment that we can live on equal (non-dominating) terms in circumstances of political disagreement by finding workable ways to agree even though we disagree.

Unless the constitution can claim to be based on terms none could rea-sonably reject, and judges can be said to be faithful interpreters of its pre-scriptions, then judicial review of legislation can only claim legitimacy as non-dominating if it has similar procedural credentials to democracy and can meet the two criteria given above for acceptable collective decision-making in circumstances of political disagreement. It is unclear that it can. Judges do seem to be claiming a different status to ordinary citizens.

---

[39] See R. Dworkin, *Freedom's Law: The Moral Reading of the American Constitution*, Oxford: Oxford University Press, 1996 p. 364.
[40] R. Wollheim, 'A Paradox in the Theory of Democracy', in P. Laslett and W. G. Runciman (eds.), *Philosophy, Politics and Society*, second series, Oxford: Blackwell, 1969, p. 84.
[41] J. Waldron, *Law and Disagreement*, Oxford: Clarendon Press, 1999, p. 246.

After all, their role as constitutional guardians is often justified in terms of their being a check on irrational, self-interested or plain myopic populist sentiments.[42] Yet it is uncertain what grounds these claims. True, they rarely allege superior moral wisdom to ordinary citizens. Their credentials lie in their legal expertise as upholders of the constitution. However, we have now seen the constitution cannot be viewed as an objective fount of moral and political wisdom. Even if it could, we know judges and legal scholars more generally differ on how any given constitution should be interpreted and its implications for particular cases. Moreover, their divisions are often as much ideological and moral as legal, even if they feel obliged to treat them as disagreements about the nature of the law rather than politics and morality.

As I noted in chapter 1, far from being above democracy, multimember courts typically resolve their not uncommon disagreements by the very democratic procedures they claim to supersede. Yet, the citizen is entitled then to ask why his or her views have counted for less than those of the nine or so figures on the bench. By contrast to elected politicians, judges have no incentives to heed the views of their fellow citizens. The winning majority on the court is simply imposing its opinion over everyone else's because of their status as members of a constitutional court. They do have to give reasons for their decision, but citizens and their political representatives have reasons too. Meanwhile, as I observed, the reasons offered by the majority of justices may differ widely from those of a significant minority of their fellow jurists. So, the reasons behind a given judgement are rarely uncontested and immune to reasonable disagreement even among legal experts.

Of course, courts claim to offer a fair and impartial process, where all are treated as equals. But when it comes to the making of decisions about our collective life, they lack the intrinsic fairness and impartiality of the democratic process – that of treating each person's views equally. For constitutional judicial review seems premised on an unjustified assertion that those on the bench are more equal than the rest. Given their freedom to interpret the law in diverse and inconsistent ways, according to the moral and legal positions they hold, with no more authority than any other legal interpreter apart from the mere fact that they are in a position to impose their opinion, their rule cannot be other than arbitrary and

---

[42] E.g. C. R. Sunstein, 'Approaching Democracy: A New Legal Order for Eastern Europe – Constitutionalism and Secession', in C. Brown (ed.), *Political Restructuring in Europe*, London: Routledge, 1994, pp. 16–18.

hence dominating. Almost in recognition of this fact, many arguments for improving the legitimacy of judicial review turn on making the judges subject to some form of idealised democratic process of selection, such as having them mirror the racial and gender balance of the wider community, and viewing their deliberations as ideal forms of public reason. However, there can be no guarantee that such artificial attempts to produce a microcosm of society will reflect the same balance of opinions as would result from all citizens having an equal voice. At best, it will amount to a rough approximation that involves the selectors and those selected deciding which issues are most salient for particular groups of people, with many of these groupings being somewhat arbitrary categorisations so far as their diverse membership is concerned. Moreover, such apolitical schemes miss the important point that we value real democracy not because it necessarily produces an answer with which we agree but for the way it respects our disagreements by giving us all an equal voice. They also remove the key mechanism possessed by electors for ensuring the elected respond to their evolving concerns – the capacity to remove them from office should they fail.

Does the possibility of contestation get around these difficulties? Not in the form Pettit envisages it. He has distinguished what he calls 'authorial' from 'editorial' democracy.[43] The former suggests the people in some way propose public policies, while the latter simply allows them to ensure rulers adhere to publicly declared rules and standards. Thus, editorial democracy might be satisfied by having some sort of statutory watchdog, such as an ombudsman, to whom citizens could appeal. Yet, this account assumes that the constitutional rules are uncontroversially in the public interest and a consensus exists as to their meaning – the problem lies with the odd rogue judge or mistaken judgement. However, we have seen the difficulty to lie deeper than this. The problem is that we disagree about both rules and judgements. In which case, we need a process of the kind described above that treats all views as deserving equal respect in the authorising, if not literally in the authorship, of the decision.

If we had good constitutional rules and virtuous and sagacious judges to enforce them, then arguably the domination of arbitrary rule might be overcome. Whereas the enlightened despot is enlightened only at his or her pleasure, the good laws bind the upright and wise judges. Of course, even such paragons might have the odd off day – hence the need for a

---

[43] Pettit, 'Democracy, Electoral and Contestatory' and his 'Democracy, National and International', *The Monist*, 89 (2006), pp. 302–25.

negative, contestatory check on their actions. But we now see the problem requires more than mere prudential guarantees. We simply do not have fail-safe ways of ascertaining whether the laws are good and the judges have the requisite expertise, for there is no commonly recognised method for doing so.

The failings of Pettit's view of the constitution as the product of a hypothetical democratic process are an instance of the weakness of objectivist views of arbitrary power more generally. If an objective account of the public good was available to us, it would be reasonable to assume that some are better at tracking it than others. If they could be counted on to do so, no domination would arise. However, as R. A. Dahl has observed, a central rationale for democracy lies in the absence of any compelling justification for such Platonic arguments for guardianship: the doctrine that those who possess knowledge of the 'royal science' of government should rule. Two claims underpin guardianship theory: first, that 'knowledge of the public good and the best means to achieve it is a "science" composed of objectively valid and vindicated truths, as the laws of physics or (in a very different way on most accounts) mathematical proofs are usually thought to be "objective". Second this knowledge can be acquired only by a minority of adults.'[44] In the world of natural science, these two claims may be met in ways that allow for expertise about the physical world without its producing domination. With regard to the first, there are complex and widely (if not universally) acknowledged means for testing a scientist's views that ground their claims to 'objectivity'. As to the second, scientists may be given a suitable training that places them on equal terms with fellow scientists in the pursuit of scientific knowledge. So long as such an education is open to all, then no inequality of status results from accepting the trained scientist's views as better informed than one's own on relevant matters – or indeed, in acknowledging that certain people may be more adept at scientific reasoning than others. For this acknowledgement is not deference to someone as a 'superior' simply because of who they are – a scientist's standing and opinions only carry weight to the extent they can pass muster before his or her peers according to commonly recognised processes of review that are applied equally to all.[45] By contrast, when, say, Nobel prize-winning scientists yield to the temptation to believe they are 'noble' individuals, whose views on fields other than their

---

[44] R. A. Dahl, *Democracy and its Critics*, New Haven: Yale University Press, 1989, pp. 65–6.

[45] Here I disagree with Richardson who suggests even a well-grounded notion of guardianship would be dominating. See Richardson, *Democratic Autonomy*, p. 41.

own should be listened to simply because they are famous and intelligent persons, then they do dominate. In this case, no independent foundation exists for their claims other than their unsubstantiated assertion of general superiority.

The risk of domination always arises when the putatively 'great and the good' trespass into the moral and political sphere, for no more or less agreed epistemology equivalent to that of the natural sciences exists for adjudicating the claims of rival moral and political theorists. Their methodologies tend to be more or less explicitly internal to the approach they advocate. At best, they offer ways of adjudicating a dispute between proponents of similar views, but not one between those with a wholly different approach. A post-modernist, a utilitarian and a deontologist apply different and incommensurable criteria to the evaluation of moral and political decision-making, each highlighting considerations that are deemed less important or of no importance at all by the others.[46] Much the same is true of rival social scientific theories, such as disputes between economists over different approaches to monetary policy. It might be argued that some political decisions are purely technical, regarding the choice of the most appropriate means to agreed ends. However, putting to one side the fact that experts frequently disagree even in quite technical areas, such as nuclear power, most policy assessments tend to involve potentially contentious moral and ideological judgements at some level or another.[47]

None of the above means no reasoned argument between alternative options is possible. Indeed, I shall discuss the role of public reason in voting and legislation in the next two chapters. But it does provide a *prima facie* reason for believing that the only peers entitled to choose between alternative collective moral and political policies are not the community of experts in these fields but the community of all moral and political reasoners. To do otherwise would be to risk domination by unjustifiably treating some as having higher status than others. Moreover, it also suggests that the method used for making the decision will not solely or even primarily have an epistemic purpose – at least not one that extends to producing the correct or the most justified answer. Its role will be more a matter of legitimacy – of giving everyone a say. As we saw, it is this quality that the process of democratic voting possesses and judicial review lacks.

Without a well-founded theory of legal guardianship, the ability of judges to trump the decisions of the democratic process will be

---

[46] Waldron, *Law and Disagreement*, p. 179.   [47] Dahl, *Democracy and its Critics*, pp. 67–70.

dominating in much the same way as that of any other member of 'the great and the good'. However, a judge's legal training does not ground his or her claims in the ways the natural scientist's does. As we noted, though all judges are legally qualified they may still differ in their views of the constitution. Some may be liberals, others conservatives; some see themselves as originalists, others as interpretists, and so on. Of course scientists also hold rival hypotheses, but unlike natural science no agreed view exists for the law (other than a vote in the highest court) of how differences of legal opinion might be resolved. For parallel reasons, we have no sure method for adjudicating on the judge's substantive credentials to rule. When we choose political representatives we are not electing experts on governing so much as professional advocates for our values and concerns – albeit with leeway to apply them to situations or in ways we have not foreseen, though with the ability to oust them should we dislike what they do in our name. However, the selection of constitutional judges *is* supposed to be a matter of judicial expertise. Yet, be it the open, politicised selection process used in the United States or the relatively closed, peer-group process employed in the UK, neither of these or any other method in use offers a way of agreeing on the credentials of the judge as a legal and moral expert in the manner of the available means for approving the physicist's expertise in his or her field.

Note, this argument is neutral as to whether some form of moral realism or objectivity ultimately grounds legal morality or not. Some theorists assume such criticisms involve moral scepticism and could be got around if judges were moral realists or objectivists of some kind.[48] However, such pretensions to be philosopher kings would arguably risk further delegitimising them. As Jeremy Waldron has observed, the objectivity or not of morality is an irrelevance.[49] Not only do objectivists and realists differ widely but also they too have no epistemology to ground their rival ontological claims (or, indeed, to answer the sceptic or the emotivist). Moreover, an additional argument still needs to be made for why their arguments should override the rival moral expertise of other moral realists in society – be they church leaders or ordinary citizens. Some version of moral realism may or may not be true, but for practical purposes its truth (if it is true) does not validate any particular judge's beliefs. The judge is still imposing his opinion of what the nature of moral facts is

[48] E.g. M. Moore, 'Moral Reality', *Wisconsin Law Review* (1982), p. 1064 and the discussion in Waldron, *Law and Disagreement*, p. 181.
[49] Waldron, *Law and Disagreement*, ch. 8.

without being able to offer generally acceptable reasons for why litigants and others affected by the decisions who hold differing views – including alternative versions of moral realism – should accept them as true. As such, the rulings of a judge holding objectivist views about morality will be every bit as arbitrary as those of a moral sceptic or emotivist.

Of course, there are certain branches of physics where reasonable disagreements persist and it is simply accepted that as yet no adequate test exists for choosing between rival theories. Scientists, though, have the luxury of not having to choose at this point, and they can still agree on what an adequate test would be like. By contrast, collective legal and political decisions have to be made in conditions where differences persist and no agreed test exists. In this case, domination will result because, in the absence of a convincing process of authorisation that shows equal concern and respect to citizens as autonomous reasoners holding different views, imposing the view of judges on the rest of us will be arbitrary.

Republicanism and procedural legal constitutionalism

At this point, a process-based version of legal constitutionalism comes into play. For it will be objected that none of the above rules out the need to have a constitution that ensures that the democratic process is itself fair and open. Indeed, some republican theorists, such as Frank Michelman and Cass Sunstein, have made a concern with the constitutionalisation of such matters as voting rights and campaign finance the touchstone of a republican approach to legal constitutionalism.[50] However, we observed in chapter 3 that a major difficulty exists with a procedural approach: namely, that when policies are reviewed on procedural grounds, such review either proves vacuous or involves a hypothetical account of what policy ought to have been adopted in ideal procedural circumstances. In other words, it turns into the outcome or results-based substantive approach. Some theorists have concluded that nothing distinctive can be said about procedures, therefore. Whatever the problems, we simply have no choice but to defend certain outcomes as desirable and attempt to secure them in as efficient a way as possible.[51]

---

[50] E.g. F. Michelman, 'Law's Republic', pp. 1493–537 and 'Conceptions of Democracy in American Constitutional Argument: Voting Rights', *Florida Law Review*, 41 (1989), pp. 443–90; C. R. Sunstein, 'Beyond the Republican Revival', *Yale Law Journal*, 97 (1988), pp. 1548–58.

[51] E.g. J. Raz, 'Disagreement in Politics', *American Journal of Jurisprudence*, 43 (1998), pp. 45–6.

If true, this would make a procedural form of republican constitution-alism of any kind a non-starter. However, this argument moves too fast, for several distinctively procedural issues remain. Indeed, even the outcome approach begs the resolution of certain procedural considerations. Why is this? For a start, it will be impossible to specify all outcomes in advance and detail the most suitable procedures for each of them. Rather, it will be necessary to guide institutional design by certain general considerations about how given procedures are likely to work in reaching their conclu-sions – their capacity to canvass all relevant views, to sift the evidence in an impartial manner, to be decisive and so on. Even if we assume no poten-tial disagreement about outcomes, at least some of these issues will have to be settled in relative ignorance of the particular outcomes we might want to secure. Of course, once we factor in disagreement, then the need to abstract even further from specific outcomes and focus on notions of procedural equity, efficiency and effectiveness becomes even greater.

Second, precisely because we cannot specify all the outcomes in advance and so have to merely propose procedures likely to produce good results, whatever procedures we choose will almost certainly throw up a bad outcome at some time or other. In these circumstances, we will have to give the legitimacy of the procedures an independent normative weight with regard to outcomes. This will be true even if we hand such questions to a constitutional court. Of course, that does not mean we need accept the outcome as the right one. But we will still have to accept the prevailing procedure as the legitimate means for overturning it.

Finally, we have seen the avoidance of domination gives us a reason to prefer procedures that instantiate a right to participate over those that do not. From this perspective, even if judges could be relied on to reach good outcomes when deciding constitutional questions, it would be procedu-rally illegitimate for them to do so. As we saw, this would be so not just for prudential or instrumental reasons, but for intrinsic ones relating to equality of respect.

These considerations get round a further objection from theorists of the substantive view. They point out that even if we do not necessarily disagree about procedures for the same reasons as we disagree about out-comes, as some accounts make it appear, we nevertheless can disagree just as fervently about procedures as we do about outcomes.[52] After all, differ-ent procedural concerns underlie arguments for different voting arrange-ments, prioritising parliamentary or presidential systems, the merits and

---

[52] Raz, 'Disagreement in Politics', p. 47.

demerits of unicameralism as opposed to bicameralism and so on. Again, outcome theorists argue that if our disagreements on procedures are on all fours with those about outcomes, why not pass on to the interesting topic straight away? However, we can now see we have no choice but to prioritise procedures over outcomes because we have no way of knowing what all these last will be.[53] We have to settle our disagreements over the former at least in part as a way for deciding future disagreements about the latter. Though outcome considerations will be relevant to the design of procedures, these will need to be general rather than specific. To the extent they raise distinct issues concerning the legitimacy of the process, then the avoidance of domination points clearly towards those that allow citizens' views to be counted on an equal basis.

These arguments might seem to be compatible with a constitution that explicitly enshrines only procedures. For example, the Australian Constitution contains no bill of rights. It merely describes the machinery of federal decision-making, outlining the processes to be used and the competences of the different levels of government. Although a standing temptation exists to read rights into such a procedural constitution and employ them for the judicial review of legislation, that can be – and for long periods has been – resisted. Meanwhile, a procedural legal constitutionalist might maintain that having some fixed account of procedures is necessary to prevent an otherwise infinite regress. For, if we prioritise procedures, then which procedures do we employ to select the procedures and so on?[54] Some procedure will be needed to set up the preferred procedure, which will itself be contentious in certain aspects. Yet, this problem will bedevil the writing of the constitution itself. Seeing the constitution as the product of constitutional politics will not get around the problem. Some republican theorists, such as Michelman and (when in republican mode) Habermas, get tempted back into a hypothetical 'ideal' procedure to resolve this issue. In different ways, they argue that democracy itself assumes certain norms. However, we saw how such 'substantive' proceduralism proves purely circular. The 'method' used to ground the approved political rights builds those rights into its very design. As such, from the perspective of those who hold alternative views, it will appear arbitrary.

---

[53] See J. Waldron, 'The Core Case Against Judicial Review', *Yale Law Journal*, 115 (2006), pp. 1345–6.

[54] F. Michelman, 'How Can the People Ever Make the Laws? A Critique of Deliberative Democracy', in J. Bohman and W. Rehg (eds.), *Deliberative Democracy: Essays on Reasons and Politics*, Cambridge, MA: MIT Press, 1997, pp. 162–5 and Richardson, *Democratic Autonomy*, p. 67.

We simply have to grasp this procedural nettle and start from some-where – be that the 'already existing' political system, or – in the case of new regimes emerging from war or revolution – with whatever arrange-ments can be cobbled together to get the process of designing a regime off to a start. But having done so, the very fact that disagreements about process will be ongoing argues against constitutionalising these proce-dures. Rather, they must be left open so we may rebuild the ship at sea – employing, as we must, the prevailing procedures to renew and reform those self-same procedures. We saw in chapter 3 how critics allege such arrangements will be self-serving and risk being highly unstable. They claim a role for the courts as neutral third-party arbitrators in such areas. However, we noted that not only is the claimed neutrality contentious, but also that, in the US at least, the Supreme Court has been highly reluctant to act in this area and remove the abuses most of these critics correctly identify in the American political system. That record of judicial inac-tion compares unfavourably with the slow, incremental yet profound and progressive constitutional reforms achieved by normal political processes in Britain and New Zealand, say. So there would appear to be no over-whelming empirical objections to disturb the basic normative case for a thorough-going proceduralism that goes all the way down.

Conclusion

In this chapter I have related the critique of legal constitutionalism in Part I and the alternative political constitutionalism defended in Part II, to the republican ideal of non-domination. The first section criticised two depoliticising strategies associated with legal constitutionalism – the setting of boundaries to politics, and the use of an idealised non-political politics. Both proved not only incoherent but also productive of domina-tion, which is itself as great a potential source of injustice as the oppression legal constitutionalists aspire to tackle. The second section then explored why avoiding domination required a political constitution in which all citizens play an equal part in an ongoing process that is both constitu-tional and constitutive.

As we also saw, though the concept of non-domination has been cen-tral to the republican tradition, it captures key aspects of the two liberal values that largely motivate legal constitutionalism – the notion of neg-ative liberty, and the need to show autonomous individuals equal con-cern and respect. However, it reveals how these core values only prove consistent with avoiding domination if they are detached from the two depoliticising strategies with which legal constitutionalists associate them and are realised through a democratic political constitutionalism.

Negative liberty understood as non-interference suggests that limited government must be less government, with politics kept at bay. Only a dubiously metaphysical notion of positive liberty can account for why individuals might wish to participate in making collective decisions – a position with sinister overtones of being 'forced to be free'. As such, it feeds into the first depoliticising strategy of setting boundaries to politics. Yet, the reduction of interference *per se* proves an incoherent notion as well as dominating. By contrast, negative liberty understood as freedom from domination allows us to distinguish between legitimate and illegitimate interference. In this case, limited government need not involve reduced government – merely government that is constrained so as not to dominate those whom it rules.

Equality of concern and respect come in here. Non-domination is inherently egalitarian. Some republicans, notably Philip Pettit, have supposed that a legal constitution offers the best means of ensuring governments pursue policies that treat all with equal concern and respect. But this thesis turns out to rely on the second depoliticising strategy of an idealised politics from which all the sources of reasonable disagreement have been removed. In the ideal circumstances of actual social and political life, then such a result-based strategy proves a source of judicial domination. Instead, we need a process of a certain kind that allows all citizens to count equally, even if they disagree with the actual decision. Democracy seems a better candidate for this role than the courts. Moreover, even a procedural constitution, as advocated by republicans such as Michelman, will dominate in giving the final word to its guardians and allowing them to impose their view of the process on others. Consequently, we must accept a continual process of rebuilding the constitutional ship at sea.

This chapter has stated what might be called the basic case for a political constitution in terms of non-domination. Nevertheless, critics might argue that it in its turn has idealised politics. We need a legal constitution not because it is ideally the best, but to avoid the pitfalls of real politics – the tyranny of the majority, the undermining of the rule of law, the danger that democracy might subvert itself. The next two chapters address these concerns head on, filling out the constitutional qualities of the democratic process.

5

The forms of political constitutionalism: public reason and the balance of power

Non-domination not only provides republicanism's basic case for establishing a system of self-rule, but also dictates how this system should operate and be organised. The key quality republicans have looked for in this regard is that the political process obliges decision-makers to 'hear the other side' ('*audi alterem partem*').[1] Historically, they have associated 'hearing the other side' with a particular conception of public reason, on the one hand, and political arrangements that embody a balance of power, on the other. The former characterises the civic attitudes and types of deliberation citizens and politicians should adopt when making decisions, the latter the way decision-making power needs to be divided to encourage these virtues and facilitate access to the political process. Republicans claim that only political systems embodying these two elements will treat all as equals and so avoid domination through arbitrary rule.

This chapter has three aims. First, it criticises those versions of these two features of republican politics that have come to be associated with constitutional judicial review and somewhat depoliticised or apolitical forms of deliberative democracy. On the one side, reasoning by the public is distinguished from a stipulative form of public reason. On the other side, the balance of power so as to encourage all citizens to give equal consideration to each other's views and interests is contrasted with the separation of power, which is revealed to have the perverse effect of removing such incentives. Second, setting the scene for chapter 6, it defends accounts of public reason and the balance of power that turn out to accord well with the processes of normal democratic politics. Finally, it shows how these accounts provide appropriate ways for 'hearing the other side' within the circumstances of politics, and do so in a manner that promotes rights and the rule of law. I start with some general considerations on the role of

---

[1] P. Pettit, *Republicanism: A Theory of Freedom and Government*, Oxford: Clarendon Press, 1997, p. 189. See also S. Hampshire, *Justice is Conflict*, London: Duckworth, 1999, p. 21.

public reason and the balance of power in mediating political disagreements, before turning to examine each in turn.

I The political forms of republicanism and the 'circumstances of politics'

Public reasoning has figured prominently in the recent literature on judicial review and democracy, especially with regard to decisions involving constitutional rights.[2] Most of these accounts aim at establishing – and claim to be oriented by – a supposedly objective view of what rights we have. However, if they specify the ideal character such public reasoning should take, they pay relatively little attention to the real institutional forms and social circumstances required to give rise to it. In particular, considerations of power and disagreement tend to be absent. Indeed, public reasoning of the approved kind is typically regarded as occurring only in situations where the power dynamics, conflicts of interest and ideological divisions characteristic of all actually existing democratic political processes have allegedly been removed or overcome.[3] As a result, constitutional courts, exceptional moments of popular deliberation (as are supposedly obtained at moments of crisis), or specialised deliberative bodies, such as citizens' juries, have come to be seen as the exemplary forums of public reasoning.[4]

Though these accounts have proved particularly attractive to legal constitutionalist defences of rights-based judicial review, they have also been employed by theorists influenced by republicanism to characterise democratic deliberation, at least on constitutional matters.[5] The version of this latter argument that applies specifically to a supposedly distinct form of 'constitutional' democratic politics, that occurs when drafting or agreeing

[2] Much of the discussion in this regard is sparked off by J. Rawls, *Political Liberalism*, New York: Columbia University Press, 1993, Lecture 6.

[3] For example, such considerations guide the elaboration of Rawls's 'original position' (*A Theory of Justice*, Oxford: Clarendon Press, 1971, ch. 3) or Habermas's 'ideal speech situation' ('Discourse Ethics: Notes on a Programe of Philosophical Justification', in his *Moral Consciousness and Communicative Action*, Cambridge: Polity, 1990, pp. 43–115).

[4] Rawls, *Political Liberalism*, pp. 231–40 and A. Gutmann and D. Thompson, *Democracy and Disagreement*, Cambridge, MA: Harvard University Press, 1996.

[5] E.g. C. R. Sunstein, 'The Enduring Legacy of Republicanism', in S. E. Elkin and K. E. Soltan (eds.), *A New Constitutionalism: Designing Political Institutions for a Good Society*, Chicago: Chicago University Press, 1993.

to a constitution,[6] was criticised in chapter 3. This chapter, and especially the next section, mounts a more general challenge to the epistemic claims and the institutional assumptions underlying all such accounts of public reason. For the likelihood of reasonable disagreement on constitutional issues seriously constrains the possibilities of any sort of public reasoning producing convergence on the 'right' answer. In the face of such differences, attempts to forge consensus are more likely to solidify domination than dissolve it.

The principal rationale for a genuinely public form of reasoning – that is, one involving the public in such a way that 'all sides are heard' – stems from this circumstance of political disagreement. According to this view, public reasoning serves less as a mode of justification and more as a means for legitimating decisions by offering a due process that acknowledges the equal moral right of all citizens to be regarded as autonomous reasoners. On this account, the showing of equality of concern and respect cannot arise from public reason establishing and being informed by a substantive view of those rights that are assumed by their proponents to be necessary to realise this goal. For these rights are themselves at issue and the attempts to provide objective means to ground them by imagining hypothetical ideal procedures for which they might be both the basis and the result prove solipsistic exercises. Instead, we need procedures that are fair and impartial simply because they weigh all views equally. In other words, the aim is to provide opportunities for the public to reason rather than specifying a rarefied type of public reasoning.

This procedural account of public reasoning addresses the constitutionalists' desire to uphold rights and the rule of law by treating all as equals and obliging them to recognise each other as such. To secure this goal the issue of power has to be grasped rather than sidestepped. The balance of power comes in here as a crucial quality of a political constitution, guiding the form its procedures need to take if all sides are to be heard. Section III contrasts the 'balancing' of the power of the parties in play, so that they must attend to each other's reasons, to attempts to remove power from the scene altogether by 'separating' the discussion of certain issues into a judicial or other forum where it supposedly no longer operates. These latter mechanisms fail to provide appropriate incentives for ensuring decision-makers track the interests of those they govern. Moreover, as the last chapter revealed, such depoliticisations not only risk entrenching

---

[6] E.g. B. Ackerman, *We the People: Foundations*, Cambridge, MA: Harvard University Press, 1991, ch. 1, a view endorsed by Rawls, *Political Liberalism*, pp. 233–4.

domination, but also involve it. Non-domination only operates where everyone has equal status. So long as any person or persons can exercise unaccountable power over others – even if their decisions are made without regard to considerations of power – then they will dominate even if they do not coercively interfere.

II Public reason: substance or procedure?

Reasoning can be public in a number of different ways. First, it can be open and transparent. Second, it can be undertaken in a public-spirited as opposed to a self-interested manner. Third, it can employ a set of public rules, reasons and conventions that are deemed to be intrinsic to participation in the relevant 'public' activity, and so are implicitly agreed to by all who do so, be they public officials or the public at large. Fourth, it can be focused on the public rather than any private good. Fifth, it can be reasoning that is accessible to all members of the public. Sixth, it can be reasoning undertaken by the public. Finally, it can endeavour to produce decisions all members of the public will find mutually acceptable.

Each of these seven notions of publicness – either on their own or in combination with some or all of the others – can be seen as offering preconditions for different forms and aspects of 'hearing the other side'. These forms and aspects have differing purposes and are appropriate to tackling diverse sorts of problems. My claim shall be that when reasoning about the legal protection of rights we need all seven notions and should interpret them in procedural terms. Only then will law be both of and for the public, and thereby treat all as equals. However, legal constitutionalists have generally operated with more substantive and restricted forms of public reasoning. These restricted forms often exclude many of the notions of publicness listed above and it is to them that I'll turn first.

Substantive accounts of public reasoning

There are stronger and weaker accounts of public reasoning. Some assume a clear method or epistemology for arriving at truth or objectivity in a given area. Others make the weaker claim that regardless of whether public reasons are objective and true, a specific set of such reasons can be identified as being intrinsic to any account of reasoning about or by the public in which individuals are treated with equal concern and respect. I shall dispute both accounts. In different ways, each unduly restricts the degree to which public reasoning needs to allow the public to express their views themselves if all sides are to be heard. In particular, they overdetermine the requirements of a fair process in ways that are arbitrary and hence dominating.

Objectivity and public reasoning

The two most widely accepted accounts of strong substantive public reasoning are the formal deductions and proofs of mathematics and the experimental method in natural science. In both cases, they can generate substantive public results that can claim a degree of objectivity and truth without necessarily involving or engaging with the public. However, there are clear and instructive disanalogies between these widely accepted models of public reasoning and those employed in law and politics.

Valid reasoning in maths can be public without being undertaken by or for the public. Certainly, mathematicians must employ clear and transparent modes of logical argumentation of kinds that are publicly acknowledged as belonging to maths and open to scrutiny and contestation by other mathematicians. Even if the motivations of those involved are a self-interested desire for prestige, they must address objective, necessary mathematical truths rather than the particular concerns of individual mathematicians, and do so in a way that will pass muster with their peers. Yet, it is not intrinsically necessary for the endeavour of maths that any but a small group of mathematical experts engage in it – after all many people will neither possess the talent nor wish to devote the time to the requisite training to be able to take part. Nor need this group be in principle open to all who might happen to have the potential to become mathematicians. Mathematics could be restricted to a small caste, such as the sons of mathematicians. Some brilliant mathematical minds might possibly be lost to the discipline that would advance it more than the closed caste will manage. However, that possible loss would not in itself detract from those advances that are achieved. In other words, such reasoning need not be carried out by the public nor be made accessible to all for it to produce valid results. Indeed, in some respects that may not be possible or desirable. Nor is there any need 'to hear the other side' in the sense of engaging with different ways of reasoning about maths that yield different conclusions – all discussions have to be framed within a given mathematical language. Likewise, though its proven conclusions can be regarded as objective and true, at least in mathematical terms, that does not mean they are all necessarily matters of public interest – at least *per se*. Thus, the relevant aspects in which reasoning in this context needs to be public are not ones that require it to be either democratic or to treat all citizens equally.

Although natural science works in a slightly different way, a parallel logic obtains. It too employs methods that are public only for 'the community of scientists', rather than everybody, and that are believed by most within that group to ground their rival claims. When different experimental physicists test a hypothesis, they 'hear the other side' to the extent of seeking to eliminate other possible explanations for the phenomena under investigation. However, only certain types of publicness seem inherent to this process: namely, some variant of the first, second and third notions listed above. Openness in experimental design, an absence of any massaging of the figures when presenting the data so as to obscure or exclude inconvenient results, and the use of publicly recognised methods that can be assessed by one's peers – all these elements are necessary. But science need not serve the public good, nor be accessible to, or undertaken by, anyone but other scientists. And since the experimental method endeavours to reveal at the very least that certain hypotheses are ungrounded, it has no need to conciliate different views. As with mathematics, so within pure science (though not its public applications) public reasoning need not be *of, by* or even *for* the public.

If, to adapt Rawls,[7] maths and experimental science aspire to be 'perfect' forms of public reasoning, a criminal court represents an 'imperfect' version. As a result, it adopts all seven notions of publicness and interprets the first three in a different, somewhat broader, way. To give a criminal a 'fair' hearing the prosecution has to be presented in a manner that allows the defence to challenge it. The defence also has to be allowed to make its own positive case for viewing the defendant as innocent – though this defence must in its turn be challengeable by the prosecution. Openness is important, therefore, as is the absence of any malice, self-interest or other bias in those conducting the proceedings which might prejudice the trial. Adherence to the public norms for conducting a trial, and to specific legal rather than general moral or other reasons, is similarly essential to ensure the integrity of the proceedings and preserve the rule of law. Only certain sorts of evidence are admissible, and acts do not become criminal simply because the prosecution, judge or jury believe them distasteful or dangerous – even if their views are well-founded. Though the law may protect various private goods, it does so for the public good. To a degree,

---

[7] Rawls, *A Theory of Justice*, pp. 85–6.

certain aspects of the trial, such as sentencing, must reflect that general goal rather than the ideals and interests of the parties to the particular case alone. Likewise, the reasoning has to be accessible to all, albeit partly through professional intermediaries. Not only must those accused be able to understand the case being made against them and capable of responding to it, but also so must the jury – for the accused are tried by their peers (at least in those cases relevant to this example). In this regard, reasoning is undertaken by the public to some extent. Finally, some combining of the different perspectives of defence and prosecution is not uncommon – for example, when accepting there may have been mitigating factors that warrant more lenient sentencing.

In certain respects this third form of public reasoning employs weaker elements of the previous two. As with mathematical reasoning, it involves a restricted set of reasons – in this case, those found in the criminal law. Appeal cannot be made to people's own moral views as to what is right or wrong or an appropriate punishment. Like experimental reasoning, the court setting is intended to sift the evidence and test the arguments of defence and prosecution. Yet, neither has the reliability or objectivity of a mathematical proof or a crucial experiment in natural science. These limitations, along with the fact that a criminal court addresses a public matter, broaden the degree to which it is accepted there may be at least two sides to the argument, each of which may enjoy a degree of plausibility, and justify the inclusion of the public in the process. As a result, such courts embody a more procedural view of publicness and employ all seven of the notions listed above. Given the guilt of a criminal often may not be clear-cut – perhaps the applicability of the law in this case may be subject to competing interpretations, or his or her involvement in the crime be open to doubt, or some element of both, among other reasons – the qualities of the process in themselves play a major part in legitimating the decision rather than the outcome *per se*. For not only can one not know the 'right' decision outside of this process, one also cannot know for sure that the process will secure it. All we can say is that by subjecting the accused to judgement by his or her peers in a public process, he or she is treated fairly: that is, as an equal. However, though this last form of public reasoning comes close, I shall argue neither it nor the previous two forms are suitable models for how we should reason about legislating on rights.

For a start, *pace* the claims of some moral philosophers, there can be no moral or political mathematics. Certain philosophers, such as those in the natural law tradition or a number of utilitarians, have argued that one can deduce objectively true moral judgements from various independent principles or facts inherent to human nature or society. At their most ambitious, they have maintained that our moral reasoning only proves logically coherent and well-founded when it assumes such facts or principles. Some theorists have even claimed that judges can engage in public reasoning in the manner of mathematicians or scientists – that is independently of the public, employing the allegedly public (though not necessarily publicly accessible) language of natural law or utility.[8] However, as we saw in the last chapter, they have to contend with the problem that there is considerable controversy about what these facts or principles might be and what follows from them. Meanwhile, no publicly agreed method exists for adjudicating between the substantive claims of rival views so as to treat some as more objective or true than others. Yet, without an epistemological theory which explains why their deliberations are likely to be more accurate or track the moral truth, their ontological claims provide no basis for their assertions of judicial expertise. Regardless of whether there are objective moral facts or not, the judiciary's beliefs about morality will be on a par with those of citizens and legislators, and as likely to be as diverse and prone to error as theirs. To treat judges' views as superior will therefore be arbitrary from their perspective. Worse, by basing their arguments in a largely ungrounded appeal to moral objectivity judges would be risking making opinions that were both capricious and subjective.[9]

Does the weaker model of public reasoning exemplified by a criminal court get around these problems? Stuart Hampshire, who sees the judicial process as a model of a procedural form of justice focused on 'hearing the other side', regards constitutional judicial review as justified for this reason.[10] But perhaps the most significant feature to note is how *different* constitutional courts are to this model, so that the analogy fails. Constitutional courts generally operate with a stronger – in the sense of a more substantive – notion of public reasoning than criminal courts. For a start, they do not involve a jury. Indeed, in legal constitutionalists' eyes it is to their advantage that they are isolated from the biases and prejudices that supposedly afflict the public at large. True, the constitution may have emerged from a special democratic process that claims to give voice to the will or reasons of the public in a more accurate way

---

[8] E.g. M. Moore, 'Moral Reality', *Wisconsin Law Review* (1982), pp. 1089–90, 1064.
[9] J. Waldron, *Law and Disagreement*, Oxford: Clarendon Press, 1999, p. 181.
[10] Hampshire, *Justice Conflict*, pp. 89–90.

than normal democratic legislation (though I disputed this latter claim in chapter 3). But even if this argument is valid and the reason of the public as entrenched in the constitution constrains the constitutional court, that constraint is comparatively weak. Constitutions tend to be considerably more abstract and open-textured than most criminal law statutes aspire to be, though many are poorly drafted, and unlike ordinary statutes can only be amended by an extraordinary political process. Nor does a criminal court offer an entirely self-sufficient model of public reasoning. In part, its standing rests on its publicly applying (and being the servant of) the public reason of both normal democratic legislation and other criminal courts. This is not to deny that judges always have to interpret law when applying it to particular cases, especially when the language of the law is extremely loose. But, as I argued in chapter 2, they have incentives to do so in ways that are subservient to the general aims of the legislature – not least because the law can be altered when the courts seem to be applying it in ways that conflict with the policy aims of elected governments. They also have reason to align their own interpretation with those of other courts, citing precedent to do so. As we saw, the incentives for constitutional courts are far fewer in this regard because they are at the top of the hierarchy and will only consider a single 'hard' example of a given issue rather than a number of analogous cases. Moreover, the central claim of legal constitutionalists is that both the legislation and the proceedings of criminal courts need to be subject in their turn to a superior form of public reasoning contained within the 'higher law' of the constitution. Yet the crucial difficulty remains of what grounds the claims of these reasons to be 'public' if they do not involve the public in either their formulation or application.

Rawls and the public reason of the constitution

As we saw in chapter 3, Rawls has offered one highly influential attempt to respond to this dilemma while avoiding the contentious metaphysics of natural law or other comprehensive moral theories. He argued that 'public reasons' are those persons of differing metaphysical beliefs would agree to in their 'public' capacity as democratic citizens as governing the 'public' sphere.[11] On this account, public reasons are limited to '"constitutional essentials" and matters of basic justice',[12] where he believed agreement is both possible and necessary. Regardless of their other views,

---

[11] Rawls, *Political Liberalism*, p. 213.   [12] Ibid., p. 214.

he thought people in their quality as citizens can share a common interest in securing equal rights to express and promote their different ideals and to pursue whatever their conception of the good life might be on the same basis as everyone else. He acknowledged that on most public policy issues, such as taxation or environmental protection, consensual decision-making is unlikely because it will be impossible for people to bracket off their broader – and often divergent and conflicting – ideological, metaphysical and practical considerations.[13] In these cases, standard democratic bargaining and majoritarian voting are appropriate mechanisms for reaching a collective decision. However, people will still want to ensure these contentious decisions are made and applied in ways that do not subvert the fundamental principles of political justice so that the system as a whole remains fair. Given that he thought public reason 'complete' and self-sufficient when it comes to political values,[14] he believed it plausible, and possibly prudent,[15] to entrust their protection to a select body of impartial, expert umpires, namely a constitutional court, who could act as 'exemplars of public reason' and ensure neither the process nor content of legislative decision-making offended basic political norms.[16]

Famously, Rawls provided a public method – the original position – which he hoped would show how people should be moved to agree on his political conception of justice as a logical entailment of their equal status as democratic citizens.[17] However, like all such methods – including rival variations of the idea of a founding contract such as Habermas's 'ideal speech situation' – it has struck all but its supporters as either too indeterminate to produce its favoured conclusions, or somewhat circular – building its results into its premises. A successful method, like those employed by experimental physicists, would have to rely on rather different and less controversial claims to those that it seeks to adjudicate.

---

[13] Ibid., pp. 214–15.

[14] Ibid., pp. 225, 244. See too his 'The Idea of Public Reason Revisited' in J. Rawls, *The Law of Peoples*, Cambridge, MA: Harvard University Press, 1999, pp. 144–5.

[15] Although Rawls's detailed discussion suggests that he thinks the United States' constitutional arrangements best accord with his scheme, he does not claim – like certain legal constitutionalists – that they are the only way of embodying his ideas. He argues that so long as public reason as he understands it is applied to the discussion of constitutional essentials, then the legislature – or indeed the people as a whole – could also operate as a suitable deliberative body to discuss these questions. See Rawls, *Political Liberalism*, pp. 234–5, though see, pp. 233–4 and 240. To this extent, his argument is not so much in support of judicial review *per se*, though he does believe it provides a powerful defence of the US version, as of a particularly pure kind of deliberative democracy. I deal with both these arguments in turn.

[16] Ibid., pp. 231–40.   [17] Ibid., pp. 226–7.

But Rawls's method exemplifies and draws on the very theory it aims to ground, being itself a hypothetical model of his form of public reasoning.

Rawls's attempt to identify a discrete realm of consensual public reasons that can act as a sort of constitutional maths – a language of political justice that trained lawyers can employ with a similar clarity and certainty to the way mathematicians use mathematical reasoning – proves a chimera. As I remarked in chapter 1, the 'burdens of judgement' apply as much to his list of basic rights and liberties as they do to different conceptions of the good. Outside the most abstract of formulations, we differ as much over our interpretations of the sources, subjects, sphere and scope of rights as we do on substantive policy issues – and for much the same reasons. Rawls's proposed demarcation of a limited 'public' sphere is itself deeply contentious, therefore. As he himself concedes, his chosen 'exemplars', the Supreme Court Justices, often – in his view, anyway – get it 'wrong',[18] offering alternative interpretations of constitutional rights to his and, he might have added, frequently draw on their deeper beliefs to ground their views, are rarely unanimous and typically resolve their disputes by majority vote.

In his last version of his theory, Rawls did appear to accept that there can be alternative conceptions of political justice, but contended these were constrained by the content of public reason itself.[19] Yet, if – as he once put it – the basic 'concept' of justice or a right may to some degree constrain the 'conceptions' we may hold of it, so it is at least the case that we are all trying to account for the same phenomena,[20] that still leaves room for a range of reasonable yet essentially contestable and incommensurable views.[21] Meanwhile, he spelt out an implication of his earlier account of 'political justice' as the product of an 'overlapping consensus' between reasonable comprehensive conceptions of the good. He admitted that these deeper commitments might provide the motivating force and rationale for most people's adherence to the constitutional norms he associated with public reason and that they are likely to want to express them in these terms. However, he added the 'proviso' that such expressions could only count

---

[18] Ibid., pp. 233, n. 18, and pp. 359–63 on *Buckley v Valeo* 424 US 1 (1976).

[19] Rawls, 'The Idea of Public Reason', p. 145, n. 35.   [20] Rawls, *A Theory of Justice*, p. 5.

[21] For example, MacCallum's famous account of liberty (G. MacCallum, 'Negative and Positive Freedom', *Philosophical Review*, 76 (1967), pp. 312–34), as a three term relation of an agent from some constraint(s) to perform certain acts, may describe the linguistic contours of the basic concept, yet is capable of being given both negative and positive readings depending on one's view of what counts as a constraint or the degree to which one believes freedom entails the availability of certain options or the actual performance of certain acts.

to the extent the resulting arguments were ultimately translated into the terms of public reason – they carry no weight in themselves.[22]

That might be a good defensive strategy for a group, such as Muslims today, who find themselves widely accused of holding views incompatible with liberal democracy. But, as I remarked in chapter 3, it misses the point that at least one motive for wanting to express the full reasoning behind one's commitment to the political system might also be to show how the prevailing interpretation of the public political culture excludes or potentially harms particular categories of citizens. Take the case of Martin Luther King, who Rawls acknowledged made effective use of Christian arguments in the civil rights campaign.[23] He was not simply affirming that even though a Christian he still upheld political values as understood by public reason. He was employing his comprehensive Christian beliefs – that formed part of the background culture of many of his opponents as well as his supporters – to challenge the way the political class in the US south understood political values, chiding his opponents for a failure to acknowledge both black and white as being 'created' equal.

Making this kind of argument involves a rather different approach to public reasoning to the one Rawls advocated. In this approach, it is accepted that there can be competing conceptions of political values and that it is important – indeed required – that we allow these alternative and potentially conflicting views to be voiced in order to 'hear the other side'. Indeed, where possible there can also be grounds for seeking a mutually acceptable accommodation between them. In this version of public reasoning, it becomes important that the public shape the language of politics, so that it reflects the balance of concerns of citizens. Judges cannot be 'exemplars' of such an account of public reason because it does not consist of seeking the 'correct' mixture of 'pure' political concepts removed from the comprehensive and other concerns of citizens. Rather, those concerns are entitled to mould and inform the political concepts, indicating how they relate to each other and are to be interpreted. In this account, public reasoning needs to be not only open, public-spirited, concerned with public issues and bound by public rules, but also publicly accessible and responsive to, and in some sense be undertaken by, the public. Consequently, a much more direct link has to be established between the public and those who frame laws and decide constitutional questions than the judiciary ever should have if they are to apply impartially,

[22] Rawls, 'The Idea of Public Reason', pp. 144, 152–6.
[23] Rawls, *Political Liberalism*, pp. 247–54.

not surreptitiously make, the law. Indeed, arguably the electoral linkage between legislators and the public exists precisely to allow citizens to influence the contours of the overlapping consensus and, crucially, reject those who do not frame it in ways that track their views. As I noted, Rawls admits that the judiciary can make poor judgements but claims that the ensuing uproar improves public reason.[24] How much more improving, though, if citizens can play a direct part in this reasoning and oust those who fail accurately to gauge the public interest.

Democratic deliberation through public reason

Some more participatory accounts of deliberative democracy, including many associated with republicanism, appear to move in this direction. Against Rawls, these stress the importance of actual dialogue and reasoning by the public as they work through the potential implications of their regarding each other as free and equal citizens. The aspiration is towards dialogue producing a convergence on an overlapping consensus of a more extensive kind than Rawls allows – both in terms of its scope and substance. Thus, they conceive the political public sphere to encompass what Rawls called the 'background culture' of civil society as well as the political forum proper, and allow the expression of comprehensive viewpoints to explicate political values.[25] However, they also believe agreement is more likely on constitutional essentials and that these – conceived as the preconditions of democratic communication – offer both a framework for, and the content of, public reasoning about most political issues, funnelling deliberators not just to a mutually acceptable but arguably the correct answer.

Yet, these epistemic claims are even more ambitious, and so less convincing, than Rawls's. Certainly, deliberating can lead to a better appreciation of all dimensions of a problem and produce a pooling of views. It can also force any proposal to meet criticisms from proponents of alternative positions. Self-interest and partiality are likely to be dampened as a result. At the very least, deliberators have to adopt the semblance of addressing the interests and concerns of others, or of employing impartial

---

[24] Ibid., p. 237.
[25] E.g. J. Habermas, *Between Facts and Norms: Contributions to a Discourse Theory of Law and Democracy*, Cambridge: Polity, 1996, pp. 107–9 and S. Benhabib, 'Liberal Dialogue versus a Critical Theory of Discursive Legitimation', in N. Rosenblum (ed.), *Liberalism and the Moral Life*, Cambridge, MA: Harvard University Press, 1989 and Rawls's comment in 'The Idea of Public Reason', p. 142, n. 28.

arguments. Finally, deliberation may cause a pause for thought, guarding against overly impulsive reactions to events or problems. However, these potential benefits may in practice fail to materialise, and even where they do may not produce any consensus on a position all could see as true.[26]

For a start, multiplying views can muddy the waters and make decision-making more complex, conflictual or plain confused, potentially overloading the system or producing stalemates that for one reason or another stymie a decision and certainly prevent consensus. Far from narrowing differences, deliberation may bring them to light – particularly in culturally divided or factionalised societies.[27] This result will be particularly likely where the viewpoints or interests involved prove incommensurable and incompatible, but may equally arise when they are simply too many and varied to be easily processed – greatly upping the transaction costs. Likewise, the pressures to address common concerns may lead to a certain pandering to popular prejudices rather than fostering impartiality and an orientation to the public interest. Rather than serving truth, it may merely lead groups to hide their real intentions in pleasing rhetoric. Indeed, deliberation may offer opportunities for demagogical oratory or the use of sophisticated spin that heightens rather than diminishes emotive reactions to issues, driving out cool dispassionate reasoning.[28] As a consequence, the convergence experienced by such groups may equally be the product of 'groupthink',[29] or persuasive and emotive rhetoric by the most articulate, which may induce weaker parties to concede too much.[30] After all, as I noted in chapter 1, the 'burdens of judgement' may mean reasonable disagreement can legitimately persist over the principles and facts involved in any issue.

These problems – particularly the first, which reveals how even calm, responsible reasoning may merely clarify rather than resolve disagreements – suggest the rationale for public reasoning to 'hear the other side' must lie elsewhere than the search for truth *per se*. Much the same goes for the purely prudential argument, whereby people are said to be the best judges of their own interest, with public deliberation the only heuristic

---

[26] H. Richardson, *Democratic Autonomy: Public Reasoning about the Ends of Policy*, Oxford: Oxford University Press, 2002, pp. 77–8.

[27] See C. Sunstein, 'The Law of Group Polarization', *Journal of Political Philosophy*, 10 (2002), pp. 175–95.

[28] D. Gambetta, '"Claro": An Essay on Discursive Machismo', in J. Elster (ed.), *Deliberative Democracy*, Cambridge: Cambridge University Press, 1998, pp. 19–43.

[29] I. L. Janis, *Groupthink*, Boston: Houghton Mifflin, 1982.

[30] This phenomenon is documented in D. Amy, *The Politics of Environmental Mediation*, New York: Columbia University Press, 1987.

for showing that something is in the public interest. Again, some of the same potential shortcomings of deliberation may lead citizens to misconstrue their interests because of the oratorical manipulation of others, or confusion resulting from the sheer weight of information. Deliberation can have substantive qualities – it may help legitimise a decision among the participants by giving them a degree of ownership over it, and it often possesses many of the positive epistemic qualities its proponents claim for it of airing information, forcing rational arguments to the fore and so on.[31] Yet, even in the best circumstances, as most political philosophy seminars reveal all too vividly, deliberation does not offer a 'method' that parallels the mathematician's proof or the natural scientist's experiment that enables us to ground a given ontological position.

This last weakness poses an obvious limitation to the proposal of some theorists that deliberation be located in special settings in order to diminish some of the above-mentioned difficulties. For example, certain theorists advocate the construction of relatively small citizens' juries composed of a carefully sampled cross-section of the community.[32] They propose that these bodies deliberate away from the full glare of publicity on the basis of a 'balanced' selection of views presented by experts. These measures aim at reducing the temptation to grandstand or to appeal to prejudiced, uninformed or unreasoned arguments. Even so, as the seminar example illustrates, they may not produce agreement. Worse, the possibility for domination remains. For the proponents of these schemes leave the selection of the topic, jury members and the expert opinions to somewhat mysterious, if presumably benign and knowledgeable, figures – no doubt the theorists themselves, or people like them. Yet, such paternalism is not only dominating in itself, it incorporates no adequate mechanism to encourage and certify that the deliberators, the agenda and menu of reasons they are offered track the interests and concerns of citizens at large. Without addressing these issues, citizens have no good reason to defer to the decisions of these bodies – no matter how deliberative and consensual they may be.[33]

The failure of these various forms of substantive public reasoning suggests that our task must be to search for a form citizens can recognise as

[31] J. Bohman, *Public Deliberation: Pluralism, Complexity and Democracy*, Cambridge, MA: MIT Press, 1996, p. 27.

[32] J. Fishkin, *Democracy and Deliberation: New Directions for Democratic Reform*, New Haven: Yale University Press, 1991.

[33] I. Shapiro, *The State of Democratic Theory*, Princeton: Princeton University Press, 2003, p. 33.

fair, balanced and supportive of rights and the rule of law, notwithstanding their reasonable substantive differences as to the character of these constitutional goods. It is to the squaring of this circle that I now turn.

Procedural accounts of public reasoning

The procedural approach to public reason enters at this point. Given that we lack a process all can acknowledge as offering a means for grounding the truth of moral, legal and political decisions, our reasons for adopting any process will have more to do with its legitimating than its epistemic properties. Even when we dispute the decision, we will need to feel that we should accept it all the same. However, that is not to say that such procedures possess no substantive merit, merely that these substantive qualities relate primarily to the character of the process itself and only secondarily, and not always infallibly, to the substantive worth of the decisions they produce. Indeed, it is to be expected that some will always have reasonable grounds for disagreeing with the outcome of the process. The point is that they do not disagree that it was rightfully made.

The republican injunction that we 'hear the other side' needs to be read in this procedural spirit. Its normative basis – its animating principle, if you like – lies in showing citizens equal concern and respect as autonomous reasoners and the consequent need to avoid domination.[34] As we saw in chapter 4, it is this argument that underpins the basic case for some form of democratic decision-making as the only legitimate authority for a government's imposing collective duties and burdens on citizens. There I concentrated on the mechanics of a democratic vote, a point to which I return in chapter 6. However, it also has implications for the sort of public reasoning that should precede voting and frame the conduct of elections, the devising of legislation and so on. For domination will not be avoided simply by allowing citizens to vote on proposals they have played no role in influencing or debating and that are just presented by technocrats or political leaders for their acceptance or rejection.

To be non-dominating, public reasoning will need to be 'public' in all seven of the senses outlined at the outset. Openness is necessary so that justice is seen to be done by fair means rather than arbitrarily imposed. Public-spiritedness ensures a willingness to give reasons, to which others can respond, rather than just asserting prejudices or interests, and to hear and respond to their reasons in turn. Again, not to give reasons risks

---

[34] Richardson, *Democratic Autonomy*, pp. 78–83.

rule being arbitrarily whimsical or self-serving. Likewise, a public, rather than a private, focus guards against factionalism. That does not mean that reasons cannot be offered for treating some groups differently to others. But the rationale should be based on a publicly defensible norm, such as equality, rather than purely private advantage. Finally, and most importantly, reasoning needs to be accessible to the public and conducted by them. Since all citizens can and do reason morally and politically, and no well-grounded moral or political science exists of the kind that entitles some to claim their reasoning offers a securer guide to people's own moral and political welfare than their own, all should be involved in collective deliberation on matters of public concern.

However, this goal entails more than just a process of any sort whereby what touches all is decided by all. It also conditions the character of this process. For, if it is to qualify as a form of public reasoning, then we need to frame our different reasons about the public good in ways that can be understood by, and address the rival reasons of, others. Nevertheless, that requirement falls short of obliging all citizens to adopt a putative set of canonical public reasons, as Rawls insists. We respect the autonomous reasoning power of our fellow citizens not by adopting reasons that enshrine a given understanding of respect, since disagreement about the relevant principles may be implicated in the issue we are attempting to resolve, but through attending to the actual arguments and reasons they employ. So individuals must be allowed to base their reasoning and arguments on their personal moral or religious views while accepting the need, as a matter of civility within a democracy where all citizens are respected as autonomous reasoners, to couch them in terms others can be expected to recognise as reasons and argumentation. Indeed, as we shall see below, the balance of power inherent in a democratic regime plays an important role in providing incentives to encourage such civic attitudes.

How far this constraint requires citizens to modify their views will depend on the character of the issue to be decided and the nature and degree of diversity of the beliefs of those involved. Such a public reasoning process is unlikely to funnel all opinion towards a consensus on the truth of certain principles of political morality or of particular policies. As I noted above, even if public deliberation is undistorted, there will still be room for reasonable disagreements, including between conflicting and incommensurable positions. However, when public reasoning of this kind works well, it can act as a filter that weeds out the most blatantly unjust and self-serving positions that fail to treat others with equal concern and respect. The result of such filtering is likely to be a compromise rather than consensus. Compromises need not be seen as 'shoddy' or 'unprincipled'. Instead, they can be seen as products of the mutual recognition by citizens of the reasonableness of their often divergent points of view by seeking to accommodate these various perspectives within a coherent programme of government. In other words, compromises are a natural part of a process that 'hears the other side' and seeks to avoid dominating citizens by failing to treat the reasons they offer equally.[35]

There is an intrinsic link between such a process of public reasoning and both rights and the rule of law. The link with rights is first and foremost through recognising all citizens as equal autonomous rights-bearers, able and entitled to reason for themselves about how they should lead their lives. However, that mutual recognition conditions the process of public reasoning and the character of its results. Democracy is sometimes portrayed as inimical to rights on the grounds that it aggregates preferences in a utilitarian manner. This portrayal mischaracterises the democratic process. As we shall see, the balance of power between different groupings within society means that majorities generally have to be constructed. Such constructions involve mutual compromises that effectively attempt to weigh and balance the various rights claimed by different individuals. Thus, collective decisions are not so much a crude sum of various positions as an attempt to regulate and render compatible a range of rights claims.

Legal constitutionalists standardly attack compromise as a mere bargain to give everyone a bit of the action in ways that can be incoherent and unjust – Dworkin's example of 'chequer-board' compromises being a prime instance of this critique.[36] Yet, compromise often goes deeper than such simple attempts to 'split the difference'. Instead, there is a genuine effort to integrate the different concerns and the various weightings they have for those involved.[37] Thus, abortion statutes drawn up by legislatures have not taken the form of a 'chequer-board' compromise whereby, say, abortions are permissible for women born on odd numbered days of the month and disallowed for those whose date of birth is an even number. Rather, they have attempted to balance the different considerations coming from those who stress the right to life of the unborn child and those

---

[35] See too R. Bellamy, *Liberalism and Pluralism: Towards a Politics of Compromise*, London: Routledge, 1999, chs. 4 and 5.

[36] R. Dworkin, *Law's Empire*, London: Fontana, 1986, p. 179.

[37] In *Liberalism and Pluralism*, pp. 101–11 I characterise such compromises as the product of negotiation.

wishing to protect the rights of the pregnant mother.[38] Thus, most of those favouring abortion have nonetheless taken very seriously the worries of the anti-abortionists regarding the sanctity of life, accepting that some account has to be taken of when embryos become viable or develop nervous systems and so on. Likewise, many pro-life advocates make exceptions for cases such as rape, particularly when the woman is under the age of consent, or where the mother's life may be at risk and so on. Henry Richardson has described the granting of gay relationships the status of civil unions if not marriage as a similar 'deep' compromise,[39] in which a mutually acceptable position has been found by a large proportion of proponents and opponents of gay marriage alike.

In both these cases, there has been a certain modification of the substantive position put forward by each of the parties so as to include at least some elements of their adversaries. We can see this effect as resulting from a process of public reasoning that explicitly seeks to canvass all opinions on an issue and encourage the different parties to take them into account and adapt their own views accordingly. For a genuine process of 'hearing the other side' produces compromises that are not only strategic alterations of the means to better pursue self-interested ends but also promote changes to these ends. In this way, the various sides are shown not only a formal equal respect as rights-bearers, but also equal concern with regard to their substantive views of what their rights are and the ways they wish to exercise them.

In so doing, a process of public reasoning of this kind also reinforces the 'rule of law'. As I noted in chapter 2, the essence of the rule of law is the avoidance of arbitrary rule through treating all as equal before the law. I also showed how rule by law is no guarantee of the rule of law in this more demanding sense. Even tyrannical rulers can have an interest in making their rule reasonably predictable in order to create a regime – albeit of an authoritarian kind. Likewise, rich and influential groups can desire to have their privileges secured against both the rulers and the less well-off and powerful. Because rulers need their cooperation and support most of all, and they are best situated to get what they want by extra-legal means if necessary, the wealthy and well-organised will be the first to be provided with legal protection. Hence the primacy, both chronologically and, certainly in the past and in many respects today,

[38] Bellamy, *Liberalism and Pluralism*, p. 113 and the debate in the British House of Commons, 732 *Parliamentary Debates*, HC (5th ser.) (1966) 1067–1166.
[39] Richardson, *Democratic Autonomy*, pp. 147–8.

substantively, of property over other rights. Legality in these cases helps stabilise the position of those concerned and incorporates potential rivals to the ruler's power and authority into the system. However, it also skews the law against the poor and less well-placed. If the law is to serve all citizens equally, therefore, we need something like the process of 'hearing the other side' described above.

This process corresponds to what Habermas has called the radical democratic 'hunch' that in an age of 'completely secularised politics . . . private legal subjects cannot come to enjoy equal individual liberties if they do not *themselves*, in the common exercise of their political autonomy, achieve clarity about justified interests and standards. They themselves must agree on the relevant aspects under which equals should be treated equally and unequals unequally.'[40] Given rival religious and secular claims, no appeal to God or any other conception of the good can overcome the 'circumstances of politics', so that the grounding for equal treatment before the law must come from within politics itself. However, in chapter 3 I dissented from Habermas's own attempt to cash out this insight because he fails fully to apply his radical democratic hunch to the constitution itself. That does not mean nothing can be said about the institutional form of democracy most likely to bring about this result, though. The balance of power, the second quality of political processes looked for by republicans, comes in here.

III The balance of power

Legal constitutionalists have typically conceived the division of power in negative terms, as a way of limiting government. Moreover, they see the chief mechanism for this purpose to be a vertical or hierarchically organised allocation of various competences between either different governmental functions (as in the separation of powers) or levels of government (as in most versions of federalism), with judicial review closely associated with both.[41] By contrast, while republicans acknowledge that constraining the power of any single actor plays a part in avoiding 'arbitrary rule', they also stress the positive role of dividing power in ensuring decision-makers 'hear the other side' – most particularly those of their principals,

---

[40] Habermas, *Between Facts and Norms*, p. xlii.
[41] E.g. E. Barendt, *An Introduction to Constitutional Law*, Oxford: Oxford University Press, 1998, pp. 17, 58.

the citizens.[42] As a result, they have traditionally emphasised the horizontal dispersal of power, achieved to some degree by arrangements that share executive and legislative functions between different and competing groups. It is this horizontal division of power that I shall designate as the 'balance of power'. As we shall see, it supports the procedural account of public reason given above, fostering rights and the rule of law far more effectively than the traditional notion of the 'separation of power'. For while this last works by multiplying veto points to minimise interferences with particular liberties or privileges that nonetheless may entrench domination in the manner outlined in the previous chapter,[43] the balance of power offers incentives to employ political rule in non-dominating ways by being responsive to the interests of citizens. Moreover, it does so in ways closely associated with the workings of actual democracies.

The terms 'balance of power' and 'separation of power' are often used interchangeably today, with the former largely assimilated to the latter. However, though historically aspects of the two have been intertwined, as in certain theories of 'mixed government',[44] not all 'separations' of power serve to 'balance' power in the manner outlined above. Though this is not the place for a full history of either doctrine,[45] a few brief historical details of their origins and the relationship of the one to the other prove helpful in illuminating their different rationales.

From Polybius onwards, the key purpose of the classical doctrine of 'mixed government' was to secure a mixture of the different social classes in a polity.[46] The theory derived from the classification of different political systems into rule by the One, or monarchy, the Few, or aristocracy, and the Many, or democracy. The argument ran that when any one of these three potential power holders ruled alone they would be tempted to do so in arbitrary and self-interested ways, producing a degeneration into tyranny, oligarchy or anarchy respectively. The solution lay in involving

---

[42] Pettit, *Republicanism*, pp. 188–90, Q. Skinner, *Reason and Rhetoric in the Philosophy of Hobbes*, Cambridge: Cambridge University Press, 1996, pp. 15–16.

[43] G. Tsebelis, *Veto Players: How Political Institutions Work*, Princeton: Princeton University Press, 2002.

[44] M. J. C. Vile, *Constitutionalism and the Separation of Powers*, second edition, Indianapolis: Liberty Fund, 1998, pp. 19–20, 36–8.

[45] In addition to Vile, *Constitutionalism*, see W. B. Gwyn, *The Meaning of the Separation of Powers: An Analysis of the Doctrine from its Origin to the Adoption of the United States Constitution*, The Hague: Martinus Nijhoff, 1965.

[46] Vile, *Constitutionalism*, pp. 37, 38; R. Bellamy, 'The Political Form of the Constitution: The Separation of Powers, Rights and Representative Democracy', *Political Studies*, 44 (1996), p. 440.

the other two groups in such a manner that each had to consult the interests of the other. In some versions of the theory, such as Aristotle's, this strategy took the form of ensuring the political officers came from a mixture of social groups,[47] in others, such as Polybius's scheme, the favoured mechanism involved having different political bodies representing different classes and in part performing different functions, so that each had a share in some aspect of the governing process.[48] Either way, the arrangements were aimed at getting a 'balance' between the various interests represented by the different social classes within the polity so as to promote the common good.

A number of assumptions underlay this thesis, many of which few people hold today – or only partially and on somewhat different grounds, thereby restricting the degree and manner in which this approach might be adopted now. These earlier theorists took the metaphor of the 'body politic' seriously. Developing this organic imagery, they regarded the various classes as distinct yet complementary 'parts' – be it 'organs', or in certain later versions, 'humours',[49] or some other aspect of the bodily system. As a result, the aim was to ensure each element performed its respective function and to render them harmonious. The divisions in society were segmental rather than cross-cutting, with competition and conflict viewed as pathological phenomena. A healthy and well-constituted polity would be one where each component collaborated with, and fostered the development of, the others. Balance is achieved by reaching an equilibrium between the parts – in cases of a tripartite division, by ensuring the weaker two outweigh whichever temporarily gets the upper hand.

During the seventeenth century, two intellectual changes – associated with the economic, social and political transformations of this period – introduced an alternative way of understanding 'balance'.[50] First, a mechanical metaphor, inspired by Newtonian physics, challenged and partly displaced the bodily, organic metaphor. Different views and

---

[47] Aristotle, *The Politics*, revised edition, trans. T. A Sinclair, ed. T. J. Saunders, Harmondsworth: Penguin, 1981, bk III, ch. 7, 1279a22–1279b4; bk IV, chs. 2, 3, 8, 9, 1289a26–1290a13, 1293b22–1294b41.

[48] Polybius, *The Rise of the Roman Empire*, trans. I. Scott-Kilvert, ed. F. W. Walbank, Harmondsworth: Penguin, 1979, bk VI, chs. 3, 4, 10, 11–18, pp. 303–5, 310–18.

[49] E.g. N. Machiavelli, *Discorsi sopra la prima deca di Tito Livio*, in *Il Principe e Discorsi*, ed. S. Bertelli, Milan: Feltrinelli, 1960, bk I, ch. 4, p. 137.

[50] D. Wootton, 'Liberty, Metaphor, and Mechanism: "Checks and Balances" and the Origins of Modern Constitutionalism', http://www.ucl.ac.uk/spp/download/seminars/0203/22Check_Bal.doc

interests were now conceptualised as so many forces that might check and counter each other or potentially be combined. Second, notions of ascribed status were replaced by a belief in equality. Instead of incorporating different natural 'classes' of person, the polity was conceived as the artificial creation of a 'people' composed of equal individuals, albeit with differing and often divergent interests that frequently divided them into distinct factions. Balance was no longer a matter of securing the complementary roles of each part of the system by establishing an equilibrium between them. Rather, it became the product of mutual checks between competing groups.

Thus, we have two different conceptions of balance, each based on contrasting ways of understanding social pluralism and conflict. The first view involves a pluralism of distinct parts, with balance ensuring each plays its allotted role. The aim here is to share power in some suitable way that recognises the peculiar qualities of each element. That could involve a horizontal distribution of power, but might equally entail a vertical arrangement – with the 'head' rightfully ruling over the 'body'. Such arrangements have been employed in modern democratic societies. For example, corporatist systems that seek to share power between different occupational groups contain elements of the horizontal version of this model – particularly in their aspiration to achieve a functionally efficient and socially just division of labour.[51] However, there are three problems with this approach. First, it is subject to elitism – there is no incentive for the political agents of the different groups to respond to their respective principals. Second, and relatedly, there will also be few inducements for the various groups genuinely to engage with each other, since any weakening of their position would tend to diminish the power and status of the group *qua* group. Indeed, elites, in particular, have every reason to seek to enhance differences so as to justify greater sectoral autonomy and so increase the number and importance of the positions they can occupy. Finally, such groups, and especially their leaders, will consequently have an interest in hindering the development of divisions and allegiances that cut across such sectoral divides. Often these attempts prove unsuccessful and the system of segmented pluralism collapses. However, where such arrangements continue, they tend either to favour the *status quo*, with

---

[51] The *locus classicus* for this approach is E. Durkheim, *The Division of Labour in Society* (1893), trans. W. R. Halls, London: Macmillan, 1984, e.g. p. lvi; see too his *Professional Ethics and Civic Morals*, London: Routledge, 1957.

each side vetoing measures that might weaken their position, or lead to ever more demands for group autonomy.

These difficulties might be overcome if the different parts really are both compatible and co-dependent, so that all would have an equal concern to search for the optimal form of cooperation to maximise their mutual benefits.[52] However, such social harmony appears unrealistic – at the very least, the capacity for people either to perceive or agree on how it should or could be achieved seems somewhat limited. Even in the historical theories of this model, 'balance' was fragile with a tendency to corruption as one or other of the parts always sought to get the upper hand. In real situations, such as the consociational arrangements employed to accommodate societies deeply divided along cultural and linguistic lines, many of the problems outlined above have been present[53] – even if a case can be made that in some circumstances no broadly acceptable alternative is available.[54]

The second view offers a quite different and, in many ways, more attractive conception of pluralism. On this account, diversity springs as much from the choices of individuals as from innate differences between them. As a result, there is a multiplicity of groups, many with overlapping and occasionally cross-cutting membership. For example, as well as rich and poor, there are also Catholics and Protestants, socialists and conservatives – and though there can be rich conservative Protestants and poor socialist Catholics, there are also poor Protestant socialists and rich Catholic conservatives, and so on. As Dahl has shown, pluralism of this kind has been a feature of modern dynamic societies, providing a precondition for the polyarchical distribution of power that lies behind the development of democracy.[55] For this type of pluralism both raises the issue of the tyranny of the majority in its new and distinctively modern democratic form, and provides its remedy.

---

[52] Precisely this supposition underpinned Durkheim's argument. See his *Leçons de sociologie*, Paris: Presses Universitaires de Paris, 1950, pp. 105, 137 and the critical discussion in R. Bellamy, *Liberalism and Modern Society*, Cambridge: Polity, 1992, pp. 99–102.

[53] See the criticism in B. Barry, 'Political Accommodation and Consociational Democracy', *British Journal of Political Science*, 5 (1975), pp. 502–3 and Bellamy, *Liberalism and Pluralism*, pp. 126–8.

[54] A. Lijphart, *The Politics of Accommodation: Pluralism and Democracy in the Netherlands*, Berkeley: University of California Press, 1968.

[55] R. A. Dahl, *Democracy and its Critics*, New Haven: Yale University Press, 1989, chs. 15, 17 and 18.

The notion of the majority as the 'most people' only emerged at the end of the seventeenth century.[56] Prior to that, the people – meaning either all members of the polity or, more usually, merely the 'popular' element – were treated as a single body. Thus, 'popular' tyranny within the segmental account was when the 'democratic' element predominated over the 'aristocratic'. Some accounts of republicanism took over this language to treat the 'people' as having a single will, with the aim of popular self-rule being to discover and give expression to an underlying popular consensus.[57] However, from the very beginning there have been alternative and more sophisticated accounts that acknowledged that among equal citizens different and often conflicting factions would exist of the kinds described above.[58] The solution to the new problem this circumstance posed was a novel kind of balance that exploited the new mechanical metaphor – namely that of self-correcting checks, as in a watch or some other self-regulating machine.[59] The equilibrium of the segmental model of balance is a largely static one, with collapse and corruption following should the parts get out of kilter. By contrast, this system allows for a dynamic equilibrium deriving from competition. As a famous early attempt to exploit the new mechanism for political purposes was to put it, 'ambition must be made to counteract ambition',[60] so that (as Montesquieu had remarked, without accurately explaining how) 'power checks power'.[61]

Two features of this modern republican account of balance need stressing. First, it is a horizontal distribution of power. It involves either rival aspirants for power, as in competing parties, or rival centres of power, as in competing governments in certain aspects of federal arrangements. Second, and most importantly, it offers the link between principal and agent that is lacking even in horizontal versions of the segmental model. For the rival power seekers or centres must recruit the support of a majority of the people to govern. Because the nature of pluralism within modern dynamic societies is such as to consist in coalitions of minorities, there will always be the opportunity for rivals to bid for each other's support. In this respect, as Madison noted, the operation of the political system follows that of the market – both were mechanisms for 'supplying, by opposite

---

[56] Wootton, 'Liberty, Metaphor, and Mechanism', pp. 23–5.

[57] Roughly speaking, this can be viewed as the strand found in the French republican tradition of Rousseau and Sieyes.

[58] In certain respects this is the Machiavellian strand that eventually gets picked up by Madison.

[59] Wootton, 'Liberty, Metaphor, and Mechanism', p. 19.   [60] *Federalist* 51.

[61] C.-L. de S. Montesquieu, *De l'esprit des lois*, 2 vols., Paris: Garnier-Flammarion, 1979, vol. I, bk XI, ch. 4, p. 293.

and rival interests, the defect of better motives'.[62] As Madison had learnt from Hume, the new connotations of 'balance' appeared nowhere more evident than in the economy and the dynamic equilibrium of the 'balance of trade'.[63] However, the American appreciated how just as the competition for profit drives rival producers and providers to supply the wants of customers at an optimal price, so the competition for power operates in an analogous way and encourages politicians to reduce their political rents in order to supply benefits to citizens without unduly raising taxes or imposing other costs upon them, such as reducing their liberties. Balance so conceived offers incentives for the different parties to 'hear the other side' and build winning electoral coalitions that are missing in the old, segmental, account of balance.

How does this mechanism relate to the separation of powers, on the one hand, and the rule of law and rights, on the other? In many respects, the separation of powers emerged as an adaptation of the segmental account of pluralism and balance, and shares a number of its problems.[64] Indeed, some versions of these latter accounts aligned the three orders of society with different functions of government. Elements of this genealogy can be found in Montesquieu's classic description of the separation of powers.[65] When such notions of ascribed status were overturned, the functional division was seen as a possible means of providing a system of balance within a classless society. The main rationale of this scheme was to prevent those charged with the formulation of the law from being responsible for its interpretation, enforcement and application. As a result, legislators would have an incentive to make laws that apply equally to all, with these same laws then binding the executive and judiciary. This arrangement supposedly prevents rule being exercised in an arbitrary and self-serving way. However, there are three problems that stand in the way of its performing this task, all of which relate to the shortcomings I noted above with regard to the segmental version of the balance of power.

The first, which is often commented on, is the conceptual and practical difficulty of distinguishing the different functions.[66] When judges, for example, adjudicate on which rules do or do not apply in particular cases, they also often end up setting precedents that in effect constitute new rules. Likewise, officials frequently have to create rules in the course of

---

[62] *Federalist* 51.   [63] Wootton, 'Liberty, Metaphor, and Mechanism', p. 19.

[64] Vile, *Constitutionalism*, pp. 36–52; Bellamy, 'The Political Form of the Constitution', pp. 442–7.

[65] Montesquieu, *De l'esprit des lois*, bk XI, ch. 6, pp. 294–302.

[66] Vile, *Constitutionalism*, pp. 318–21.

implementing a given law that in turn come to take on a life of their own. Legislators, too, are inevitably concerned with how the laws they frame will be interpreted and applied to specific cases. Thus, each branch of government engages in all three functions to some degree or another. Indeed, the more complex the activities of government, the more interrelated they are likely to become. As even defenders of the doctrine acknowledge, the separation of powers is at best 'partial'.[67]

Second, even if such functional separation is possible, it need not lead to a check on arbitrary power. As I observed above, the thesis originally foresaw the different functions being performed by different sections of society. However, the separation will be undermined if those controlling the various agencies all belong to the same group.[68] In parliamentary systems, where the executive emerges from the largest grouping in the legislature, separation of these two branches will prove difficult. Even in presidential systems it is not unusual for the president's party to have a majority in the legislature. Meanwhile, it may also be the case that the judiciary share the ideological convictions or interests of both president and legislature. In which case, all three functions are effectively held in the same hands even if the personnel are nominally different.

Third, and most important, the separation of powers fails to provide incentives that ensure these agents serve their principals – the citizens.[69] This functional separation involves a vertical division of power. As we saw, unlike horizontal divisions of power, there is no competitive element. In consequence, each functional part can either increase its political rents or shirk its responsibilities and displace the costs on to the others. This possibility is particularly present in the case of the judicial branch, which has almost no mechanism for rendering it accountable for its decisions. Thus, it may enhance its power through the recognition of new sets of rights, without having to bear any responsibility for the impact of its decisions on other social policies or potential increases in taxation. Indeed, to the extent each separate branch of government retains autonomy over its own separate functional sphere it remains able to act arbitrarily on matters within its competence.

[67] Barendt, *An Introduction to Constitutional Law*, p. 15.

[68] As Madison noted, it was necessary not just to have 'constitutional means' but also 'personal motives' to resist the encroachments of the others (*Federalist* 48). Yet, as Dahl observed, this call for incentives to structure the exercise of power proved more rhetoric than reality (R. A. Dahl, *A Preface to Democratic Theory*, Chicago: University of Chicago Press, 1956, pp. 30–32).

[69] See G. Brennan and A. Hamlin, 'A Revisionist View of the Separation of Powers', *Journal of Theoretical Politics*, 6 (1994), pp. 351–2.

As a result of these three weaknesses, the separation of powers provides no compelling reason of itself for the different functions of government to 'hear the other side' – be that each other, or the people they are supposed to serve. The motivation comes from outside the system, from the people themselves. Moreover, this effect is generated by the horizontal 'balancing' mechanism offered by the competition for power. To attain and stay in office, politicians need to recruit and retain quite diverse support. Even within the legislature, the executive normally has to mollify numerous factions within their own party representing a broad cross-section of public opinion. As such, they are obliged to engage in the process of public reasoning and compromise described above.

Any functional separation will dilute this 'balancing' effect. At best it will force one set of power holders to share that power with another set. In itself, that need not mean they use it well and in the interests of the generality of citizens. Indeed, given that separation creates an externality between the two or more separated bodies and prevents its internalisation, the likelihood is that it may work against their interests. For there are no incentives within this structure to ensure power holders perform better than each other – merely that they do not perform so badly that they delegitimise or break the system, or at least their role within it.[70] Each branch has the option of placing both the blame and costs for poor decisions – or those it would rather not take – on the other, while selectively ignoring those decisions when it suits their purpose.[71] When outright conflict arises, the default solution will be to a return to the *status quo*. Small wonder that exponents of this model are driven to focusing on quasi-revolutionary 'constitutional moments' rather than incremental reform as a source of progressive change.

In fact, the evolution of the US Supreme Court's decisions reveals the very disfunctionalities predicted above. On a whole range of controversial issues – from abortion to discrimination in education – Congress has shifted both responsibility and possible blame onto the Court.[72] The Court has generally assisted this process by relaxing requirements

---

[70] This is at least one reason for the Court's following the polls and more generally going with the flow of social and political opinion – for evidence see M. Tushnet, *Taking the Constitution Away from the Courts*, Princeton: Princeton University Press, 1999, pp. 134–5, 147–51.

[71] As J. M. Pickerell notes, *Constitutional Deliberation in Congress*, Durham, NC: Duke University Press, 2004, ch. 2, on the policy issues Congress is keen to decide, adverse Court decisions tend to be more like speed bumps or detours than road blocks.

[72] M. Graber, 'The Nonmajoritarian Difficulty: Legislative Deference to the Judiciary', *Studies in American Political Development*, 7 (1993), pp. 35–73.

of standing and justiciability, and allowing greater use of class actions and *amicus curiae* briefs – thereby extending its power into the broad domain of social policy.[73] However, neither those promoting the actions – be they conservative or progressive groups – nor the judges themselves have an incentive to 'hear the other side' in ways that ensure the direct and indirect impact of their proposals or decisions on other policies and people get considered. Consequently, they will be less rather than more likely to deliberate. Major issues, such as the legality of abortion, can turn on a single nominee – a rarity in any legislature. When the winner in the Court takes all, then the judicial majority may prove tyrannous indeed. For example, campaigns for welfare rights and campaign finance reform have both been derailed through adverse Court decisions declaring them 'unconstitutional'.

No doubt the Justices all believe they are conscientiously defending individual rights under the Constitution and so ought not to be responsive or accountable to popular opinion. Yet when they present competing principles and interpretations, all capable of being given a degree of reasoned defence and reflecting similar positions in the wider population, then rights prove ill-served if victory for one side can arise without considering the others. Far from being inimical to rights, the mechanism of balance encourages an attention not just to rights but also the rule of law. Rulers accept the need to make their rule both predictable and equitable – the two qualities of law-like rule – when their rule depends on the voluntary compliance of diverse groups of their citizens.[74] As we saw in chapter 2, ordinary people want predictability in the political rules so that they can act autonomously and plan ahead. However, politicians also value this quality because it allows them to govern increasingly complex societies in an efficient and regular manner. They cannot anticipate every situation and rule effectively using *ad hoc* measures. They too need a stable legal framework that can regulate the majority of social interactions. Apart from anything else, it means they can delegate the vast majority of mundane, everyday decisions to various officials – including an independent judiciary – so that they can focus on the issues that interest them or are of most salience for people. Most importantly, as the competition for power becomes institutionalised, rulers acquire an interest in the rules of the political game being similarly predictable and stable.

[73] R. J. McKeever, *Raw Judicial Power? The Supreme Court and American Society*, second edition, Manchester: Manchester University Press, 1995, pp. 18–22.

[74] S. Holmes, 'Lineages of the Rule of Law', in J. M. Maravall and A. Przeworski (eds.), *Democracy and the Rule of Law*, Cambridge: Cambridge University Press, 2003, p. 30.

Meanwhile, laws become more equitable and attentive to rights the more pluralistic a society becomes, so that rulers have to engage with a broad range of roughly equal groups all possessing a degree of political leverage.[75] It is no accident that the most progressive periods of social reform in modern times have coincided with mass mobilisation for war, when rulers had to convince citizens of the value of fighting for their country. In many countries, war also stimulated the extension of the franchise to workers and especially to women, who now became an acknowledged part of the domestic labour force. More generally, citizens are more likely to submit to an authority in which they regard themselves as having a part – however small that may be.

Of course, citizens will never have absolutely equal influence over rulers, despite acquiring equal votes. The better organised and financed will always do better than the poor and disorganised, though the desire to avoid widespread popular unrest should never be discounted. Changes in agendas, problems and resources will favour different groups and alter the political balance between the socially and economically strong and weak. The key, though, must always be to multiply the groups with which power holders have to engage, forcing them to 'hear' and 'harken to' as many sides as possible.

In many respects, it is as important, if not more so, to ensure political elites not only have to compete with each other but also with other elites in the economy and society. For example, the significance of the separation of church and state as a constraint on rulers is often lost in talk of state neutrality. In fact, its chief merit lies in preventing governments from claiming a monopoly of moral authority and forcing them to contend with criticism from competing moral elites.

The existence of a plurality of competing public and private agencies also helps overcome two worries with any system of checks and balances. The first worry is that such checking may subvert the independence of a given branch of government or institution. For example, it is often feared that checks by the executive on the judiciary undermine their neutrality, or that government regulation of higher education subverts the autonomy of universities, thereby endangering academic objectivity. Yet, as we saw when exploring the doctrine of the separation of powers, independence can also mean the body concerned remains free to exert arbitrary power within its sphere. Multiple checks overcome the dual dangers of either undermining independence or having too much of

[75] Ibid., p. 49.

it.[76] By being checked by numerous other agents and agencies, an institution is prevented from becoming so much under the sway of any one of them. It can be responsive without becoming dominated. Thus, by having a variety of sources of public and private funding, universities can be made responsive to social and student pressures about their role and research agenda, without losing the capacity to reject certain pressures or becoming dominated by any one agency.

The second worry with checking by another body is that it can be too heavy-handed, especially if it tackles a core power of the agent or agency concerned.[77] The stakes involved may be such that the penalty would have to be extreme to stand a chance of deterring the relevant behaviour. Even then – as harsh penalties in the area of crime reveal – it may not work. The key to changing behaviour is to make it habitual and to alter the moral mindset that leads to corrupt, criminal or other, lesser, kinds of undesirable and dominating behaviour in the first place. Again, multiple pressure points soften the blow but over time offer a more effective means for bringing slow but continuous pressure for change. For example, when an unelected body, such as the judiciary, checks unprofessional behaviour by politicians their action can lead to accusations of their subverting the electoral process and so undermine the legitimacy and effectiveness of their authority – especially if the penalty they impose involves removing or suspending the offenders from office. However, if their role is simply naming and shaming, with the penalty decided by the elected peers or even the electorate, then such accusations have less force. As a result, though the regulating body may be weaker, it can nonetheless make a greater impact.

What may be designated as the modern conception of the balance of powers uses the dynamic pluralism and disagreements of democratic societies to promote rather than subvert constitutional values. As we have seen, in the older, segmental, account of pluralism and balance sub-groups among the people always posed a threat to social harmony and the public interest. They formed so many potentially subversive 'factions'. The 'majority' constituted a particularly dangerous and potentially tyrannous faction, involving either the dominance of the 'popular' element over the monarchy and aristocracy, or the triumph of the 'mob' over individuals – in many accounts the allegedly most virtuous and

---

[76] See J. Braithwaite, 'On Speaking Softly and Carrying Big Sticks: Neglected Dimensions of a Republican Separation of Powers', *University of Toronto Law Journal*, 47 (1997), pp. 342–4.
[77] Ibid., pp. 314–16.

industrious part of the society, whose property the masses sought to plunder. Counter- majoritarian checks therefore seemed in order, produced above all through vertical divisions of power such as the classic doctrine of the separation of powers. Yet, if – as came to be the case – we see these groups as also so many factions, then this supposed cure may actually merely exacerbate the disease by allowing minorities to dominate. By contrast, the competitive account of balance obliges minorities to hear and combine with each other to construct majorities – as such it promotes the procedural process of public reasoning discussed in the previous section.

The key, of course, is to institutionalise this process of balance. As perceptive constitutional theorists saw, the modern democratic form of competing parties does just that. Government is obliged to confront the prospect of continuous opposition and the possibility of being ousted from power on a regular basis. The Madison of *Federalist* 10 may have provided the *locus classicus* of the attack on factions, but as he observed – and indeed helped promote – the party system in the United States, he altered his mind.[78] Reflecting back on the constitutional debates, he now remarked how 'no free Country has ever been without parties'. The 'right of suffrage' was 'a fundamental Article of Republican Constitutions' and had as its corollary 'that the vital principle of republican government is the *lex majoris partis*, the will of the majority'. The equal right to vote not only made 'the sweeping denunciation of majority Governments' something 'every friend of Republican Government ought to raise his voice against', but also rendered illegitimate his previous advocacy of multiplying veto points for what he now realised were best viewed as minority vested interests. Devices such as the Electoral College, for electing the US President, or even the separation of powers belong to the era of ascribed status. At best, they involve deference – which we saw in chapter 4 is one of the most insidious forms of domination – at worst, they hinder progressive measures to promote the public interest. Given that parties were inevitable in the age of mass politics, the most appropriate mechanism for overcoming their drawbacks was 'by making one party a check on the other'. How far contemporary party democracies offer such a system of checks, and the ways they might be improved, form the subject of the next chapter.

---

[78] R. A. Dahl, *How Democratic is the American Constitution?*, New Haven: Yale University Press, 2002, pp. 31–7, from which the following quotes from Madison come.

Conclusion

This chapter has explored the underlying rationale behind the two main political mechanisms for promoting constitutional values in a manner consistent with showing citizens equal concern and respect in circumstances of reasonable political disagreement: public reason and the balance of power. I have argued that a procedural version of the first and a competitive and horizontal version of the second prove the only plausible candidates. Moreover, both have a *prima facie* fit with actually existing democratic party politics. The topic of the next and final chapter is appropriately a fuller examination of the constitutional and constitutive role played by real democracy.

6

Bringing together norms and forms: the democratic constitution

Chapters 4 and 5 described respectively the underlying norms of a political constitutionalism and the most appropriate forms for it to take. In each case, I suggested that the norms and related forms are best met through procedures similar to those associated with democracy. This chapter takes this suggestion further and argues that actually existing democracies prove both constitutional and constitutive through embodying the republican principles of non-domination and political equality, on the one hand, and political mechanisms that ensure suitable kinds of public reasoning and the balance of power, on the other.

I noted in the opening section of chapter 3 how legal constitutionalists have tended to advocate apolitical models of deliberative democracy. Indeed, there has been a propensity among normative theorists more generally to dismiss the democratic systems that actually govern us as at best devoid of normative value, and at worst positively perilous to the norms most democrats espouse.[1] Hence the desire to constitutionalise these norms and to advocate deliberative conceptions of democracy that reflect highly idealised conceptions of judicial reasoning.[2] However, a running theme of this book has been the unavoidability of the political dimension of legal and constitutional decision-making. By contrast to much contemporary political theory, therefore, I want to explore and

---

[1] As I noted in the Introduction, Roberto Unger has spoken eloquently of the 'discomfort with democracy' – by which he means real, party based majoritarian democracy rather than the deliberative ideal of a 'polite conversation among gentlemen in an eighteenth-century drawing room' – as being one of the 'dirty little secrets of contemporary jurisprudence' in *What Should Legal Analysis Become?*, London: Verso, 1996, p. 72. See too J. Waldron, 'Dirty Little Secret', *Columbia Law Review*, 98 (1998), pp. 510–30.

[2] E.g. J. Rawls, *Political Liberalism*, New York: Columbia University Press, 1993, Lecture 6 and J. Cohen, 'Deliberation and Democratic Legitimacy', in S. Benhabib (ed.), *Democracy and Difference: Contesting the Boundaries of the Political*, Princeton: Princeton University Press, 1996, pp. 98–9, 105.

extol the normative qualities of real democracy. Indeed, the very aspects many legal and political theorists are apt to denigrate – its adversarial and competitive qualities, its use of compromise and majority rule to generate agreement, the role of political parties – are those I seek to praise. Deliberation, consensus, direct citizen participation through social movements, consultative juries and other mechanisms besides the ballot box – these all have their place, but a secondary one. If constitutional values are to be adequately realised and protected in the everyday circumstances of political disagreement that confront us, then we need to adopt the methods of real rather than ideal democratic politics.

The constitutional claims of actually existing democratic processes lie in their consistency with the norms and forms outlined in chapters 4 and 5 respectively. To assess how far they do meet these standards, I shall explore each in turn, summarising relevant elements of the argument thus far along the way. I conclude by looking at how electoral democracy relates to the process of law-making and executive scrutiny in legislatures.

I Non-domination and political equality

Chapter 4 showed how political equality was an intrinsic component of freedom as non-domination and could only be realised fully within some form of democracy. As I noted, this argument for linking individual freedom and democracy needs to be distinguished from another view popular among republicans that bases its case for democratic participation not on freedom from mastery but on freedom as self-mastery or autonomy.[3] This derivation proves problematic.[4] As we saw, liberals have challenged republicans to explain why the public liberty of participation is worth the sacrifice of numerous private liberties. After all, political junkies apart, most people tend to be more engaged with the latter. They would rather cultivate their gardens than the public good. Of course, their capacity to do so depends on a public framework of suitable private rights. Yet, without a highly unlikely complete consensus on what every particular of that public framework should be, there will always be tensions and occasional

---

[3] E.g. M. Sandel, *Democracy's Discontent: America in Search of a Public Philosophy*, Cambridge, MA: Harvard University Press, 1996, pp. 9, 274.
[4] See A. Weale, *Democracy*, Basingstoke: Macmillan, 1999, ch. 4 and T. Christiano, *The Rule of the Many: Fundamental Issues in Democratic Theory*, Oxford: Westview, 1996, ch. 1, who influence what follows.

conflicts between an individual's liberty and the collective agreements that give rise to the public arrangements necessary to secure it.[5]

As a result of these difficulties, the link between individual liberty conceived of as autonomy and democracy is a tenuous one. It could be argued that under majority rule democracy maximises autonomy because it encourages the greatest possible number of people to live under laws they have chosen.[6] But this argument implicitly acknowledges that for some, at least, democracy will limit autonomy. Indeed, we shall see how even the members of a majority coalition do not get all that they want but must necessarily compromise with others. So the argument that democracy is an expression of individual autonomy only proves coherent on the basis of a highly contested positive view of liberty, in which political participation serves as a vital component of individual self-realisation and leads to a consensus on the common good. Unsurprisingly, most liberals have regarded such linkages with suspicion.[7] They concede that 'self-government may, on the whole, provide a better guarantee of the preservation of civil liberties than other regimes' but they claim there is 'no necessary connection between individual liberty and democracy', at least so far as negative liberty is concerned, and that a liberal-minded despot might allow his subjects more freedom, though less political and possibly other kinds of equality, than a democracy.[8]

As we saw in chapter 4, these problems and conclusions about the relationship of freedom to democracy prove unfounded in the case of freedom as non-domination.[9] The aim of this conception of liberty is to give everyone the status of a 'free person' in which nobody holds sway over them as their 'superior'. This condition involves equality between rulers and ruled when making collective decisions about the public arrangements necessary to social life. Only under some such system of collective self-rule will their interests and opinions be treated with equal concern and respect in

---

[5] This difficulty also bedevils arguments by self-styled non-republicans to derive arguments for democracy from autonomy – e.g. D. Held, *Models of Democracy*, third edition, Cambridge: Polity Press, 2006, ch. 10.

[6] R. A. Dahl, *Democracy and its Critics*, New Haven: Yale University Press, 1989, pp. 138–9.

[7] E.g. F. Oppenheim, *Political Concepts: A Reconstruction*, Oxford: Blackwell, 1981, p. 92 and Richardson, *Democratic Autonomy: Public Reasoning about the Ends of Policy*, Oxford: Oxford University Press, 2002, pp. 58–61.

[8] I. Berlin, 'Two Concepts of Liberty', in his *Four Essays on Liberty*, Oxford: Oxford University Press, 1969, pp. 129–31.

[9] See too Q. Skinner, 'The Paradoxes of Political Liberty', in S. M. McMurrin (ed.), *The Tanner Lectures on Human Values*, vol. VII, Cambridge: Cambridge University Press, 1986, pp. 225–50.

ways that are non-dominating. For only under some such system are they regarded as autonomous individuals and their different views given equal weight. Such equal weighting, though, might be interpreted as occurring in two divergent ways: either by promoting outcomes that maximise people's liberty and welfare equally, or by being an equitable process for deciding between individuals' often competing claims. Democracy has been justified in terms of both these goals. In what follows, I shall defend the latter view. It offers not only the most plausible rationale but also one that reinforces the intrinsic as opposed to merely instrumental relationship of democracy to non-domination. The scene will then have been set for showing why equal votes within majoritarian, competitive party democracies offers a compelling realisation of this ideal.

The equal consideration of interests and the circumstances of politics

The crucial reason for relating non-domination to democracy in this way lies in the need to adopt a procedural, or input, rather than a substantive, or output, approach to equality of concern and respect to meet the challenge of the 'circumstances of politics' – the condition of having to make necessary collective decisions where there is disagreement about their scope and content. The unavoidability of having at least some collective arrangements to facilitate social interaction explains why citizens have an interest in the existence of a public sphere that possesses non-dominating characteristics even if they hold a potentially competing interest in pursuing personal projects. Living in some sort of political regime is simply inescapable. However, this condition need not lead to everyone having an interest in possessing an equal share in shaping public life. If it were possible to identify criteria for organising these collective arrangements so that they unequivocally showed citizens substantive equal concern and respect, then trustworthy experts could rule. As we saw in chapter 4, having experts decide such matters might still raise the worry of enlightened despotism, where the potential for domination exists and citizens lose self-respect through their views counting for less than others. There is also the prudential fear that once appointed these guardians might abuse their position. Yet, these worries might be met by creating fair and open contestatory or consultative mechanisms rather than through giving all an equal share in the authoring of decisions.[10] It would only make sense

---

[10] As I noted, Philip Pettit, *Republicanism: A Theory of Freedom and Government*, second edition, Oxford: Clarendon Press, 1999, pp. 183–6, essentially adopts this argument.

to do the latter if it would contribute in some way to reaching the desired substantive result. Developing points made in chapter 4, I shall argue that reasonable disagreement about which collective arrangements might achieve this outcome makes such approaches unworkable. Consequently, the link between democracy and non-domination rests on its being an equitable process rather than because it necessarily produces decisions that all consider substantively equitable.

Let's work through this argument step by step.[11] We need collective decisions because we share a world with others, many of whose activities have knock-on effects for our own. As a result, all but anarchists accept we have an interest in there being certain collective arrangements to regulate our social interaction and promote various public goods. However, relative scarcity means these goods will be unable to be so organised that they can satisfy everyone's interest in a given form of collective provision. Therefore, to the extent citizens view each other as social equals, as non-domination requires, they will want these arrangements to treat their interests with equal consideration. Now, if we can show that the only way in which our interest in collective arrangements can be married with all citizens being shown equal concern and respect is through giving them an equal share in decision-making, we will have linked democracy and non-domination.

I noted above that some theorists suggest this condition can be met by ensuring governments only promote those arrangements and policies that aim at the common good.[12] The underlying rationale behind this proposal is that power holders ought to be concerned with the public welfare rather than their own. On the one hand, this limitation aims at protecting a realm of privacy. On the other hand, citizens want governments to focus on fostering everyone's welfare rather than that of the power holders and their influential friends. Both limitations seem well designed to protect against arbitrary rule. The first protects against purely 'nosy' preferences, whereby we could be allowed to interfere in another's activities not because our well-being is affected but simply because we think they ought to act differently. The second tries to guard against rulers using their position in a self-interested way. Yet, as we shall see, pervasive reasonable disagreement about the collective good makes each of these arguments deeply problematic, rendering it impossible to show in

---

[11] What follows draws on the excellent discussion in Christiano, *The Rule of the Many*, ch. 2 and his 'The Authority of Democracy', *Journal of Political Philosophy*, 12 (2004), pp. 266–90.

[12] Notably Pettit, *Republicanism*, p. 56.

a non-arbitrary manner which arrangements are truly collective in either of these senses.

All attempts at defining the collective good in an appropriate sense, including those that employ some version of democracy to do so, face overwhelming technical and normative difficulties.[13] The size, dynamism and diversity of modern societies make such decisions technically problematic because social activity is so complex, open and hard to predict. Even when experts agree on ends they will invariably disagree about the appropriate means. Indeed, unless they are omniscient about people's present and future interests and the ways they might be most efficiently met, then – as critics of economic planning have remarked – their interferences may actually inhibit rather than foster the individual initiatives whereby people discover and elaborate upon their ends and the ways they might be satisfied. Normative disagreements about which ends and means are morally desirable or acceptable prove even more intractable. Within pluralist societies, people are going to have very varied life experiences. In any case, humans are diverse and flourish in different ways and environments. Consequently, they bring very different judgements to bear when considering how society might be best organised, and will often have extraordinarily dissimilar interests. These assorted views and interests may frequently prove either logically or, given the relative scarcity of resources and the limits of human knowledge and ingenuity, contingently incompatible. Moreover, because of the variety of conflicting plausible moral and empirical judgements we may bring to these clashes, these contesting judgements will frequently appear incommensurable as well. As a result, it will often be impossible to come up with a non-controversial formula for ensuring the interests of each and every person receive equal concern and respect in a given conception of the collective good. Indeed, all but procedural views of democracy offer arbitrary accounts of equal concern and respect.

Equal outcomes: democracy and welfarist views of non-arbitrary rule

These difficulties clearly arise in what might be seen as the simplest version of avoiding domination by pursuing a collective good that gives equal consideration to the interests of each individual – namely, the promotion of equal well-being.[14] The difficulty with this argument is that it depends

---

[13] See Christiano, *The Rule of the Many*, pp. 61–71 and 'The Authority of Democracy', pp. 272–3; Weale, *Democracy*, p. 57.

[14] Christiano, *The Rule of the Many*, pp. 62–9.

on making interpersonal comparisons that, because of the problems given above, are likely to arouse considerable disagreement. For a start, it is going to be impossible technically to grasp all the interests involved in any given set of complex circumstances. Their sheer number and diversity makes matters hard enough, straining the capacity of anyone to understand what the overall interests of all individuals might be. Add to this technical dilemma the normative problems noted earlier. No matter how unbiased, people will always be inclined to view the interests of others through their own. Each person's experience is necessarily limited, and however hard they try to put themselves in the shoes of others they will tend to do so in ways that assume they are more or less similar to themselves. Likewise, they will be liable to underestimate the damage caused by the curtailment or suppression of interests different to theirs. Even if one could get round this difficulty, the fact that individuals are constantly learning about and refining their understanding of the good, redefining their interests and altering their preferences accordingly, means that our knowledge will always be incomplete. As the Austrian market theorists noted,[15] ensuring equal well-being may also involve continuous and intrusive interferences with others in order to redistribute the benefits of one individual's activities to others, undermining individual responsibility and incentives in the process.

Note that these problems arise with both arguments for limiting government to the pursuit of the collective good outlined earlier – that of securing a realm of privacy as well as the promotion of everyone's welfare, not just power holders. Think of the controversies surrounding the application of Mill's harm principle.[16] These involve both the technical difficulties alluded to, which make it hard to know what the consequences of any action might be for others, and the normative problems when agreeing on what constitutes harm in the first place. As I remarked, people with different moral experiences often fail to appreciate the impact their activities may have on others. Thus, religious believers often criticise secularists (no doubt correctly) for ignoring the hurt caused by attacks on their faith, yet they in their turn rarely acknowledge the offence the teaching or expression of religious views may cause those who do not share them.

Several theorists have tried to avoid these problems by advocating apparently less demanding views of how governments might be brought

---

[15] A. Shand, *Free Market Morality: The Political Economy of the Austrian School*, New York: Routledge, 1990.
[16] J. S. Mill, 'On Liberty', in *Utilitarianism, On Liberty and Representative Government*, London: Dent, 1972, p. 72.

to track each individual's interests via an account of the collective welfare. These accounts depend not so much on the content of the public good as the form it takes. Moreover, some have proposed variants of democracy for achieving this purpose. These arguments include having governments maximise the collective welfare, limiting them so they act only to advance each person's interests or welfare, or ensuring they consider solely those aspects of people's views or interests that can be generalised.[17] That all these proposals could count as plausible ways of linking the equal consideration of interests with the collective good is in itself an indication of the difficulties such a project faces. However, that they fail to prevent arbitrary rule also means that they cannot serve as convincing arguments for why non-domination involves an equal share in democratic decision-making.

The first argument is essentially utilitarian, and like the attempt to pursue equal well-being involves making inevitably contentious interpersonal comparisons. Using democratic voting as a method for determining those policies that favour the greatest good of the greatest number potentially offers a rough and ready way round this quandary.[18] However, there are notorious problems – discussed in the next section – in aggregating the preferences of individuals into a social preference. There is also the difficulty that the utilitarian goals of maximising total or average welfare can be compatible with sacrificing a few to the greater good of the many, thereby dominating some – potentially even enslaving them – for the benefit of the rest. This possibility serves as the basis for fears of the tyranny of the majority, to which we shall also return.

Some social choice theorists have proposed avoiding this dilemma by insisting on all public decisions being made unanimously, thereby ensuring that no collective measure gets adopted the advantages of which did not outweigh the costs no matter how they might end up being distributed.[19] At one level, unanimity might appear to be a very pure form of democracy. However, as I have remarked in earlier chapters, counter-majoritarian devices such as this are biased towards the *status quo*. Unless we provide for pre-existing baseline conditions that involve no domination that favours,

---

[17] See the useful discussion in Richardson, *Democratic Autonomy*, pp. 42–7, on which what follows draws.

[18] Most famously, this utilitarian defence is that offered by James Mill's *Essay on Government* (1820).

[19] J. M. Buchanan and G. Tullock, *The Calculus of Consent: Logical Foundations of Constitutional Democracy*, Ann Arbor: University of Michigan Press, 1965, pp. 12, 14 and J. M. Buchanan and R. A. Musgrave, *Public Finance and Public Choice: Two Contrasting Visions of the State*, Cambridge, MA: MIT Press, 1999, p. 21.

either directly or indirectly, private agents or agencies, and which the proposed government action may be directed at removing, then unanimity will entrench rather than guard against arbitrary rule.[20] Meanwhile, the unanimity requirement also overlooks one of the central dilemmas of pluralism – the impossibility, given the problems of incompatibility and incommensurability, of accommodating all worthwhile values and interests in a single social world.

Finally, the common good has been identified with some form of generality. Rousseau offers the *locus classicus* for the democratic and egalitarian version of this argument.[21] Whereas the 'will of all', being the product of self-interest and factionalism, could give rise to the tyranny of the majority, he claimed the 'general will' produces decisions that treat all as equals by serving their common interests. A public good, like the environment, can appear to have this structure, at least in principle. If, for example, citizens consider when voting what it would be like should a given piece of self-serving polluting behaviour, such as being able to drive their car in the inner city at rush hour, be generally adopted, then it would probably lose its attraction as a collective as opposed to a purely personal option. By contrast, promoting clean air offers a general benefit that can be enjoyed equally by all. Even so, as Rousseau conceded, to reach such happy results it will almost certainly be necessary to screen out quite a lot of potentially conflicting considerations of the kind any full account of such decisions invariably raises, and assume a background of rough social equality that excludes free-riding.

On the whole, the generality requirement rules out either too little or too much to be a reliable and non-contestable way of identifying the common good. As we saw in chapter 2, generality often serves as a formal criterion for the rule of law. The idea is to ensure laws apply equally to all and are not aimed at persecuting particular individuals. The difficulty is that rules can be general in form and still discriminate against groups, such as Jews in Nazi Germany. Yet, sometimes discrimination is warranted because there can be relevant differences that mean some people may need to be treated differently in certain circumstances. As a result, more

---

[20] As Douglas Rae has shown, given that for all sorts of reasons we may be as likely to want to change the *status quo* as maintain it, majority rule rather than a unanimity rule offers a more accurate solution to Buchanan and Tullock's choice problem. See D. Rae, 'Decision-Rules and Individual Values in Constitutional Choice', *American Political Science Review*, 63 (1969), pp. 40–56 and 'The Limits of Consensual Decision', *American Political Science Review*, 69 (1975), pp. 1270–94.

[21] J. J. Rousseau, *The Social Contract and Discourses*, trans. G. D. H. Cole, London: Dent, 1973, p. 185.

substantive versions of the generality requirement, that try to tackle the problem with formal accounts by explicitly ruling out discrimination against particular groups, go too far. Thus, libertarians have seen generality as an alternative to the unanimity view as a way of preventing collectively financed programmes that benefit some rather than others.[22] However, this would exclude measures where equal treatment may require discrimination, such as special access arrangements for the disabled or maternity leave for women. Moreover, it would be wrong to regard such policies as self-interested moves on the part of these groups – many able-bodied or male citizens respectively would support these measures because they thought them just and certainly generalisable in form.

Equal process: democratic participation as non-arbitrariness

The argument so far suggests that the reasons behind linking democracy with non-domination cannot be that it produces a version of the common good that is of itself non-arbitrary because it tracks the interests of every citizen in some relevantly egalitarian manner. If democracy is to count as a non-arbitrary form of rule, therefore, the rationale must reside in the process it offers for making collective decisions rather than the content or form those decisions take. As we saw in chapter 4, Philip Pettit grants democracy value as a heuristic device for determining whether a given policy on the collective good actually does track the interests of all concerned by allowing the contestation of those politicians and policies that fail to do so.[23] By contrast, this approach sees equal participation in the collective decision-making process as constitutive of non-arbitrary rule.

According to this account, we guard against domination through arbitrary rule so long as all citizens have an equal and ongoing chance of having their interests considered in the collective decision. In other words, the way to achieve non-domination lies in giving substance to people's quality as equal citizens by securing political equality in some form of popular rule.[24] To say the people rule is not to say that decisions reflect their common will – merely that all citizens have participated on equal terms in a common political process in order to determine the collective policy goals of the polity. On this view, democracy does not serve so much to

---

[22] J. M. Buchanan and R. D. Congleton, *Politics by Principle, Not Interest*, Cambridge: Cambridge University Press, 1998, p. 44.

[23] Pettit, *Republicanism*, pp. 56–7.   [24] Richardson, *Democratic Autonomy*, pp. 47–8, 62–3.

construct the common good, something we have seen to be improbable and contentious, as to fairly and equitably resolve disagreements as to what it is given that we have to make some decisions on collective arrangements.[25] So long as these decisions remain open to contestation and change by a like process, so that they stay continuously subject to popular rule, then citizens retain their status as political equals and a condition of non-domination – whereby they cannot be ruled without giving equal consideration to their interests – obtains.

The key determinants of political equality so conceived are that rule of the people be by the people according to some mechanism that gives them all an equal say. The next stage of the argument entails showing the basic components of such an arrangement consist in citizens having an equal vote in common elections where political parties compete for the people's vote and electoral and legislative decisions are made by majority rule. A familiar objection will be raised at this point. It will be contended that to ensure these basic components do indeed satisfy political equality we shall need principles of political justice that set the frame, determining precisely how political resources should be equalised by protecting a range of basic civil and political freedoms, possibly even certain related social and economic rights. In other words, political equality will need to be protected by the full panoply of constitutional rights and rules.[26]

This argument has been extensively criticised in the body of this book. It assumes that disagreements about justice differ from those relating to interests in being susceptible to rational resolution. Interests may be genuinely opposed, with none of the parties involved being mistaken about where their interests lie, so that conflicts cannot be resolved except through some equitable decision-making procedure that can, at best, only achieve a reasonable accommodation between them. But justice is the product of judgements that may or may not be mistaken and that we all have a common interest in getting right. However, we have seen that judgements about justice are just as prone to disagreements. Chapter 5 revealed how reasoning about justice is not like persuading someone of a proof in mathematics. It involves many of the same uncertainties involved in identifying and weighing our interests.[27] Moreover, our conceptions of justice are likely to be biased towards our own interests, or at least our own experiences, with competing views on justice being implicated in conflicts

[25] In linking democracy to political equality in this way, I follow Christiano, *The Rule of the Many*, p. 70 and Weale, *Democracy*, pp. 58–9.
[26] Richardson, *Democratic Autonomy*, pp. 11, 16, 47–8.
[27] See Christiano, 'The Authority of Democracy', pp. 275–7.

of interest in similar ways to those noted above with regard to Mill's harm principle. As a result, the self-same arguments that recommend a procedural resolution of competing interests when making collective decisions also suggest a similar solution to controversies about justice.

To try and settle decisions concerning the justice of political institutions by enshrining a particular conception within a constitution undermines rather than reinforces equal concern and respect between citizens.[28] On the one hand, the aforementioned cognitive bias, whereby we tend to assimilate the moral and other experiences of others to our own, means that the constitutionalised judgements concerning the requirements of political justice may ignore important concerns of particular groups. On the other hand, citizens are not being treated with equal moral standing if their views on what political justice requires do not count because this topic has been taken out of the political arena. If their views are treated as of little or no consequence, their self-respect gets undermined.

Thus, we cannot rely on a constitution to secure the participatory conditions of equal concern and respect. Not only is there no clear way, including that of a special democratic process, whereby we might reliably frame such a constitution, but there is also no legitimate expertise for interpreting such a framework with unfailing reliability so 'it tracks the interests' of those concerned. Consequently, people's interest in having their concerns fairly judged and in being recognised as having something worth saying cannot be satisfied without giving them an equal say in the rules of the political game. Moreover, to do so will help bolster their allegiance to those rules. Citizens are unlikely to feel a sense of belonging within a political society that fails to respond to their sense of justice, as the alienation of many politically marginalised groups – such as indigenous or immigrant communities – attests. True, some of their views may be muddled or prejudiced, but it is doubtful they could be won over if they do not have an opportunity to be part of a discussion that addresses and engages with those failings.

The only route to promoting equal recognition among citizens, there-fore, lies in having democracy police itself. So long as a system of equal votes, majority rule and party competition – however interpreted – offers a plausible system for giving citizens an equal say in the ways collective arrangements are organised – including those of the democratic process – then a self-constituting democratic constitution that avoids dominating

---

[28] For a useful discussion of this point, see Christiano, *The Rule of the Many*, pp. 71–5.

through arbitrary rule will have been secured. That does not mean I and many others will not think, say, that some electoral systems perform better than others. However, such disagreements are no different to those among legal constitutionalists as to which rights ought to be in a constitution, what the best modes of judicial interpretation are and so on. Just as these differences do not disturb their general view that having a constitution frame democracy is preferable to not having one, so it may be argued that as long as the basic components of a working and responsive democratic system can be shown to be adequate for the tasks they need to perform, then if these are in place – even if they could be improved – citizens will enjoy a non-dominating environment that treats them with equal concern and respect.

In what follows, I shall argue that real democracy does operate in these non-dominating ways by satisfying the criteria for public reason and the balance of power outlined in the last chapter. As we shall see, equal voting and majority rule offer impartial and open processes for the fair weighing of different views, thereby possessing the attributes of a procedural account of public reasoning. At the same time, these qualities are reinforced through party competition balancing power in ways that ensure the representation of a wide range of views, promoting their discussion, accommodation and criticism, and securing the responsiveness and accountability of politicians.

II Public reason

Chapter 5 defended the following seven qualities as necessary attributes of public reasoning on political issues: openness and transparency; public-spiritedness; regulation by a set of public rules, reasons and conventions; focus on the public good; public accessibility; public participation; and mutual acceptability. In theory at least, publicity in these senses is important in avoiding arbitrary rule. They constrain rulers, including citizens when operating within various forms of popular rule, from acting in their own interests and oblige them to address the reasons and interests of others – thereby 'hearing the other side'. They also fulfil a basic rule of law requirement of enabling citizens, politicians and public servants to know where they stand with regard to political institutions by providing rules of the game that are open, reasonably settled, fair and impartial.

The claim that in laying out the principles behind political institutions written constitutions promote and buttress public reason provides one of the strongest arguments for legal constitutionalism. However, as chapter 5 also noted, substantive accounts, such as Rawls proposes,[29] do not meet the seven criteria noted above, whereas a procedural account does. To recall, Rawls argued that public reason involves all citizens in their various public capacities adopting the same principles of political justice when considering the public good, with these being enshrined in the institutions of the political community. Like others who adopt this approach, he contends the best way to conceptualise these principles is to regard them as the products of an ideal democratic process that filters out self-serving or prejudiced arguments by placing all on an equal footing. As a result, the ensuing principles ostensibly embody a substantive form of impartial public reasoning that leads to outcomes that treat all with equal concern and respect. Unfortunately, we saw such models rest on contentious premises about human nature and social causality that in any case invariably prove too indeterminate to generate their claimed results. Similar difficulties bedevil the resulting principles that are themselves controversial and often too abstract to offer clear and consistent guides to decision-making, making it hard for a constitutional court (or anyone else) to fulfil the role of 'exemplars' of public reason that he accords them. These problems arise less from cultural or social differences or faulty or biased thinking *per se*, than the very limits of our moral reasoning that Rawls himself has highlighted under the heading 'the burdens of judgement'. For, contra Rawls, these limitations make reasonable disagreement about justice inevitable – witness the diversity of views even among the various practitioners of this approach.

As a result, the capacity of his or similar principles to satisfy criteria Rawls by and large endorses for public reasoning also becomes constrained. For a start, openness and transparency get undermined by the contestability, vagueness and indeterminacy of his list of basic liberties, which may be interpreted, balanced and applied in numerous and often conflicting ways to particular cases. The publicity of rules also gets weakened, because their force may not be clear and publicly accessible. These shortcomings may well lead the public-spiritedness of their enforcers, the judiciary, to be called into question, along with the degree to which they generally address the public good. These worries are likely to be exacerbated if there is no public participation in considering how

---

[29] Rawls, *Political Liberalism*, Lecture 6 but see too Buchanan and Tullock, *The Calculus of Consent*, B. Barry, *Justice as Impartiality*, Oxford: Oxford University Press, 1995 and J. Habermas, 'Discourse Ethics: Notes on a Programme of Philosophical Justification', in his *Moral Consciousness and Communicative Action*, Cambridge: Polity, 1990, pp. 43–115.

these public rules should be understood as to encourage their mutual acceptability and render those charged with their enforcement publicly accountable.

A procedural approach gets around these difficulties by not requiring all to agree on principles of justice or to believe that the basic institutions are just in their preferred sense. On the contrary, it takes as its starting point that people reasonably disagree about these matters, and that even when they agree will encounter problems in implementing any given theory of justice in an equitable manner. As we saw, this dilemma leads to citizens having an interest in possessing an equal say in determining the nature of the collective goods to be provided by their political community – including the sources, subjects, sphere and scope of the principles of political justice it will uphold – since this is the least controversial way to show them equal concern and respect. By extension, they also have an interest in being able to see that their views are being equally weighted alongside others. In other words, they will want the procedures to publicly show that all sides get an equal hearing and can be challenged for not doing so – hence the need for a procedural reading of the seven qualities of public reason.

How far, then, do equal votes and majority rule meet these standards, and to what extent are they promoted by general elections involving competing parties? These two issues occupy the remainder of this section and the next respectively.

Equal votes

Giving each and every citizen one (and only one) vote in a general election offers a rough and ready and easy to verify form of ensuring all citizens' views carry the same weight in collective decision-making. As such, the system provides an open and transparent set of public rules that are easily understood, and so publicly accessible, involve – indeed, facilitate – public participation, and all can regard as fair, given the circumstances of politics and the resulting disagreements that divide them. Though who we vote for is usually treated as a private matter to prevent citizens being intimidated into supporting the rich and powerful, the conduct of elections is in all other respects public in all seven senses: bound by public rules and open to public scrutiny, with all the adult public able to play an equal part.[30]

---

[30] On equal votes as a 'public' way of providing citizens with equal political resources, see Christiano, 'The Authority of Democracy', pp. 274–7.

Of course, even if all are entitled and formally able to vote, with the votes being scrupulously and openly counted, there remain many ways in which a bare system of one person one vote may still fail to measure up to what many would regard as an adequate standard of either publicity or a substantively equal say. Polling can be held at times that constrain the opportunities to vote of those in certain occupations or holding particular religious views, ballot boxes may be few and far between and located in places that certain sections of the community will find intimidating, constituency boundaries can be drawn in ways that favour particular groups and so on. For example, most of these tactics have been employed at times in the southern states of the United States to intimidate black voters. Legal constitutionalists argue that at the very least we will need constitutional judicial review to ensure equality in voting.[31]

As we saw in discussing such proposals in chapter 3, the difficulty is that such procedural decisions are hard to distinguish from the contentious substantive judgements associated with the outcome approach, and so in practice involve either too little and/or too much, rarely having a progressive effect.[32] For example, in the eyes of most who have advocated this policy, the US Supreme Court has usually done too little. Even with regard to ensuring a purely formal equality of the vote, it has allowed a number of states to permanently disenfranchise over a million voters who have served custodial sentences (i.e. depriving them of the vote not simply for the duration of their prison sentence but forever afterwards) – a policy that disproportionately affects minority and disadvantaged groups, with African-American men constituting over a third of those so disenfranchised. Yet in doing too little, the Court has also done too much. Thus, a decision such as *Buckley*,[33] that held limits on campaign expenditures in the Election Act Amendment of 1974 were unconstitutional on the grounds that they restricted free political speech, not only took an extremely formalist view of electoral equality, but also entrenched that formal view by overriding a legislative attempt to reach a more egalitarian position.

It has been the inherently inclusive and egalitarian logic behind one person one vote (and, as we shall see, majority rule) that has prompted

---

[31] For example, we noted in chapter 3 how it is the key concern of J. H. Ely, *Democracy and Distrust: A Theory of Judicial Review*, Cambridge, MA: Harvard University Press, 1980, notwithstanding his criticism of Dworkin's and Rawls's 'outcome' approach to judicial review.

[32] See M. Tushnet, *Taking the Constitution Away from the Courts*, Princeton: Princeton University Press, 1999, pp. 158–60.

[33] *Buckley v Valeo* 424 US 424 (1976).

conservatives in the past to advocate the counter-majoritarian constitutional mechanisms that progressives now seek to employ for their own purposes. By and large, the historical record suggests such attempts to be misguided. Campaigns by disenfranchised and disadvantaged groups to acquire the vote and render its deployment more effective have been far more effective in extending and reforming democracy than judicial action.[34] For the one embodies a commitment to equality of status that we have seen the other lacks – no matter how even-handed and impartial the holders of judicial power may seek to be.

Most progressive democratic reforms have been made with the support of existing voters acting to undermine their own privileged position – itself a testimony to the public-spiritedness of voting. However, doubts about democracy, such as the 'tyranny of the majority', are typically premised on the belief that most voting is self-interested, with personal rather than public reasons predominating. As the 'rational voter paradox' reveals, though, the rationally self-interested voter stays at home – the likelihood that his or her vote will make a difference is so minuscule that the costs in time and shoe leather of going to vote invariably outweigh the probability of any benefit accruing from having done so.[35] Consequently, it makes little sense to see voting in terms of trying to satisfy certain wants or achieve particular outcomes. Voting is more like expressing a judgement or set of value commitments – a view that is not only more empirically accurate as a way of explaining voting behaviour but also more normatively attractive, though the vote offers the opportunity to express nasty as well as nice values.[36] This account has implications too for how we understand majority rule and the representative role of parties, our next two topics.

Majority rule

Democratic voting can appear mechanical, yet this aspect may well prove an advantage rather than a drawback. Everyone is assumed to be equally

---

[34] See the comparative assessment in R. A. Dahl, *How Democratic is the American Constitution?*, New Haven: Yale University Press, 2002, ch. 5.

[35] A. Downs, *An Economic Theory of Democracy*, New York: Basic Books, 1957, p. 265. For an empirical critique of the public choice account of democratic politics, see L. Lewin, *Self-Interest and Public Interest in Western Politics*, Oxford: Oxford University Press, 1991, especially ch. 2.

[36] For the 'expressive' account of voting, see G. Brennan and L. Lomasky, *Democracy and Decision*, Cambridge: Cambridge University Press, 1993. For political choice as a 'judgement' see P. Jones, 'Intense Preferences, Strong Beliefs and Democratic Decision-Making', *Political Studies*, 36 (1988), pp. 7–29.

entitled to express a view and the process itself is neutral as regards the content of those views. As a means of settling substantive disagreements for which no agreed criteria exist as to what the substantively best view is, these are both appealing features. The winners do not claim victory on the grounds that their judgement is superior in some way to that of the losers. Their success merely reflects their view having been endorsed by the majority of the political community. If voting was less mechanical, then it would raise the very issue it seeks to resolve by appearing to promote one or other of the views in contention on substantive grounds, and hence become as contentious as them. In the process, it would also cease to treat voters with equal respect and acknowledging the reasonableness of their disagreements.[37] Nevertheless, voting is not arbitrary. Though sometimes condemned as a lottery, it precisely is not that. Simply tossing a coin or spinning a bottle to make a choice may treat all the options equally but it treats the supporters of those positions unequally by giving an option favoured by a single person the same chance as one favoured by many more. By contrast, as Jeremy Waldron has noted,[38] majority rule offers a method that accords respect to millions of individuals by giving equal weight to each person's views. Of course, this weight will be minimal and to those in the minority may appear to carry no weight at all. However, in the case of decisions that affect millions of people, no individual person could fairly claim to count more than minimally in the collective process. Moreover, as Condorcet revealed,[39] it may also be more likely to be right than individual judgement.

---

[37] In this regard, Dworkin is mistaken to argue that 'true democracy is not just *statistical* democracy, in which anything a majority or plurality wants is democratic for that reason, but *communal* democracy, in which a majority decision is legitimate only if it is a majority within a community of equals' (R. Dworkin, *Freedom's Law: The Moral Reading of the American Constitution*, Oxford: Oxford University Press, 1996, 'Introduction: The Moral Reading and the Majoritarian Premise', p. 364). What he overlooks is that the very statistical character of voting is an intrinsic part of treating people as members of a community of equals. Dworkin goes on to argue (pp. 364–5) that the communal quality comes not from the democratic process showing citizens equality of concern and respect so much as the outcomes. Yet it is the merits of any given outcome which may be what is in dispute. For this reason, the communal aspect can only come from the procedures being fair and inclusive. Thus, to the extent the statistical quality of democracy promotes equality of respect, by not judging any view to be less worthy than any other, it contributes to democracy's communal quality. See too J. Waldron, *Law and Disagreement*, Oxford: Oxford University Press, 1999, p. 113.

[38] Waldron, *Law and Disagreement*, pp. 108–10, 114.

[39] Marquis de Condorcet, 'Essay on the Application of Mathematics to the Theory of Decision-Making', in K. M. Baker (ed.), *Condorcet: Selected Writings*, Indianapolis: Bobbs Merrill, 1976.

The claims for majority rule as coinciding with public reason correspond roughly with the defence made by Kenneth May. May argued that majority rule was a necessary consequence of four reasonable requirements for a decision rule within a democratic society.[40] The first requirement is anonymity, in that the outcome must not favour one voter more than another or depend on whether specific persons have supported or opposed it. This criterion supports voter equality. The second is neutrality with regard to alternatives. In particular, there must be no bias towards the *status quo*, such as all counter-majoritarian schemes involve. Such bias is usually justified on the grounds that stability requires we avoid precipitate or radical reforms – particularly in areas that are deemed important for the protection of individual rights against myopic and misguided understandings of the collective welfare. However, institutional inertia and a small 'c' conservative predisposition among most people to stick to what they know tend to favour existing arrangements in any case. If public reason is to give equal weight to the views of the public, there can be no legitimate argument for giving extra influence to the views of those who favour existing arrangements, potentially hindering justified change in the process. After all, as I noted in chapter 1, there is as much if not more reason to fear individual rights will be damaged by not reforming dominating policies and systems as in altering a good set-up for a worse. At the very least, the two dangers need to be treated even-handedly.

May's third requirement comes in here – he argued that a decision rule should be positively responsive. By this he meant that if a group was evenly divided between two options, A and B, then if one citizen came to alter his or her preference from A to B, then the decision should favour B over A. The previous two conditions could be met by simply tossing a coin, which in the case of a even split would be non-dominating and consistent with a procedural conception of public reason, but if all are indifferent about A or B apart from one person, then it is legitimate that person's view should hold sway. Finally, and implicit in the foregoing, a decision-making rule must be decisive, producing a clear result. When there is disagreement this is all-important – we need a fair closure device and in satisfying the preceding three requirements, majority rule operates as just that.

However, matters get more complex once the number of choices and choosers rises above two. In this regard, public choice theorists have

---

[40] K. May, 'A Set of Independent Necessary and Sufficient Conditions for Simple Majority Decision', *Econometrica*, 10 (1952), pp. 680–84.

argued democracy is faced with an intractable problem. They have developed Kenneth Arrow's famous demonstration that no aggregation rule can produce a determinate outcome while satisfying five seemingly reasonable normative conditions: Pareto optimality, non-dictatorship, independence of irrelevant alternatives, unlimited domain and transitivity of preference orderings.[41] The best known instance of the problem, is that of majority cycles (in which, for example, option A beats B beats C beats A). Arrow's Impossibility Theorem showed this to be merely a specific case of a general problem bedevilling any rule for aggregating preferences where there are more than two alternatives. As a result, theorists such as William H. Riker have argued that democratic decision-making is not only incoherent but also arbitrary and dominating. In particular, it is open to either instability, as in cycles, or hidden elite manipulation, notably through strategic voting, log-rolling and especially agenda setting, in order to get round these problems and produce a stable outcome.[42]

Though much of the literature is targeted at majoritarianism, it should be noted that Arrow's theorem and the problems it raises applies to any social choice function that aspires to produce a social ordering from a given set of individual preferences. Nevertheless, it has been widely interpreted as rendering majoritarian democracy in particular irrational. There are two responses to be made to this challenge. First, as Gerry Mackie has shown, though Riker's arguments concerning incoherence, instability and manipulation are all logical possibilities, counter to his claims they are empirically improbable.[43] By and large, socialisation and other behavioural constraints – including those of competitive elections explored below – serve to make individual preferences resemble each other sufficiently for cycling to be rare and eliminable by fair voting rules. Nor is manipulation so frequent or irremediable, or disequilibrium that common. The preferences of others are harder to know than the model assumes, and the possibility of a monopoly agenda setter largely unknown – meanwhile strategic voting and agenda setting tend to cancel each other out. Indeed, Mackie reveals Riker's famous examples of these phenomena to be largely misdescribed.[44] Again, though different voting

[41] K. J. Arrow, *Social Choice and Individual Values*, second edition, New Haven: Yale University Press, 1963.

[42] W. H. Riker, *Liberalism Against Populism: A Confrontation Between the Theory of Democracy and the Theory of Social Choice*, San Francisco: Freeman and Co., 1982, pp. 137, 239. For a careful outline of Riker's main arguments, see G. Mackie, *Democracy Defended*, Cambridge: Cambridge University Press, 2003, pp. 5–9 and ch. 2.

[43] Mackie, *Democracy Defended*, ch. 3.   [44] Ibid., pp. 18–19 for a summary of his findings.

rules may theoretically produce different definitions of the majority, in practice the mild homogeneity among voters that usually obtains means they rarely do.[45] Moreover, just because different voting rules can produce different results does not make the choice of any given voting rule in itself arbitrary, as Riker claims. Rather, it makes possible their comparison for different purposes and settings.[46] After all, the only voting systems considered either by Riker or in the public domain are those that offer reasonable interpretations of giving all an equal vote. They are versions of either plurality or PR systems, rather than say 'Bellamy's vote is always equal to all votes cast + 1 on any issue'.

This last point is also important because some republican theorists have assumed equal voting can only be achieved through some form of PR, and that their desired version should be enshrined in a constitution as a result.[47] Clearly, the various types of PR offer a *prima facie* better fit than plurality systems with the general defence of democracy as an equal say.[48] In particular, the greater representativeness of PR systems can be a good reason for adopting them in circumstances where there are diffuse minorities and the sort of segmental cleavage associated with cultural difference.[49] Likewise, when it comes to counting votes, then in terms of accuracy and fairness in reflecting the distribution of preferences, a Borda count probably performs best.[50] However, it would be wrong for that reason to suggest that PR combined with a Borda count was the only system compatible with non-domination. There are pros and cons for most of the generally accepted systems. In fact, none of the standard options, including first past the post, perform so badly that they give rise to Arrovian problems or produce tyrannous majorities on a regular basis. For example, plurality systems do more or less the same as PR in terms of rights protection.[51] In reducing the incentives for groups to change their views, though, PR tends to favour the *status quo* more than plurality systems, which are apt to promote change and reform. As we saw in chapter 5, pluralism and diversity make the kinds of compromise likely to emerge from PR and the resulting coalitions justified, but in certain

[45] Ibid., ch. 2 and H. Nurmi, *Comparing Voting Systems*, Dordrecht: D. Reidel, 1987.
[46] Mackie, *Democracy Defended*, p. 69 citing and commenting on Nurmi, *Comparing Voting Systems*, p. 191.
[47] E.g. Richardson, *Democratic Autonomy*, pp. 199–202.
[48] See Christiano, *The Rule of the Many*, pp. 224–40.
[49] A. Lijphart, *Democracy in Plural Societies*, New Haven: Yale University Press, 1977.
[50] Mackie, *Democracy Defended*, pp. 67–8.
[51] See J. Foweraker and T. Landman, 'Constitutional Design and Democratic Performance', *Democratization*, 9 (2002), p. 55.

circumstances that can also increase conflict by entrenching divisions. There can be losses in the coherence of policy, efficiency and especially accountability.[52] In sum, democratic decision-making can be both a form of public reason, offering an intelligible and rational way for aggregating preferences, and subject to public reasoning as to its most appropriate form in given social circumstances.

A second response to the Arrovian-inspired critique develops the underlying reason these social choice analyses fail in practice and argues that they also miss the point of democratic decision-making, at least as it has been conceived here.[53] The Arrow/Riker argument makes it seem that the prime rationale for democratic decision-making is aggregation to achieve maximal social utility, pointing out the dilemmas raised for this goal by any intransitivity of preference orderings. However, I have disputed welfare maximisation as an appropriate justification for democracy. Rather, its basis is the equal distribution of decision-making power. It is the commitment to this goal that provides a backdrop to aggregation by producing a concern to have equitable procedures for agenda setting, deal-making and debate. Above all, what makes elections and legislation forms of public reason is their capacity to be of the public in the seven ways described above. That arises in part because of equal votes and majority rule, as explored in this section, but also by the context of real politics as provided by party competition and the balance of power, to be examined in the next. As we shall see, it is this competition that frames the construction of majorities and maintains a commitment to an open and equitable process.

III The balance of power

Chapter 5 detailed how the balance of power provides the crucial mechanism for ensuring democracy operates in a way that promotes non-domination through forms of public reasoning that 'hear the other side'. As we noted, the key aspect of this mechanism is competition between rival rulers. On the one hand, such competition promotes inclusion by providing incentives for incumbents to address a wide range of disparate concerns in order to build a broad coalition of supporters. On the other hand, it institutionalises contestation. Inclusiveness and permanent

---

[52] For a useful up-to-date summary of the evidence, which tends to be somewhat mixed, see P. Norris, *Electoral Engineering: Voting Rules and Political Behavior*, Cambridge: Cambridge University Press, 2004.

[53] Richardson, *Democratic Autonomy*, p. 51, Christiano, *The Rule of the Many*, p. 96.

opposition also serve to promote adherence to the system and encourage a degree of solidarity and trust among citizens. They begin to relate their interests to those of others in reciprocal ways, while acknowledging the legitimacy and utility of dissent to highlight problems. By contrast, non-competitive forms of distributing power, such as the classic doctrine of the separation of powers, were shown to possess neither of these qualities. In being counter-majoritarian, they are also inegalitarian – entrenching vested interests rather than producing reciprocal accommodations that seek to balance the various reasons in play.

Within actually existing democracies the central instruments for securing such forms of competitive balance and their attendant benefits are political parties. As Schattschneider famously remarked, 'modern democracy is unthinkable save in terms of political parties'.[54] They are the essential components of what Joseph Schumpeter had contemporaneously identified as his 'other model' of democracy: namely, 'that institutional arrangement for arriving at political decisions by means of a competitive struggle for the people's vote'.[55] Yet, while acknowledging the descriptive force of Schumpeter's definition, the main efforts of most normative political theorists have been aimed at thinking the unthinkable and seeking to rehabilitate various aspects of what Schumpeter called the 'classical theory' of democracy.[56] The prime features of the various theories Schumpeter somewhat incongruously grouped under this heading were popular participation in decision-making to produce a collective rational will on the common good. In other words, such classical theories reflect the highly contentious substantive form of public reasoning criticised above and in the previous chapter. By contrast, the normative and not simply descriptive force of the Schumpeterian model derives from its bolstering a procedural form of public reason suited to circumstances where we reasonably disagree about our common interests and the collective arrangements needed to pursue them, and practically cannot take decisions but only choose decision-makers to act on our behalf.[57]

---

[54] E. E. Schattschneider, *Party Government*, New York: Holt, Reinhart & Winston, 1942, p. 1.

[55] J. A. Schumpeter, *Capitalism, Socialism and Democracy* [1942], London: Allen and Unwin, 1976, p. 269.

[56] Ibid., p. 250. For a measured lament at this state of affairs, see I. Shapiro, *The State of Democratic Theory*, Princeton: Princeton University Press, 2003, especially ch. 3.

[57] For a detailed discussion of Schumpeter, see my *Rethinking Liberalism*, London: Pinter, 2000, ch. 5.

How does this system of party competition work to bolster non-dominating forms of public reason?[58] Parties bring together broad coalitions of opinions and interests within a general programme of government. As a result, they oblige citizens to relate their concerns to those of others as part of a comprehensive set of policies for the people as a whole. These qualities encourage three of the elements of public reason: namely, public-spiritedness, focus on the public good and mutual acceptability. By offering alternative manifestos, parties also foster deliberation about the collective good in both elections and during the legislative process. Electoral competition promotes the scrutiny of rival views, and places incumbents under a continuous obligation to address the criticisms posed by their potential successors in office. These processes serve three more aspects of public reason: openness and transparency, public accessibility and public participation. Finally, in providing mechanisms through which citizens can simultaneously pursue a wide range of disparate interests, parties support the final aspect of public reasoning – regulation by a set of public rules, reasons and conventions. When citizens organise simply to pursue a single issue that concerns them above all others, as is the case with anti-abortion campaigners in the United States, for example, then they are apt to have less concern with the overall fairness of the system as a whole. They have one overriding goal which they seek to pursue by any available means. Parties, though, have an interest in maintaining the rules of the game. They compete over time, anticipating that they will spend periods out of as well as in office. They need to hold together coalitions of voters with a wide range of concerns whose support is conditional on their views being given a fair hearing within the policy mix.

Proponents of deliberative democracy have been apt to doubt these virtues of actually existing democratic processes and to criticise them for simply producing coalitions of self-interested groups that combine solely for mutual advantage so as to maximise the rents they can extract from

---

[58] There is of course a vast literature on parties charting their rise, fall, virtues and vices. For a recent survey of the current literature, see R. Gunther, José Ramon-Montero and Juan J. Linz (eds.), *Political Parties: Old Concepts and New Challenges*, Oxford: Oxford University Press, 2002. What follows draws on the important work of H.-D. Klingemann, R. I. Hoffer-bert and I. Budge, *Parties, Policies and Democracy*, Oxford: Westview Press, 1994 – a study based on data over forty years for ten advanced democracies that explicitly (and positively) assesses the theme explored here: namely, the democratic role of parties as mechanisms of representation and accountability, whereby policy preferences get translated into policy priorities.

their fellow citizens through controlling the state apparatus.[59] However, if that was the case we would expect the party system to be far more fluid than it actually is, with parties leapfrogging each other to maximise votes and politicians forming new parties in their jockeying for power.[60] Meanwhile, we noted above that rational self-interest offers an implausible explanatory account of voters' motivation. Although single-issue parties tied to a particular grievance or interest occasionally surface, especially in PR systems in which a party can obtain seats with a very low percentage of the vote, within most established democracies these are the exception. In fact, the main divisions between the major parties are ideological.[61] As a result, parties tend to relate their policy differences across the whole range of issues to differences of political principle. Though all parties typically claim citizens will be 'better off' as a result of their policies, they offer different normative accounts of well-being against which such improvements might be measured and stress the legitimacy as well as efficiency of the alternative means they propose for reaching their goals.

An appropriate, public reason inducing, balance of power is achieved through parties competing across certain pivotal ideological cleavages that capture the main political divisions within contemporary societies. Though parties have developed in various ways in different countries, two forms of cleavage have come to dominate: centre and periphery, and left and right.[62] While competition along both dimensions can serve to advance equal votes and ensure that majority rule operates in ways that promote rather than subvert rights and the rule of law, the first proves more problematic in this regard than the second.

Centre–periphery cleavages tend to arise out of resistance by certain territorially based cultural, religious, ethnic and socio-economic

---

[59] E.g. the criticisms of the 'aggregative' model in Cohen, 'Deliberation and Democratic Legitimacy'. Of course, these arguments repeat the criticisms of public choice theorists while offering up deliberation as a panacea. Yet, these criticisms are overstated, as we have seen – not least because they ignore the deliberative elements of real democracy. As I noted in chapter 5, they also overstate the likelihood and virtues of consensus (on this point see too Weale, *Democracy*, pp. 142–3 and Shapiro, *The State of Democratic Theory*, pp. 21–34). To a remarkable degree, their ideas resemble what Hans Daalder calls 'the denial of party' by left- and right-wing critics from the eighteenth century onwards. See H. Daalder, 'Parties: Denied, Dismissed, or Redundant? A Critique', in Gunther, Ramon-Montero and Linz, *Political Parties*, pp. 39–42.

[60] Klingemann, Hofferbert and Budge, *Parties, Policies and Democracy*, pp. 23, 246.

[61] Ibid., pp. 246–54.

[62] The classic account of the origins of party alignments is S. M. Lipset and S. Rokkan, 'Cleavage Structures, Party Systems and Voter Alignments', in S. M. Lipset and S. Rokkan (eds.), *Party Systems and Voter Alignments*, New York: Free Press, 1967, pp. 1–64.

minorities to rule by a national majority. As such, they are sometimes seen as evidence for fears about the tyranny of the majority. That risk is somewhat belied by the success of many such minorities getting regional issues onto the political agenda – witness the success of the Scots and Welsh over the past decade notwithstanding the UK's plurality system. However, it is certainly true that regional differences heighten worries that simply giving everyone an equal vote may not be sufficient to ensure a consistent minority's view being given equal consideration. That concern is particularly strong where there are sub-national groups with a distinctive political culture to the rest of the population. In such cases, the absence of a common political identity with their fellow citizens within the cultural majority may undercut a minority's ability to form alliances with them on particular policy areas – even when they share certain other interests. Such cultural differences increase the need for more proportional representative electoral systems and, in the case of territorially concentrated minorities, can significantly add to the standard functional reasons for a degree of local government, giving grounds for a substantial degree of regional autonomy. However, though both measures tend to favour the *status quo* by raising the transaction costs of decision-making and giving greater sway to veto players, neither should be regarded as anti-majoritarian *per se*. The first simply aims at a more effective way of calculating the majority suitable for diverse societies. The second is best construed as a concern with which majority is appropriate for what decisions. After all, the resulting sub-units generally employ majoritarian voting mechanisms in their turn.

At one level, therefore, the institutionalisation of centre–periphery politics can be seen as a fruitful balancing of power that generates a procedural form of public reasoning by giving each side an equal voice. Central policies will only be successfully constructed through giving some recognition to local economic, social and cultural differences. As a result, different groups will have to enter into dialogue with each other and search for fruitful compromises based on mutual accommodation. Regional autonomy can also stimulate efficiencies and improved public structures through regions offering citizens competing tax and services regimes. Indeed, debates about the correct balance between centre and periphery show how the character of the polity and the identity of its demos or demoi can arise and be tackled through normal democratic politics.

At another level, however, as the example of Belgium to some degree illustrates,[63] there is a danger that contests over the definition of the

---

[63] Klingemann, Hofferbert and Budge, *Parties, Policies and Democracy*, ch. 13.

political community can come so to dominate competition over how to use government power that the democratic accountability of rulers to the ruled gets undermined. As I observed in chapter 5, arrangements that institutionalise community divisions, such as consociational and analogous segmental forms of dividing power, not only divide responsibility but also entrench the positions of elites, thereby removing their incentives to either better serve the public interest or accommodate others. To a degree, a working democracy is pre-constituted by agreement between a given body of people possessing enough of a collective identity and interests to be able to share common decision rules. *Pace* those who see a constitutional patriotism as a means for creating a demos,[64] constitutions are no different. They too are constituted as well as constitutive of their people, and can be forced to adapt to the point of being unworkable if there is such a deep degree of polity disagreement among rival peoples as can only be resolved through war or the peaceful secession of one of the groups.

Fortunately, such diametrically opposed positions are rare in democratic politics. Left and right has proven an even more pervasive and enduring political division. Yet it has rarely led to polarised opposition, even in multiparty systems where it might be thought incentives existed for many parties to take up extreme positions.[65] That is partly because of the difficulties we have noted in either defining our interests or formulating the policies best suited to pursuing them. Not only is the chain of cause and effect so complex in highly differentiated, large-scale societies that it is hard to know what the consequences of particular actions might be, and hence how a given interest or value might best be pursued, but also the normative considerations that shape our interests have an internal complexity of their own that defies the giving of simple answers as to what justice requires in particular circumstances. Meanwhile, our interests and value commitments are themselves complicated. People tend to belong to many different kinds of social, economic and cultural groups. Alongside, and in most cases more prominently than, the segmental cleavages typical of ethnic and cultural diversity, plural societies are characterised by cross-cutting cleavages due to citizens having a wide variety of different interests and values that result in them allying with different groups on different issues. Rather than being consistently left and right across

---

[64] E.g. J. Habermas, *Between Facts and Norms*, Cambridge: Polity Press, 1996, Appendix II: 'Citizenship and National Identity', p. 500.
[65] Klingemann, Hofferbert and Budge, *Parties, Policies and Democracy*, pp. 247–9.

the board, people find themselves having elements of leftish and right-ish thinking depending on the topic – even, given the above-mentioned intricacies of practical and normative reasoning about most matters, on a single topic.[66]

The tendency we noted earlier for parties to offer programmatic statements within a broad ideological framework can be seen as a response to this situation. For a start, it enables them to build coalitions of supporters. Instead of being confronted by choices on single issues that might polarise opinion, and be hard to make in any case, voters are offered competing bundles of policy areas that each party highlights as being particularly salient for its agenda.[67] However, even if the headline aspects of their agendas are distinct, considerable overlap exists as parties seek to hold on to their core ideological supporters while attracting additional voters from the centre. PR has sometimes been said to reduce this effect by encouraging a large number of parties. The incentives in this structure are said to be for them strongly to differentiate themselves from each other and develop a core support.[68] Yet there is little evidence of such centre-fleeing. Though extremist and single-issue parties are more likely to arise in such systems, parties that hope to enter the government as coalition partners must inevitably have an eye to how their programmes will link up with those of others.[69]

These features of left–right party competition have important implications for some of the dilemmas surrounding majority rule. For a start, it minimises the likelihood of cycles. By boiling down choice to competing packages along a single dimension it avoids some of the problems associated with choosing between a plethora of specific policy options. Even when more dimensions are involved it is possible for voters to use relatively simple decision-making rules whereby they can identify which party package contains most of their favoured options.[70] Empirical evidence indicates electorates employ both these strategies. Competition in a single

[66] See W. B. Gallie, 'Liberal Morality and Socialist Morality', in P. Laslett (ed.), *Philosophy, Politics and Society*, Oxford: Blackwell, 1956, pp. 116–33. I owe this point and reference to A. Weale, *Democratic Citizenship and the European Union*, Manchester: Manchester University Press, 2005, pp. 130–31.

[67] Klingemann, Hofferbert and Budge, *Parties, Policies and Democracy*, ch. 2, develop David Robertson's 'saliency theory' (*A Theory of Party Competition*, London: Wiley, 1976), modifying Downs's 'spatial' model of party competition in *Economic Theory*.

[68] G. Sartori, *Parties and Party Systems: A Framework for Analysis*, Cambridge: Cambridge University Press, 1976.

[69] Klingemann, Hofferbert and Budge, *Parties, Policies and Democracy*, p. 249.

[70] Ibid., pp. 25–6, 254–5.

dimension also leads parties to converge on the median voter,[71] which will generally prove to be the Condorcet winner – the option that can beat all others under majority rule when placed in a pair-wise comparison with the alternatives.[72] Meanwhile, because parties tend to define themselves as having a distinctive view and policy agenda to their opponents rather than as diametric opposites, scope exists for winners to accommodate elements of the programmes of others. Such scope is essential in the coalition systems which predominate in modern democracies. However, selective borrowing occurs even from the programmes of losers. To the extent they are articulating genuine concerns, future electoral advantage will move governments to steal their opponents' clothes and even concede that in certain areas they do indeed have the best policies.[73]

However, such convergence can raise worries of a different kind – namely that in various ways parties fail to respond to citizens, colluding to set the agenda and keep certain items off it. As a result, parties are charged with being instruments of domination rather than mechanisms for overcoming it. It is certainly true that because party identities often reflect historic trends, they have a tendency to freeze in certain traditional political divisions and issues, freezing out others in the process.[74] This propensity makes it harder for new concerns to get onto the political agenda. Feminist, cultural and environmental issues were initially frozen out in this way, becoming the focus of social movements and, in PR systems, small political parties. Yet, however unsatisfactorily from the point of view of many dedicated to these causes, it remains undeniable that such issues have become increasingly mainstreamed within the traditional left–right ideological cleavage. Indeed, it is through the main traditional parties developing distinctive yet, from their perspective, proactive and often complementary positions on these matters, that they have been linked with other interests in ways that can command majority support.[75]

---

[71] M. D. McDonald, S. M. Mendes and I. Budge, 'What Are Elections For? Conferring the Median Mandate', *British Journal of Political Science*, 34 (2004), pp. 1–26.

[72] P. C. Ordeshook, *Game Theory and Political Theory*, Cambridge: Cambridge University Press, 1986, pp. 245–57.

[73] Klingemann, Hofferbert and Budge, *Parties, Policies and Democracy*, pp. 30–31, 243–4.

[74] Lipset and Rokkan, 'Cleavage Structures'.

[75] This is not to deny that the proliferation of single-interest groups represents a growing challenge to the party system that parties have increasingly sought to sidestep rather than to meet – for example by becoming cartel parties increasingly insulated from the need for a mass base (see R. Katz and P. Mair, 'Changing Models of Party Organisation: The Emergence of the Cartel Party', *Party Politics*, 1 (1995), pp. 5–28) – even if such challenges have arguably been overstated (see P. Norris, *Democratic Phoenix: Political*

For partly related reasons, parties are sometimes criticised as being the creatures of powerful social and economic interests, well-organised political elites, or some combination of both. This criticism reaches back to the 1880s and the founding fathers of political sociology keen to dispel the 'myth', as they often saw it, of mass popular democracy.[76] Yet, the claim that a cohesive and well-organised minority can consistently control the agenda has proved hard to substantiate.[77] Party programmes have changed over time and not consistently in ways that suit entrenched social and economic groups – witness the development of the post-war welfare states.[78] Moreover, though behind the scenes removal of certain issues from the political agenda is possible, if by its very nature hard to prove, the policies enacted by governments reflect the agenda set by parties in open election campaigns to a remarkable degree. Meanwhile, though there are common trends in the way the agenda has evolved, doctrinal differences between parties remain clear.

In fact, the tendency of competing parties to converge in a system of majority rule reflects the various ways it protects minorities. Because an electoral majority is built from minorities and is prone to cycling coalitions, a ruling group will do well not to rely on a minimal winning coalition and to exclude other groups completely – thereby reducing the possibility of such cycles. Hence the need to build a broad-based programme that overlaps with that of the main opposition. As a result, any given minority either has a good chance of being part of a future winning coalition, or – for that very reason – is likely not to be entirely excluded by any winning coalition keen to retain its long-term power. By contrast, counter-majoritarian blocks on majority rule advantage ideologically concentrated over more

---

Activism Worldwide, Cambridge: Cambridge University Press, 2003, chs. 6 and 7). However, such developments are not just challenges to parties but to the constitutional mechanisms of democracy that the various alternatives do not begin to address. A typical example is R. J. Dalton, *Democratic Challenges, Democratic Choices: The Erosion of Political Support in Advanced Industrial Democracies*, Oxford: Oxford University Press, 2004, whose analysis of the challenges outstrips by far his portrayal of the choices, which while big on promoting participation for all kinds of groups contains no mention of how their disparate views might be fairly aggregated into coherent policy programmes that show all sides equal concern and respect.

[76] E.g. R. Michels, *Political Parties: A Sociological Study of the Oligarchical Tendencies of Modern Democracy* (1911), New York: Dover, 1959, G. Mosca, *The Ruling Class* (1896, 1923), New York: McGraw-Hill, 1939 and C. W. Mills, *The Power Elite*, Oxford: Oxford University Press, 1956.

[77] See R. A. Dahl, 'A Critique of the Ruling Elite Model', *American Political Science Review*, 52 (1958), pp. 463–9.

[78] Klingemann, Hofferbert and Budge, *Parties, Policies and Democracy*, p. 255.

dispersed majorities, even allowing extremes to muster strategic blocking points, and far from protecting minorities, can lead to their complete exclusion.[79]

Meanwhile, the agenda-setting character of elections points to another important respect in which parties make votes count. If votes in elections are to influence legislation and government policy, then representatives must regard themselves more like mandated delegates than as trustees.[80] Party discipline ties politicians to the programme selected by voters. Obviously, a manifesto simply indicates the general policy areas parties seek to concentrate on and the broad approaches they intend to take. They do not specify in detail all the decisions a government will take. However, that is necessarily the case. The future cannot be predicted and governments always have to confront unanticipated events – including those created by unexpected consequences of some of their own policies. Moreover, much policy-making gets handed down to delegated bodies and administrators. What the electorate can expect, though, is that what governments do is consistent with the overall range of policy aims outlined in the election. To a remarkable degree that is the case, with the dynamics of electoral politics passing over to the legislative process.[81]

IV The constitutionality of legislative politics

The analysis of real democracy has focused so far on electoral politics. However, the crucial point, which I have already indicated to be the case, is that elections influence legislation. As Juan Linz has shown, the representative functions of parties are enhanced in parliamentary as opposed to presidential systems.[82] A similar finding can be found with unitary, as opposed to federal, and PR by contrast to plurality systems.[83] Even more important for our purposes is the related result that parliamentary and unitary systems perform best in terms of fostering participation

---

[79] A. J. McGann, 'The Tyranny of the Supermajority: How Majority Rule Protects Minorities', *Journal of Theoretical Politics*, 16 (2004), pp. 56, 71.

[80] Christiano, *The Rule of the Many*, pp. 213–15.

[81] Klingemann, Hofferbert and Budge, *Parties, Policies and Democracy*, pp. 240–43.

[82] J. Linz, 'Presidential or Parliamentary Democracy: Does it Make a Difference?', in J. Linz and A. Valenzuela (eds.), *The Failure of Presidential Democracy*, Baltimore: Johns Hopkins University Press, 1994, pp. 3–90.

[83] G. Tsebelis, 'Decision-Making in Political Systems: Veto-Players in Multicameralism, Presidentialism and Multipartyism', *British Journal of Political Science*, 25 (1995), pp. 289–325.

and political, civil and minority rights, though the advantages of PR over plurality systems in these respects are less clear-cut.[84]

The reasons for these differences are threefold, and relate to the ways different types of democratic system promote the basic virtues of democracy as a system of non-domination involving public reason and a competitive balance of power. First, the election of a single candidate is far more likely to be subject to the problems of majority rule – enjoying either only a plurality of support that is less than an actual majority of voters, or – where there are more than two candidates – getting elected through an arbitrary resolution of a cycle (as arguably occurred in the 2002 French presidential election, when the National Front candidate Le Pen surprisingly emerged as higher ranked than the Socialist Lionel Jospin, and was then massively defeated in a run-off with Jacques Chirac). Second, presidential and federal systems are subject to the problems we noted in chapter 5 with regard to the separation of power. The executive and legislature may compete for power, and may even become deadlocked, but not necessarily in ways that serve the interests of their principals, the electors. While seeking to increase their respective power, the one can simply shift the costs and blame for their actions onto the other. This tendency is only modified when candidates for both the presidency and the legislature arise from the same sets of parties and compete on similar programmes. As I also observed in chapter 5, similar pathologies can attend the tensions between federal and state governments, especially when federalism is linked to a bicameral chamber representing the states.[85] Third, within parliamentary and unitary systems there is a more direct link between the executive and the legislative programme chosen by the electorate. That linkage is sometimes said to be attenuated in PR systems, where governments can often emerge through post-electoral bargaining among party groups.[86] However, these negotiations standardly reflect the electoral policy commitments made by the parties involved, often in anticipation of forging coalitions following the election.[87] Such bargaining is no different to the way politicians within a party with an overall majority employ their delegated authority to respond to unforeseen events. In each case, they act within a general framework of broad value commitments and policy goals. Moreover, coalition governments are likely to be more representative

---

[84] See Foweraker and Landman, 'Constitutional Design and Democratic Performance'.
[85] G. Tsebelis and J. Money, *Bicameralism*, Cambridge: Cambridge University Press, 1997.
[86] Downs, *Economic Theory*, p. 156.
[87] A. Lijphart, *Democracies: Patterns of Majoritarian and Consensus Government in Twenty-One Countries*, New Haven: Yale University Press, 1984, ch. 4.

of the range of citizen concerns than those based on an outright parliamentary majority, which in first past the post systems may actually
result from getting a minority of votes among the electorate at large. Still,
the two may be less different than is supposed. After all, the two main
parties in two-party plurality systems tend to be broad coalitions.

The result of combining public reasoning with the balance of power
is that most legislation is not the product of a homogeneous majority
imposing its will upon a consistent minority, but of a series of compromises brokered by winning coalitions of different minorities. Compromise
is standardly attributed to pure bargaining in which the parties involved
look out for themselves and seek to get as much of what they desire as they
can. Critics claim they only take account of the interests of others to the
extent they are obliged to. Given the strong and rich generally need concede less to the weak and poor than to other rich and strong groups, pure
bargaining seems unlikely to produce equitable or stable compromises.
There are also questions of integrity and the incommensurability and
incompatibility of what different groups want. Certain values are integral
to a given group's identity and could not be bargained away without a
sense of deep loss. In neither case does mutual adjustment in order to
arrive at a mutually beneficial compromise seem likely.

So interpreted, democratic compromise appears either a shoddy capit-
ulation, whereby principle gets sacrificed to self-interest, or simply incoherent. Yet, as we saw in chapter 5, compromise can also indicate a laudable
willingness to see another's point of view, thereby showing a decent respect
for difference.[88] If there are divergent and competing views and interests,
all each of which are well-founded, then, if a collective agreement is necessary, it seems both prudent and justified to seek an accommodation
between them.[89] Indeed, in practice compromise proves more sophisticated than simply 'splitting the difference' or giving everyone a turn.
More common is a trade-off. Most political parties have to engage in a
degree of log-rolling to get elected and in multiparty systems to get legislation enacted. This procedure gets various groups that may disagree
over many issues yet prioritise them differently to back a common programme. If three groups are split over the possession of nuclear weapons,
development aid and a graduate tax, say, but each values a different one
of these more than the others, it may be possible for them to agree to

---

[88] What follows draws on and develops R. Bellamy, *Liberalism and Pluralism: Towards a
Politics of Compromise*, London: Routledge, 1999, ch. 4.
[89] M. Benjamin, *Splitting the Difference: Compromise and Integrity in Ethics and Politics*,
Lawrence: University Press of Kansas, 1990, pp. 26–32.

a package giving each the policy they value most while putting up with another they disagree with in an area that matters less to them. Of course, sometimes the result can be a programme that is too inconsistent to be tenable or attractive. Here, it might be better for the groups to shift to an agreed second best. A notion adapted from economics, the basic idea is that modifications to one's preferred option may be less desirable than obtaining one's next best or even lower ranked choice. For example, a cheap sports car that pretends to be an expensive one may be less appealing than a solid family estate. Individuals and groups with conflicting first preferences may even have a shared second preference. Sometimes it may appear that people's concerns are simply incommensurable, irreconcilable or talk past each other. Appeals by religious groups for special treatment have sometimes been portrayed in such terms. However, it may be possible to appeal by analogy to a shared norm or precedent and argue casuistically towards a common position. Thus, within a largely secular political culture, a religious group might be able to point to some humanist analogue to religious belief, such as state support for the arts, to justify protection of their religion on grounds of equity.

These more developed forms of compromise share a common desire not so much to compare different positions as to give each one its due and to seek reciprocal solutions. They adopt a problem-solving approach to conflicts, rather than viewing them as a battle to be won or lost.[90] The aim is an integrative rather than a distributive compromise, with the interests and values of others being matters to be met rather than constraints to be overcome through minimal, tactical concessions. Such compromises try to include the moral reasons of each side. Conflicts can often appear intractable at the level of abstract principle because radically under-described. Democratic deliberation in both the electoral campaign and the legislature often plays a role in this regard, though a more realistic one than is sometimes claimed for it. Debate may not transform preferences but, by allowing the concerns of the parties involved to be fully articulated, the specific force of the various reasons they invoke can be appreciated. Thick description may help clarify the distinctive weight of each person's or group's demands, revealing that reasons of different weight or involving different sorts of consideration are involved. When described in detail, it may prove possible to address the main preoccupations of each party and aggregate them in a coherent way.

[90] J. H. Carens, 'Compromises in Politics', in J. R. Pennock and J. W. Chapman (eds.), *Compromise in Ethics, Law and Politics*, New York: New York University Press, 1979, pp. 126–9.

Controlling the executive: courts versus legislatures

These points need to be remembered when addressing a common and important criticism to the effect that party discipline makes parliamentary majorities the mere creatures of the executive. The British parliament comes in for especial attack in this regard given that, as mentioned, in plurality systems an executive can arrogate considerable power on the basis of a minority of the popular vote. For example, Margaret Thatcher and more recently Tony Blair have both enjoyed large parliamentary majorities despite securing the support of under 35% of the electorate and less than 50% of votes cast (ranging from a high of almost 46% for Mrs Thatcher in the 1983 election, to a low of just over 35% for Mr Blair in 2005). Their administrations have also been criticised for steadily eroding civil liberties – either for reasons of perceived administrative convenience and efficiency, such as can tempt any executive keen to pursue its programme with a minimum of what it may regard as carping criticism, or by overreacting to terrorism and other potential threats to security. Legal constitutionalists have argued that in these circumstances judicial review forms an essential check against executive arrogance and carelessness, especially with regard to individual rights. For, it is precisely when issues of the collective welfare are most prominent that the entitlements of the individual are likely to be neglected.[91]

How justified are these worries and does judicial review offer an appropriate response? At one level, these criticisms are simply misguided. It is not arbitrary that governments possess a legislative majority to implement policy goals that have won the support of (and been influenced by) an electoral plurality or majority in a free and fair election. Rather, given that, as we have seen, the electoral process itself operates as a model of public reasoning in which citizens are shown equal concern and respect as rights holders when deciding on their collective arrangements, it is arbitrary for a certain individuals to have their rights or views on rights given an extra or overwhelming weight with regard to those of others. To characterise majority rule as producing a clash between the collective welfare and individual rights is misconceived within a system that weighs individual rights equitably and fairly. This is especially true given

[91] E.g. R. Dworkin, 'Does Britain Need a Bill of Rights?', in his *Freedom's Law*, ch. 18. For a corrective, stressing the long history of judicial inaction relative to democratic struggle on these issues, see K. Ewing and C. Gearty, *Freedom under Thatcher: Civil Liberties in Modern Britain*, Oxford: Oxford University Press, 1990 and *The Struggle for Civil Liberties: Political Freedom and the Rule of Law in Britain 1914–1945*, Oxford: Oxford University Press, 2001.

that most majorities are actually winning coalitions of minorities, with legislative programmes reflecting a compromise between them. Despite her large majority, Margaret Thatcher always had to accommodate a reasonably broad church within her own party, suffered increasingly serious backbench revolts as she became more dogmatic towards the end of her administration, ultimately being removed from office by her own party in anticipation of a probable electoral defeat had she remained. More generally, it is sometimes overlooked how the vast majority of a citizen's rights derive not from the constitution but ordinary legislation. To the extent they exist, voting, welfare, employment and environmental rights, for example, have all been implemented by executives backed by legislative majorities – often in the face of challenges in the courts by powerful vested interests.[92]

In what may be called the normal circumstances of democratic disagreement, seeking judicial review of a decision that has been taken according to the due democratic procedures could only be legitimate if it could somehow be shown that the legal procedures were fairer and more attentive to the principles at issue. Yet, once the democratic process is no longer misrepresented as an irrational form of self-interested rent seeking, this case proves hard to make. When it comes to the procedural virtues of equality of participation, equity in representation and influence, accountability and contestation – all of which we have seen are vital for rights to be taken seriously and the rule of law upheld – then competitive party, parliamentary democracy with majority rule outperforms courts significantly without their having substantive advantages.[93]

Though courts do have procedures for hearing both sides of those cases that come before them, there is neither equality in access to justice nor in the range of views that may be applied to considering the cases at hand. Litigation before the courts is extremely costly and constrained by rules of standing that restrict the possibility of judicial redress to a small number of cases.[94] These costs can be a major problem for the

---

[92] For example, Ewing and Gearty, *The Struggle for Civil Liberties*, pp. 17–21, report how the Representation of the People Acts 1918 and 1928 were enacted against judicial hostility, while acts such as the National Assistance Act 1948 or the Sex Discrimination Act 1975 were legislative not judicial initiatives.

[93] See J. Waldron, 'The Core of the Case Against Judicial Review', *Yale Law Journal*, 115 (2006), pp. 1346–406.

[94] For the UK, see Lord Woolf's Report *Access to Justice: Final Report*, London: HMSO, 1996, and Appendix III that details the lack of proportionality between the value of claims and the expense of pursuing them, particularly in the sorts of cases that relate to most ordinary people involving relatively small sums.

poor when challenging irregularities due to corruption, injustice or sheer carelessness by public (or private) bureaucracies. By and large, legal action favours those with the deepest pockets – particularly big business, not least because they possess the resources to use the law to pursue objectives beyond the winning of a particular case.[95] Of course, pressure groups have to some degree democratised this process by sponsoring public-interest litigation and class actions.[96] However, the groups able to mobilise in appropriate ways are necessarily highly selective. In the short term, their actions may help overcome the above-mentioned tendency of established party divisions to freeze out certain new issues and concerns. Yet, as I remarked in chapter 1, they can also distort the political agenda by giving unequal weight to particular well-organised voices prepared to pursue a single issue above all others.[97] In sum, because it lacks the equalising effect offered by a system of fair voting, the legal process can be even more open to the very distortions of interest group politics that have led legal constitutionalists to criticise democracy.[98]

These defects are increased by the deficiencies of courts as a forum of public reason. Their shortcomings from a procedural point of view follow straightforwardly from limited access to justice, on the one hand, which we saw restricts the public setting of the agenda as well as the obtaining of redress, and the limited representativeness of the judiciary. Many legislatures may fare little better than the judiciary at fairly representing the population in terms of gender, class, culture and ethnicity.[99] However, while symbolically important, representation in terms of presence offers an imperfect indicator of the representation of ideas, interests and ideals, which tend to cut across many gender, ethnic and cultural divisions.[100] The dynamics of electoral competition under a free vote mean that legislatures perform far better in this last respect. No similarly effective mechanism

---

[95] M. Galanter, 'Why the Haves Come Out Ahead: Speculations on the Limits of Legal Change', *Law and Society*, 9 (1974), pp. 95–160.

[96] C. Harlow and R. Rawlings, *Pressure Through Law*, London: Routledge, 1992.

[97] For the various ways this has occurred in the US, see Tushnet, *Taking the Constitution Away from the Courts*, pp. 135–41.

[98] See P. H. Rubbin, C. Curran and J. F. Curran, 'Litigation versus Legislation: Forum Shopping by Rent Seekers', *Public Choice*, 107 (2001), pp. 295–310.

[99] In fact, those countries, such as Norway and Sweden, that have more representative legislatures, in the sense of their reflecting more accurately the social composition of the political community, also fare much better so far as the make-up of their judiciary is concerned. The UK and especially the US perform particularly badly by this measure among advanced democracies.

[100] For a discussion of this issue, see A. Phillips, *The Politics of Presence*, Oxford: Clarendon Press, 1995.

operates for courts – indeed, usually their selection procedures are deliberately designed with the aim of removing ideological bias. Given the notorious lack of success of these measures,[101] the failure to fairly select representative views becomes all-important. When judges vote on constitutional cases, majority rule cannot be seen as a fair procedural device for identifying the reason of the public as it can within a legislature. Rather, as C. Herman Pritchett famously put it, 'private attitudes . . . become public law'.[102] Moreover, whereas voters can challenge the decisions of legislatures at the next election, they have little or no redress against the judgements of a constitutional court, which being at the top of the legal hierarchy is largely self-policing.

Meanwhile, the procedural norms that do exist in courts can be drawbacks rather than advantages so far as substantive public reasoning is concerned. As I observed in chapter 1, judges have to deal with those cases that come up and decide on the law in the context of the submissions made by the parties concerned. They do not consider the case as part of a general programme of government and with regard to its knock-on effects for other policy areas, while the legal grounds raised by the respective counsels may be somewhat narrower than the general moral or policy issues potentially raised by the case.[103] These constraints are ideal for ensuring legality but not for determining social and political justice more broadly conceived. Even when judges seek to assess executive action directly on the basis of constitutional standards such as proportionality, reasonableness or rights, these benchmarks prove abstract and imprecise; making it hard to be sure which policy decision best serves their purpose. After all, in most of these cases there are several rights and different sorts of moral consideration in play. As I have often remarked before, many

---

[101] For the predominantly conservative bias of the UK judiciary, see J. G. A. Griffith's classic account, *The Politics of the Judiciary*, fifth edition, London: Fontana, 1997. The literature on the influence of ideological bias on judicial decision-making in the US is huge, but for a round-up of research 1959–98 documenting the influence of party affiliation see D. R. Pinello, 'Linking Party to Judicial Ideology in American Courts', *Justice System Journal*, 20 (1999), pp. 219–54.

[102] C. Herman Pritchett, 'Division of Opinion Among Justices on the U.S. Supreme Court, 1939–41', *American Political Science Review*, 25 (1941), p. 890.

[103] See Adam Tomkins's discussion in *Our Republican Constitution*, Oxford: Hart, 2005, pp. 27–8 of *R (Prolife Alliance) v British Broadcasting Corporation* [2004] 1 AC 185, reported in chapter 1, where the respective counsels bracketed the general issue of whether the screening of pictures deemed 'offensive to public feeling', in this case images of an abortion, was in conflict with a right to freedom of speech and merely asked for a decision on whether the rules had been properly applied in this case.

rulings get made on the basis of split decisions. Yet, such disagreements return us to the above-mentioned procedural failings of courts.

Therefore, courts offer an ambiguous check on the arbitrary power of executives given that they themselves may serve as a source of arbitrary judgements. Indeed, the judicial record is mixed to say the least. We have noted the poor US judicial record with regard to organised labour and improving the democratic process in chapters 1 and 3. UK courts fare little better. As in the US,[104] for example, the 1920s and 1930s saw the judicial connivance in a significant erosion of civil and political liberties to constrain political radicalism in cases such as *Duncan v Jones*,[105] affirming that the police possess a common law power to obstruct a public meeting they contend may lead to a breach of the peace. The pattern, begun at the time of the General Strike, of a sympathetic judiciary supporting police action hindering the right to strike, continued into the 1980s under Margaret Thatcher, when her confrontation with the miners was facilitated by judges only granting bail to strikers on condition they did not become further involved and giving legal legitimacy to the police practice of stopping potential pickets at motorway exits miles from where they wanted to go and forcing them to turn back.[106] The development of judicial review reveals a similarly chequered history. Thus, the only consistent element of the application by British courts of an extremely vague test of 'reasonableness' to executive action following the *Wednesbury* ruling of Lord Greene in 1947,[107] appears to have been to block the policies of Labour administrations. How else to explain the Lords' rulings in *Secretary of State for Education v Tameside MBC*[108] that a Labour government's insistence that a Conservative local education authority change a school from a selective grammar school to a comprehensive was unlawful in the absence of an explicit manifesto commitment to do so, whereas in *Bromley v GLC*[109] the Labour controlled Greater London Council was acting unlawfully in cutting fares on the underground and raising money through an increase

---

[104] E.g. *Schenke v US* 249 US 47 (1919), *Debs v US* 249 US 211 (1919) and *Abrams v US* 259 US 616 (1919), cases where legislative restrictions on the public advocacy of socialism where deemed compatible with the First Amendment.

[105] [1936] 1 KB 218.

[106] For details see Ewing and Gearty, *Freedom under Thatcher* and *Moss v McLachlan* [1985] IRLR 76.

[107] *Associated Provincial Picture Houses v Wednesbury Corporation* [1948] 1 KB 223 at 230, later refined by Lord Diplock in *Council of Civil Service Unions v Minister for the Civil Service* [1985] AC 374 at 410. For a succinct survey of the *Wednesbury* era see A. Tomkins, *Public Law*, Oxford: Oxford University Press, 2003, pp. 176–82, whose account I follow.

[108] [1997] AC 1014.   [109] [1983] 1 AC 768.

in the rates despite such an explicit manifesto commitment? Significantly, the attempt to tighten the criteria to overcome such inconsistencies by restricting judicial redress to executive actions that were clearly 'absurd' or 'perverse' was against another Labour authority trying to escape attempts by the Conservative administration to cap its budget,[110] and subsequently refined to reject the plea of a family of four that a room in a guesthouse with no laundry or cooking facilities did not satisfy their statutory right to be housed.[111] Some commentators claimed the Human Rights Act would improve matters by providing the judiciary with clear criteria.[112] However, their faith seems misplaced given that a number of subsequent judgements on issues such as the stopping, searching and detention of protestors by the police have been held compatible with the Act,[113] often citing these earlier cases as precedents.

Some commentators have been apt to lay the blame for the judiciary's relative ineffectiveness on so many of its members being part of the social establishment.[114] To a degree, that will be true almost by definition – the judiciary simply are part of the ruling class. Yet, the suggestion that their performance might be improved by better methods of selection raises a paradox. If the aim is to make them more representative, then that would entail democratising the judiciary so that they become in effect an alternative legislature. That proposal grants the justice of democratic procedures, but raises the issue of why we should unnecessarily duplicate the task of choosing legislators. Why should a rival body have precedence over another we have all voted for? Other proposals seem to boil down to little more than somehow finding ways of choosing judges who will decide as their proponents believe they should. Quite apart from the practical difficulties that bedevil such Platonic schemes for choosing reliable Guardians, they return us to the central problem that what the 'right' decisions might be is what is at issue. Above I cited liberal criticism of British judicial decisions because, as in the US, liberals are currently the

---

[110] *Nottinghamshire County Council v Secretary of State for the Environment* [1986] AC 240 at 247.

[111] *Pulhofer v Hillingdon London Borough Council* [1986] AC 484 at 518.

[112] J. Jowell and A. Lester, 'Beyond *Wednesbury*: Substantive Principles of Administrative Law' *Public Law* (1987), pp. 368–82.

[113] E.g. *Austin v Metropolitan Police Commissioner* [2003] EWHC 480 (QB), *R (Gillen) v Metropolitan Police Commissioner* [2004] EWCA Civ 1067, and *R (Laporte) v Gloucestershire Chief Constable, Thames Valley Chief Constable and Metropolitan Police Commissioner* [2004] EWCA Civ 1639. See K. D. Ewing, 'The Futility of the Human Rights Act', *Public Law* (2004), pp. 829–52.

[114] E.g. Griffith, *The Politics of the Judiciary*.

most prominent contemporary legal constitutionalists within the UK. However, during the late 1960s and 1970s, when Labour was in office, calls for the judicial control of the executive's 'electoral dictatorship' came largely from Conservatives who would have applauded most of the judgements cited above.[115] Radical schemes for politicising the judiciary could well backfire. They also ignore the fact that a certain institutional conservatism plays an important role in maintaining the judiciary's role as upholders of the 'rule of law' in the formal sense of applying laws in a like manner to like cases.

Hard cases? States of emergency and the politically powerless

Notwithstanding these difficulties, there may be situations where the claims of executives to be the voice of fair electoral and legislative majorities are far weaker, and hence the need for, and legitimacy of, an independent check on their power to avoid rights violations is consequently stronger. Three potential scenarios come to mind. The first is when executives have to respond to an exceptional crisis that was unanticipated in any party manifesto and where, as in threats to national security, there is an especial risk that civil liberties may be overlooked as a result of precipitate action to meet an emergency. The second is when legislating on matters of private morality that nonetheless have a public dimension: issues such as abortion and gay marriage fit this category, for example. Finally, there are laws and policies involving 'discrete and insular minorities', who may be unable to build electoral coalitions with other groups and hence have no electoral clout whereby their interests might be protected. I shall examine each in turn.

Emergency legislation to fight terrorism has been a constant source of concern to human rights watchers. Be it the IRA or Al-Qaeda, the fear of governments and security services that they will be blamed for failing to adequately protect citizens in the event of a major terrorist outrage will always tempt them to overreact, sacrificing liberty to what may still be a somewhat illusory security given the difficulty of preventing rogue individuals harming ordinary people in the course of their everyday lives. There is also the worry that such measures will be employed to hinder legitimate but, for the governments concerned, inconvenient

---

[115] E.g. Quentin Hogg (later Lord Hailsham), *New Charter*, London: Conservative Political Centre, 1969. For a discussion of Labour and Conservative proposals for a Bill of Rights, and the problems they raise from a democratic point of view, see R. Bellamy, *Liberalism and Pluralism*, ch. 7.

criticism and opposition to contentious policies by non-terrorist groups, such as anti-nuclear or road protestors or trade unionists within the public services, or to exclude individuals, such as asylum seekers, with no connection to terrorist organisations beyond a shared ethnicity or religious affiliation.

A major problem for legal constitutionalists is that the courts have proved unreliable protectors of individual rights in such circumstances. To name only some of the most notorious UK cases of the past hundred odd years (1917–2003),[116] and without even mentioning Northern Ireland, from *R v Halliday, ex parte Zadig*,[117] upholding the legality of internment during the First World War, through *Council of Civil Service Unions v Minister for the Civil Service*,[118] defending Margaret Thatcher's unprovoked withdrawal of trade union rights from government employees at the listening centre GCHQ, to *Attorney-General v Guardian Newspapers*,[119] maintaining the ban on the publication of revelations found in the book *Spycatcher* by the former MI5 officer Peter Wright, and *A and others v Secretary of State for the Home Department*,[120] confirming the legality of provisions in the Anti-Terrorism, Crime and Security Act 2001, judges have been unwilling to overrule executive curtailments of civil liberties when issues of public security are involved. Again, the hope that things would change with the Human Rights Act has proved somewhat belied by subsequent rulings in *Secretary of State for the Home Department v Rehman*,[121] upholding a decision to deport a visiting Pakistani national despite concluding that there was no proof that he constituted a danger to national security, and *R v Shayler*,[122] maintaining the compatibility with the protection of freedom of speech guaranteed by Article 10 of the European Convention on Human Rights of the notorious section 1 of the Official Secrets Act 1989 banning disclosure of any information relating to security resulting from employment in the intelligence services – even if it is in the public interest to do so and no danger to public safety results.[123] Indeed, the record of the US Supreme Court in such cases, notwithstanding having long had a bill of rights, is if anything worse. When crises are held to threaten the nation's security, the Court proves substantially more likely to curtail rights and civil liberties than when peace prevails. Moreover, this finding applies not so much to the decisions related to the

---

[116] These examples are taken from Tomkins, *Our Republican Constitution*, p. 14, who provides a fuller list.
[117] [1917] AC 260.   [118] [1985] 1 AC 374.   [119] [1987] 1 WLR 1248.
[120] [2003] 2 WLR 564.   [121] [2003] 1 AC 153.   [122] [2003] 1 AC 247.
[123] See Tomkins, *Our Republican Constitution*, pp. 30–31.

emergency, though there are notorious cases like the detention without trial of Japanese Americans during the Second World War[124] or the Cold War ban on the Communist Party,[125] as to cases totally unrelated to it.[126]

Of course, there have also been judgements that a liberal-minded constitutionalist could applaud, such as *Rasul v Bush*,[127] giving a foreign national imprisoned at Guantanamo Bay access to the US federal civilian courts, or the House of Lords ruling on the incompatibility with the Human Rights Act of the indefinite detention without charge of non-national terrorist suspects in Belmarsh prison.[128] If the governments will always get their way on such matters because party discipline aligns legislative majorities closely to executives, then even an imperfect check on executive power in such cases might seem justified rather than no check at all – that way at least some abuses of power will be prevented. In fact, though, complete pessimism proves unwarranted. Most governments are coalitions, either between parties or, in systems such as the UK's that favour two parties, between groups within the governing party. Committed civil libertarians of one sort or another form an important group on both the left and right of the political spectrum, even if the salience and slant they give these issues reflects their broader ideological convictions. Moreover, party loyalty is likely to be weaker in areas falling outside a government's main agenda as set by the election and outlined in its manifesto. For example, in a detailed analysis of the debates leading up to the passing of the 2001 Anti-Terrorism, Crime and Security Act, Adam Tomkins has shown how despite the speed with which this measure was prepared and pushed through parliament in the wake of 9/11, significant changes were made to curb some of the executive powers it established.[129] Thus, safeguards were introduced regarding the collection and retention of personal data, the Home Secretary had to show an individual could be

---

[124] *Korematsu v US* 323 US 214 (1944).   [125] *Dennis v US* 341 US 494 (1951).

[126] L. Epstein, D. E. Ho, G. King and J. A. Segal, 'The Supreme Court During Crisis: How War Affects Only Non-War Cases', *New York University Law Review*, 80 (2005), pp. 1–116. They note that an emergency leads the Court to be less liberal overall when dealing with civil liberties cases, but curiously not in rulings directly related to war. They conjecture that it avoids addressing substantive issues in such cases as beyond its competence. Instead, it concentrates on the procedural issue of whether the measure was duly authorised by Congress or not, thereby leading it to overrule what it regards as unauthorised actions.

[127] 524 US 2004.

[128] By eight votes to one in *A and others v Secretary of State for the Home Department* [2004] UKHL 56, [2005] 2 WLR 87, HL. Note, though, that the Court of Appeal had earlier upheld the government's position against the detainees in *A and others v Secretary of State for the Home Department* [2003] 3 WLR 564.

[129] Tomkins, *Our Republican Constitution*, pp. 126–30.

'reasonably' suspected of terrorist activity to be detained without trial and, most importantly of all, the whole Act and especially Part IV, allowing indefinite detention without trial of those suspected of links to international terrorists, was subjected to various reviews and a sunset clause, whereby the powers would lapse and any renewal would have to obtain further parliamentary approval. Indeed, despite the brief period allowed for debate some five select committee reports were published on the Bill. These served to highlight its controversial aspects, promoted consultation with a range of relevant pressure and interest groups, and forced the government into a more focused justification of its measures than it had hitherto provided. In fact, before the House of Lords' Belmarsh decision a special all-party Committee of Privy Counsellors had published a report deeply critical of the detention regime authorised by the 2001 Act.[130] This report resulted from a provision in the Act (section 122) that was inserted as a result of parliamentary pressure. It is arguable that without it, the House of Lords would not have ruled as it did. Indeed, while the Law Lords in *A* took issue with detention against trial, the narrowness of the adjudicative process meant that they left the rest of the Act intact – wider reforms were only raised by the all-party Committee.[131]

Admittedly, much remained in the Act that a civil libertarian would find unsatisfactory. Yet, it would be inaccurate to describe the legislature, notwithstanding the government's large majority, as a mere rubber stamp of the executive's will. It should also be borne in mind that there are no easy answers in such situations. After all, a possible failure to apprehend a potential terrorist could cost the lives, and infringe the rights, of many hundreds of innocent citizens. Emergency situations do create pressures that call for swift executive action. That said, it would be wrong to assume, as legal constitutionalists are apt to, that the popular default position in such situations will always be towards ever more draconian law and order measures, or that the judiciary will invariably oppose them – in fact, most of the Law Lords in *A* conceded that they might be necessary in principle, and Lord Hope even ruled 'there was ample evidence' supporting the government's view 'that there was an emergency threatening the life of the nation'.[132] Ordinary citizens are more affected by tightened security measures than most judges will be. They cannot only find their lives inconvenienced in numerous small ways, but also have an interest in

---

[130] HC (2002–3) 100, 13 December 2003.
[131] See A. Tomkins, 'Readings of *A v Secretary of State for the Home Department*', *Public Law* (2005), pp. 259–66.
[132] Ibid., 261–2.

governments remaining open to criticism, in measures not exacerbating rather than alleviating the danger of a threat by unnecessarily alienating further certain aggrieved groups and so on. As a result, electoral incentives exist for even party loyalists to oppose their leaders on such issues. Thus, the even stronger measures introduced by the government in the Terrorism Bill in the wake of the London bombings of 7 July 2005 led to Prime Minister Blair's first defeat in the Commons since coming to power in 1997. Proposals to extend the time police could detain terrorist suspects without charge from 14 to 90 days were defeated by 31 votes, with 49 Labour MPs rebelling against the government. Moreover, in a BBC poll following the vote, 57.81% endorsed the MPs' decision. Indeed, Mr Blair's reduced majority in the 2005 election can be attributed at least in part to disaffection among some of his core voters over his support for the United States invasion of Iraq – a decision that had also prompted parliamentary opposition and scrutiny.[133]

When it comes to the second set of issues, namely legislation on matters of personal morality, then party discipline has been historically weak. In fact, in the UK Members of Parliament are usually given a free vote on such topics, which are generally introduced as private members' Bills, even if their success depends on the government being sufficiently favourable to allow them adequate parliamentary time to be debated and voted on. Jeremy Waldron has remarked how this circumstance produced a remarkably respectful and sustained discussion of abortion – covering more than a 100 pages in Hansard – during the debates on the Medical Termination of Pregnancy Bill during its passage through the Commons in 1966.[134] He attributes the degree of mutual recognition between pro-choice and pro-life MPs, who were to be found within all parties, to the fact that neither side was being forced to concede they were wrong in their interpretation of matters of fundamental political principle. Instead, the very political process in which they were engaged is one that concedes that there are two or more sides to any question that deserve to be treated equitably. As participants in a process of public reasoning, each side deserved to be heard and attended to. As Waldron notes, even when it was clear the pro-choice side would win the vote, pro-life MPs paid tribute to the respectfulness

[133] For example, the government's decision to go to war with Iraq was met by mass protests and the biggest revolt of backbenchers since the nineteenth century, with 139 Labour MPs voting against the government.

[134] J. Waldron, 'Legislating with Integrity', *Fordham Law Review*, 72 (2003), pp. 388–94, commenting on the Second Reading of the Medical Termination of Pregnancy Bill 732 Parl. Deb., HC (5th ser.) (1966), pp. 1067–1166.

with which they had been treated, praising the 'extraordinary moderation and skill' of the Bill's sponsor.[135]

It was particularly important in this regard that the vote did not involve condemning the pro-life position as wrong or misguided – merely as being out of kilter with majority opinion. As we have seen above, following the view of the majority after a free discussion can be seen as a reasonable and public way to fairly adjudicate between competing views. Given that on this issue there was little reason to doubt that the House of Commons contained a cross-section of British public opinion, then a free vote in the legislature can be seen as a fair mechanism for settling the collective view. The legislature is large enough to contain a representative sample of the range of views, yet small enough to allow debate and a degree of compromise between them. As I noted in chapter 5, though there are hardline pro-life and pro-choice views, there is also a range of views in between – sensitive to grey areas that allow modifications to the pro-life position when mother's life is at stake, say, or to the pro-choice position when at the point when a foetus becomes viable. A detailed Bill can accommodate these sorts of nuances, allowing each side to see evidence of its influence in particular provisions. By contrast, when a constitutional court settles this matter by a majority vote, as is usually the case, voting simply serves as a closure device. It cannot be seen as a procedural means for fairly giving all opinions on the matter equal due. The range of legal and moral opinion represented by the court is likely to be somewhat arbitrary with regard to the full gamut of views among the public at large. This arbitrariness of the sample means that in the case of the court but not the legislature there is a genuine danger of majority tyranny.

Some republican theorists have argued that free votes ought to be extended to more issues and become the norm for legislative debates on matters of principle.[136] However, the key to the legitimacy of parliament lies in its being both representative and accountable. Parties, as we saw, play a vital role in this regard because they make it possible for views on a range of policies to be brought together in ways that render legislators delegates of the electorate. On the rare occasions legislation relating to personal morality is necessary, then free votes seem appropriate because these issues cut across the dominant party divisions. In this case, the legislature is acting as a rough microcosm of the nation as a whole. But that

---

[135] Ibid., n. 47, citing Norman St John-Stevas, a Catholic Conservative MP who opposed the Bill.
[136] Tomkins, *Our Republican Constitution*, pp. 136–9.

is not the normal basis on which parliament operates. On most issues of public policy, the agenda has been set at the general election and parliament's role is to reflect voting in that popular arena.

What about the third scenario, that of 'discrete and insular minorities'?[137] As we saw in chapter 3, this possibility both inspired and greatly complicated the procedural approach to judicial review put forward by Ely and others.[138] As I have noted already, in the case of territorially concentrated cultural or ethnic minorities, these considerations can be met through some arrangement for devolving certain powers to specific regions. The key problem posed by this scenario is in the case of groups that are territorially dispersed yet isolated and so electorally insignificant and subject to such overwhelming prejudice from the majority of the population that they risk not having their interests considered fairly at all. The caveats entered here are important.[139] For a start, significant minorities can often be important political allies in the formation of coalitions, giving them political influence well beyond their voting strength. So the mere existence of a distinct cultural, ethnic or other minority need not mean it is politically isolated. Moreover, the test of whether minority rights are being unfairly overridden cannot be that all the rights a given group or their academic supporters believe they should have are not yet legally acknowledged. Legitimate room has to be allowed for reasonable disagreements about rights. All legislation passed by a majority vote involves some minority losing out – and some losers deserve never to win. As Mark Tushnet has observed, 'we have to distinguish between *mere* losers and minorities that lose because they cannot protect themselves in politics'.[140] Finally, one cannot assume that it will be the normal practice for majorities to override in unacceptable ways the rights of any minority lacking electoral clout. A commitment to treating one's fellow citizens as equals is an intrinsic aspect of a commitment to democracy and has stood behind successive extensions of the franchise to workers and women by electoral majorities – on occasion even at the expense of their own position.

All three points are relevant when considering the group that naturally dominates the US literature, namely, blacks in the southern states. Yet worries in their regard are at least partially belied by the Civil Rights and

---

[137] The phrase, of course, comes from Justice Stone's famous footnote in *United States v Carolene Products Co.* 304 US 144 at 152 n. 4 (1938).

[138] Ely, *Democracy and Distrust*, pp. 75–7.

[139] See Waldron, 'The Core of the Case Against Judicial Review', pp. 1403–6.

[140] Tushnet, *Taking the Constitution Away from the Courts*, p. 159.

the Voting Rights Acts, legislation passed with large legislative majorities. No doubt the Democrats anticipated acquiring new electoral partners in the south, though the losses they incurred in promoting this legislation were greater than the gains. Certainly, the southern whites felt they were an aggrieved minority, outvoted by northern elites – though few constitutional rights advocates feel great sympathy for them. However, the greatest factor in the vote was undoubtedly a widespread popular feeling that justice demanded this change. Moreover, as this legislation shows, an acknowledgement of equal citizenship rights need not be equivalent to having them incorporated within a constitutional document – merely securing them due process within the political system. Of course, this is not to deny that considerable prejudice and discrimination remains. It is to suggest, though, as has been discussed in chapters 1 and 3, that it is potentially eradicable more effectively and legitimately by electoral as opposed to judicial means.[141]

'Discrete and insular' minorities are neither frequent nor normal occurrences within democratic politics, therefore. However, two potential types that could arise come to mind. One category is that of the moral deviant, for whose activities the vast majority feel disgust and often evoke hatred – such as paedophiles. The danger here is of draconian legislation being introduced to appease popular outrage at some particularly heinous case of child abuse. Again, such groups are perhaps less isolated than might be supposed. After all, they come from all ages and classes, and with the exception of their sexual tastes are likely to be allied with significant groups within society. Moreover, tolerance here justifiably does not extend to their right to engage in their preferred sexual behaviour – merely to their receiving due process in the courts and so on. But given we could all be subject to false accusations for this or other crimes, all citizens have an interest in the courts operating fairly.

Yet, despite all those linkages that might lead the electorate at large to be fair, if not forgiving, in such cases, it remains true that moral panics have periodically lead to a vocal section of the population, often backed by the popular press, to call for hasty and myopic measures that risk infringing the rights of such minorities. In fact, it needs emphasising that such calls

---

[141] On the normative and practical importance of legislative as opposed to Court action in securing civil rights in the US south, see R. A. Burt, *The Constitution in Conflict*, Cambridge, MA: Harvard University Press, 1992, especially ch. 8 and G. Rosenberg, *The Hollow Hope: Can Courts Bring About Social Change?*, Chicago: University of Chicago Press, 1991.

have largely gone unheeded.[142] If the general population was prone to persecuting isolated minorities then its doubtful judicial review would make much difference. Even advocates of bills of rights acknowledge that their force derives from their being widely accepted within the political community as expressing the ways citizens feel they should relate to each other in the public sphere.[143] As the example of Nazi Germany reveals, if widespread popular acknowledgement of the relevant minority's rights is lacking, then the likelihood is that the prejudice will be shared by a significant majority of the elite as well.[144] So, the relevance of judicial review in this sort of case is to guard against a potential, aberrant instance of undue discrimination. That seems weak ground on which to build a general case for judicial review – especially given the historical tendency of the judiciary to support the not so moral interests of the ruling elite of which it forms a part against popular demands for greater substantive equality.

As it happens, the prime source of tension between judges and politicians in this area has concerned complaints that judges have been too lenient in sentencing. However, by and large that has resulted from them following general sentencing guidelines and resisting executive attempts to intervene in individual high-profile cases. The main bone of contention has not been over the government's right to legislate for higher sentences so much as their occasional interferences with due process. Yet the dispositions that lead judges to act in a generally scrupulous manner in this regard, namely an institutional legalism, can operate without reference to constitutional rights.

Similar considerations apply to my second category of 'discrete' minority. This type includes groups like asylum seekers or the Roma, for whom the exercise of political rights is either impossible or incompatible with their lifestyle, and who are perceived as a net cost on the wider political community and are often the subject of racism. Again, the justifiable respects in which their concerns might be treated with less regard than those of the majority have to be borne in mind. In any political system, the allocation of limited resources will produce winners and losers.

---

[142] For example, the enthusiasm of some Home Secretaries notwithstanding, British governments have so far resisted periodic calls for a UK version of Megan's Law on the grounds that it creates more problems than it solves.

[143] E.g. J. Raz, 'On the Authority and Interpretation of Constitutions', in L. Alexander (ed.), *Constitutionalism: Philosophical Foundations*, Cambridge: Cambridge University Press, 1998, p. 154.

[144] Ely, *Democracy and Distrust*, p. 181.

Democratic decision-making offers a fair method for distribution, but there will often be consistent decisional minorities who find their activities receive less public support than others, no matter how important these may be to them.[145] Even if asylum seekers and the Roma could or did exercise the vote, a legitimate gap might exist between the costs of what they ideally wish for and what the community was prepared to pay at the expense of spending that benefited the permanent resident majority. The question is whether even their rights to a fair hearing and a humanitarian regard for their safety and well-being are being ignored. Once more, a blanket presumption of a lack of popular humanitarian concern seems unwarranted. After all, ordinary people are far more likely to appreciate the struggle to survive than the wealthy few: charitable giving as a percentage of income is much higher among the poor majority than the rich minority. That is not to say that there are not exceptions where simple prejudice inexplicably and despicably blinds people to the fate of their fellows. Here too, though, elite sympathy is sadly unlikely to operate in the absence of widespread popular support. Where it does, it may backfire – causing a justified decision to be treated as illegitimate because imposed, thereby making it harder to marshal the popular support that in the long term must follow if any measures are to be effective. Yet again, more stands to be gained from formal rule of law considerations that belong to the institutional training and constraints of the judiciary and do not require reference to the grander moral considerations that surround constitutional rights. Though more limited in scope, such judgements can be very effective – as is demonstrated by the rulings in asylum cases in the pre-Human Rights Act era against Michael Howard, a UK Home Secretary particularly prone to abusing his discretionary powers in such areas.[146] As with the first so with this second category, the exceptional character of this sort of case cannot provide an all-purpose argument for judicial review.

---

[145] Legislation providing for the rights of gypsies and travellers predates the Human Rights Act. Thus, a private member's Bill led to the Caravan Sites Act 1968 that resulted in local authorities providing some 400 sites. True, this obligation was removed by the then Conservative government in the Criminal Justice and Public Order Act 1994. However, the Commission for Racial Equality (CRE) recognises gypsies and travellers as a distinct racial group and race relations legislation lays certain obligations on local authorities not to discriminate against them in areas such as education and housing.

[146] E.g. the legal blocking of his attempts to refuse entry to Rev Sun Il Moon under his powers under the Immigration Acts, *R v Secretary of State for the Home Department ex parte Moon* (1996) 8 Admin LR 477, or to deport the Saudi dissident al-Masari, *Mohammed A S Masari v Immigration Officer Gatwick and Secretary of State for the Home Department*, Appeal No. HX 75955/94, 5 March 1996.

Conclusion

This chapter has upheld the claim of actually existing democratic practices to embody constitutional values and to supply mechanisms likely to preserve them. Within the circumstances of politics, the commitment to equality of concern and respect that animates most contemporary theories of rights and the rule of law can only be met via a form of self-rule that satisfies the condition of non-domination. A system of equal votes and majority rule complies with this criterion by offering a procedural form of public reasoning that provides a fair means for 'hearing the other side'. Competition between political parties further reinforces this system by promoting the responsiveness of political agents to their citizen principals and of citizens to each other. Meanwhile, both electoral campaigns and legislative bodies can be seen as deliberative and attentive to matters of principle. Rather than crude mechanisms whereby majorities ride roughshod over the rights of minorities, democratic practices offer incentives for building compromises that are attentive to the diverse concerns of a broad range of groups in society. In sum, the strong case for judicial review discussed in Part I is aimed at a straw target. Worse, in interfering with what can now be seen as a due constitutional process, it proves both arbitrary and dominating. Far from upholding the democratic values of equal concern and respect against the perversities of actual democracy, constitutional judicial review perversely undermines their most legitimate and effective safeguard – the democratic constitution.

Conclusion

This book has defended democracy against judicial review. It has done so not on the grounds that democracy is more important than constitutionalism, rights or the rule of law, but because democracy embodies and upholds these values. The judicial constraint of democracy weakens its constitutional attributes, putting inferior mechanisms in their place. That is not to say that actually existing democracy is perfect and decisions made by judicial review necessarily imperfect, merely that the imperfections of the first cannot be perfected by the second. Though undeniably in need of improvement, the democratic arrangements found in the world's established working democracies are sufficient to satisfy the requirements of republican non-domination, whereas all efforts to improve on such arrangements through judicial intervention create conditions of domination. Judicial review undermines the equality of concern and respect between citizens that lies at the heart of the constitutional project and that democratic processes serve to secure.

It will be objected that I have praised a version of actually existing democracy that is currently passing out of existence. Party membership and voting are experiencing a steady if slow decline in all established democracies.[1] Though the picture is mixed, with occasional increases in membership and turnout as well as significant variations between countries, and not yet at the crisis point regularly predicted by commentators of left and right since the 1960s,[2] a sustained general downward trend is undeniable. Quite apart from the shortcomings of the actors involved, these developments have also been attributed to systemic failings of democracy itself. Democratic mechanisms are felt to be ill-suited to securing effective and equitable government in today's complex and globalising societies. The electorate is too vast and diverse, the problems

---

[1] For a suitably pessimistic account, see P. Mair, *Polity-Scepticism, Party Failings and the Challenge to European Democracy*, Uhlenbeck Lecture 24, Wassenaar: NIAS, 2006.

[2] See P. Norris, *Democratic Phoenix: Political Activism Worldwide*, Cambridge: Cambridge University Press, 2003, ch. 7.

too technical, the scale of government too large for citizens to be able effectively to relate to each other, the tasks of politics or the institutions and persons assigned to tackle them. If matters did indeed get so bad that the democratic system could no longer claim to be either credibly representative of political opinion or responsible and accountable for central matters of public policy, then it would cease to possess the constitutional credentials described here. The exceptional situation described in the final section of the last chapter would have become the norm. In these circumstances, it might be argued that legal constitutionalism offers the best available proxy for actual democratic decision-making. This book has also concentrated on the domestic politics of democratic states, which remains the prime political context for deciding the most salient decisions affecting the lives of citizens. Yet, to the extent globalisation is partly responsible for the contemporary attenuation of democracy, with global democracy – even in such well-developed transnational regional systems as the EU – but a pale shadow of its national counterpart,[3] the case for legal constitutionalism is arguably further strengthened, with many seeing international law as providing a necessary global legal constitutionalism to overcome the fact that all citizens now find themselves virtually or totally excluded from many of the political processes that affect their lives.[4]

Two concluding observations are relevant here. First, this defence of legal constitutionalism involves a significant shift from the main arguments of legal constitutionalists criticised in this book. These claim that constitutional judicial review offers an ideal type of democracy that involves a substantive form of public reasoning. As such, it is superior to any real popular democracy rather than a poor second best. By contrast, this argument simply suggests we need judicial review given the limited possibilities for democracy. However, the book's critique of legal constitutionalism's foundations and mechanisms remains valid even against this more modest account, regardless of the possible disappearance of the proposed political alternative. Indeed, that critique remains even more relevant given that the political fragmentation and economic liberalisation typically associated with globalisation have promoted the American style of legalism and judicial review most criticised in this

---

[3] See R. Bellamy, D. Castiglione and J. Shaw (eds.), *Making European Citizens: Civic Inclusion in a Transnational Context*, Basingstoke: Palgrave, 2006.

[4] For an influential claim of how real democracy must give way to an ideal deliberative democracy of universal rights in this context, see J. Habermas, *The Postnational Constellation*, Cambridge: Polity, 2001, especially pp. 107–12.

book.[5] In which case, the need for reliance on such a poorly based and unreliable method for preserving constitutional values can hardly be viewed as an enticing prospect.

Second, far from offering a solution, legal constitutionalism is more likely to be part of the problem – helping corrode the very democratic processes it seeks so inadequately to replace. As I noted, reports of democracy's death have been much exaggerated – it could be healthier but it is still very much alive. Instead of writing off democracy, there remains much that could be done to enhance the very mechanisms that make it work. Regrettably, as recent attempted or actual reforms in the United Kingdom and the European Union testify, the legal constitutional medicines administered to tackle the developing democratic deficits have a tendency to exacerbate rather than alleviate these problems.[6] The counter-majoritarian and dominating character of judicial review, along with the parallel drawbacks noted in chapters 5 and 6 of most forms of bicameralism and many neo-federal arrangements, erode yet further the equality of votes and the incentives towards responsibility and accountability of politicians. Ironically, many of the proposals for supposedly constitution-alising both the UK and the EU reproduce the very arrangements that have so distorted democracy in the USA.[7] Symptomatic of the confused and perverse thinking surrounding constitutional issues, is the fact that the one reform with a clear democratic rationale, namely proportional representation, remains stalled in both the United Kingdom and the United States, while being mistakenly seen by some of its supporters as an alternative to

---

[5] See R. D. Kelemen and E. C. Sibbitt, 'The Globalisation of American Law', *International Organization*, 58 (2004), pp. 103–36.

[6] For a partial critique of both these initiatives, see R. Bellamy, 'Constitutive Citizenship vs. Constitutional Rights: Republican Reflections on the EU Charter and the Human Rights Act', in T. Campbell, K. D. Ewing and A. Tomkins (eds.), *Sceptical Essays on Human Rights*, Oxford: Oxford University Press, 2001, pp. 15–39.

[7] For explicit (and positive) comparisons between constitutional developments in the EU and UK, on the one side, and the US, on the other, see S. Fabbrini, 'Transatlantic Constitutionalism: Comparing the United States and the European Union', *European Journal of Political Research*, 43 (2004), pp. 547–69 and R. Dworkin, 'Does Britain Need a Bill of Rights?' in his *Freedom's Law: The Moral Reading of the American Constitution*, Oxford: Oxford University Press, 1996, ch. 18, respectively. For a critique of these two proposals, see R. Bellamy, 'The European Constitution is Dead, Long Live European Constitutionalism', *Constellations: An International Journal of Critical and Democratic Theory*, 13:2 (2006), pp. 181–9 and *Liberalism and Pluralism: Towards a Politics of Compromise*, London: Routledge, 1999, ch. 7. The democratic limitations of the US Constitution are detailed in R. A. Dahl, *How Democratic Is the American Constitution?*, New Haven: Yale University Press, 2002 and S. Levinson, *Our Undemocratic Constitution: Where the Constitution Goes Wrong (And How We the People Can Correct It)*, New York: Oxford University Press, 2006.

majoritarianism, and so at one with other counter-majoritarian proposals, rather than as reinforcing majority rule. Meanwhile, there has been an
increasing use and advocacy of quasi-democratic inputs, such as referenda
and consultation with various pressure groups, in a vain attempt to give
a veneer of popular legitimacy to the growing deployment of delegated
regulative agencies by governments. Such pseudo-democratic processes
facilitate agenda setting by elites and offer no incentives for citizens to
engage with the concerns of others.[8] In sum, the new governance agenda
being undertaken in the name of improving democracy ends up producing the very sorts of unconstitutional democracy liberal constitutionalists
fear, even if the real danger of such systems is tyranny by unrepresentative minorities rather than a majority. To avoid this fate, constitutional
reforms need to move with the grain of democracy rather than against
it. Instead of misguidedly and often inadvertently dismantling the democratic constitution, they need to reinvigorate it. Saying precisely how to
do so lies outside this book,[9] but hopefully it has shown why we should
adopt this approach, and indicated the norms that ought to guide such
measures and the forms they must take.

---

[8] Such mechanisms have proved especially popular in the EU – for a critical assessment, see
R. Bellamy, 'Still in Deficit: Rights, Regulation and Democracy in the EU', *European Law
Journal*, 12:6 (2006), pp. 725–42.

[9] Though I plan to do so in a work in progress on democracy, constitutionalism and citizenship in the EU.

INDEX

www.ingramcontent.com/pod-product-compliance
Ingram Content Group UK Ltd.
Pitfield, Milton Keynes, MK11 3LW, UK
UKHW020451010325
455719UK00015B/536